The Political Economy of Inequality

The Political Economy of Inequality

Frank Stilwell

polity

First published in 2019 by Polity Press

Polity Press
65 Bridge Street
Cambridge CB2 1UR, UK

Polity Press
101 Station Landing
Suite 300
Medford, MA 02155, USA

ISBN-13: 978-1-5095-2864-6
ISBN-13: 978-1-5095-2865-3 (pb)

A catalogue record for this book is available from the British Library.

Library of Congress Cataloging-in-Publication Data

Names: Stilwell, Frank J. B., author.
Title: The political economy of inequality / Frank Stilwell.
Description: Cambridge, UK ; Medford, MA : Polity, 2019. | Includes
   bibliographical references and index.
Identifiers: LCCN 2018041109 (print) | LCCN 2019003438 (ebook) | ISBN
   9781509528684 (Epub) | ISBN 9781509528646 | ISBN 9781509528646(hardback)
   | ISBN 9781509528653(paperback)
Subjects: LCSH: Income distribution. | Equality.
Classification: LCC HC79.I5 (ebook) | LCC HC79.I5 S774 2019 (print) | DDC
   339.2--dc23
LC record available at https://lccn.loc.gov/2018041109

Typeset in 10.5 on 12pt Palatino LT Std by
Servis Filmsetting Ltd, Stockport, Cheshire
Printed and bound in the UK by CPI Group (UK) Ltd, Croydon

For further information on Polity, visit our website: politybooks.com

Contents

Tables and Figures

Tables

Figures

Abbreviations

AI	artificial intelligence
APC	Anti-Poverty Consensus
APCC	Anti-Poverty Counter-Consensus
BI	basic income
BRICS	Brazil, Russia, India, China and South Africa
CEOs	chief executive officers
FIRE	finance, insurance and real estate
GDP	gross domestic product
GPI	genuine progress indicator
HDI	Human Development Index
IAHDI	inequality-adjusted Human Development Index
IMF	International Monetary Fund
JINKS	Japan, India, Nigeria, the Republic of Korea and Saudi Arabia
MDGs	Millennium Development Goals
NGO	non-governmental organization
OECD	Organization for Economic Cooperation and Development
PPP	purchasing power parity
SDGs	Sustainable Development Goals
UN	United Nations

Preface

Economic inequality is a worldwide concern. During the last few decades, the gap between the incomes, wealth and living standards of rich and poor people has increased in most countries. Prominent public figures, including the Pope, the managing director of the International Monetary Fund and numerous heads of state, have described current levels of inequality as unacceptable. Whether and how public policies should seek to narrow the gap between rich and poor remains controversial, however, and governments are often unwilling to accept the challenge in practice. Vested interests are at stake. There are also widely differing views about the causes, consequences and ethics of inequality. It is pertinent to ask what role the economics profession could and should play in these circumstances. Can it contribute to progress by improving public knowledge about key aspects of inequality, its causes and consequences? I think this would require a broader perspective than most mainstream economists evidently countenance. As a political economist, I have written this book to show a more effective way forward.

The book considers the patterns of inequality, the processes that cause it, the problems that result and the public policies that could reform it, given the political will to act. It is a work of committed scholarship, setting out to coolly consider the issues, the evidence and the competing currents of analysis that offer potentially progressive solutions. The style is transdisciplinary, looking at economic, social, political and environmental issues relating to inequality. These characteristics should make the book relevant to many fields of study, not only economics and political economy, but also sociology, political science, development studies, history and economic geography. Concurrently, the book seeks to engage the interest of non-academic readers. My personal contacts with people engaged in political parties, trade unions, NGOs and social movements lead me to think that there is a strong thirst 'out there' for a clear and reasonably concise book on this subject.

There are already many other books on this topic. Since the onset of the global financial crisis over a decade ago, an impressive array of publications has included Thomas Piketty's blockbuster *Capital in the Twenty-first Century* (2014) and useful contributions by James Galbraith, Joseph Stiglitz, Branko Milanovic, Danny Dorling and the late Tony Atkinson, among others. The *World Inequality Report*, first published in 2017, has given a boost to the public dissemination of relevant data on trends in inequality of incomes and wealth. What follows here draws on these and many other contributions, seeking a synthesis, developing the analysis and sharpening its implications. It considers key concepts in political economic analysis, examines the most up-to-date information, applies insights drawn from across the social sciences and explores the implications for policies and politics. I hope that this breadth of coverage, combined with clarity of exposition, will give the book wide appeal and interest.

All scholarly work has a collective character. Personally, I have been fortunate to be at the University of Sydney for most of my academic career, working in the School of Social and Political Sciences with colleagues in a Department of Political Economy who seek to make critically constructive contributions to knowledge, education and social change. Challenging economic orthodoxy and developing progressive alternatives are central to this collective enterprise. Scholarly work has a cumulative character too, reflected here in how the book builds on my previous books and articles on the topic over more than four decades, on new ideas and on the latest information from diverse sources. Making the coverage global has been the hardest challenge this time. Due attention cannot be given to every country and the focus is somewhat biased towards the English-speaking nations, reflecting the most likely locations of readers. However, I have tried to ensure that the data, analysis and examples reflect contemporary developments worldwide.

Some people deserve special thanks. David Primrose worked on this book as my research assistant, offering many useful suggestions as well as carefully preparing the statistical tables and figures. Franklin Obeng-Odoom provided feedback on an earlier draft and encouraged me to embrace southern and post-colonial perspectives alongside the other elements of political economy that shape the book's approach. Chris Sheil, my colleague at the Evatt Foundation in Australia, deserves my appreciation for his comments on an earlier draft and for his commitment to get the best data on distributional inequality. Ben Spies-Butcher, Jim Stanford and Phil Griffiths referred me to useful information. Thanks are also due to George Owers, assisted by Julia Davies, from Polity Press, who enthusiastically drove the publishing project and arranged for four anonymous referees to provide helpful feedback on the original proposal. Rachel Moore made the production arrangements for Polity. Justin Dyer did a great job of copy-editing. Neale Towart carefully prepared the index. Finally, my partner Ann Grealis has been, as ever, a marvellous supporter of my efforts.

I hope that the book will be useful to readers seeking to know what is happening in a world of economic inequality and what could make a difference. The royalties from the sale of the book will go to support Oxfam's campaign to reduce global inequality.

Frank Stilwell
Sydney, 2018

Preliminaries

1

Mind the Gap

Imagine you are watching a parade of the whole of the world's population. There are nearly 5 billion adults and they all walk past within an hour. The height of each person is proportional to their annual income – 1 centimetre per 100 euros. The poorest people come first and the wealthiest people come last. As the parade lasts only 60 minutes, it is like watching a fantastically speeded-up video.

For the first few minutes, however, it does not seem fast because, bizarrely, almost nothing is visible. It takes four minutes before tiny figures less than 10 centimetres high appear. The height of the marchers rises slowly but, after 15 minutes, they are only 28 centimetres tall. The people who have passed by during this first quarter of the parade live in various degrees of personal poverty. Taller people keep appearing but, at the 30 minutes mark, exactly halfway through the parade, they measure only 68 centimetres, which is up to about the level of your thigh.

During the second half of the parade, the height of the marchers rises more quickly. At the 45-minute mark, they stand 1.6 metres tall, nearing the average height of real adult people like you and me. At the 50-minute mark they are 2.4 metres tall. Then, at the 55-minute mark, they are 4 metres tall, more than twice the height of average adults in the real world. These are certainly rich people but, as the saying goes, 'You ain't seen nothing yet!' A much more dramatic surge occurs in the last few minutes of the parade. At the 58-minute mark, the marchers are 7.8 metres tall. At the

59-minute mark, they are a towering 21.5 metres. With about 10 seconds to go, their height reaches 100 metres.

Then, in the last two seconds of the grand parade, a truly amazing phenomenon occurs. The height of the giants rises from 250 metres to over 3,000 metres, about as tall as the highest mountain in the UK. Anyone who blinks during the last half-second would miss seeing these massive marchers. Even the alert onlookers find it hard to visualize just how tall they are because clouds shroud the tops of their bodies.

After the parade, most of the onlookers disperse, quietly mulling over what they have seen, but a few stay behind to discuss its significance. All are amazed at the incredible contrast between the tiny figures in the first half of the parade and the enormous giants towards the end. One person who had seen a similar parade about 25 years ago says there is now a sharper contrast among the marchers because those at the end have become so much taller. Another person wryly comments that the clouds that obscure the tallest giants' height may have something to do with tax havens in which some very rich people conceal their income. A third person notes that the typical skin colours of the people in this year's parade changed a lot as the hour progressed, people of African appearance being the most numerous in the first quarter of the parade and fair-skinned people hardly seen until after halfway. The person who had seen the earlier parade says she recalls that people of Asian appearances used to be mainly in the early stages of the parade, but they now seem a little more evenly spread across the ranks. As the last onlookers drift off, all agree that it has been a remarkably thought-provoking experience to see this parade of dwarfs and giants.

Depicting economic inequality in this way is a dramatic device. It is not novel: the Dutch economist Jan Pen introduced it decades ago (Pen 1971) and it has been used to depict income inequalities within individual nations (e.g. Stilwell 1993; Stilwell & Jordan 2007). Applied here to global income inequalities, the grand parade helps set the scene by showing that the extent of inequality is much greater than people usually think.

The reasons why people are often aware of the big picture are not hard to discern. Each of us is constrained by geography and history. We grow up in households and neighbourhoods that shape our understanding of what is normal. When we are children, our horizons seldom extend beyond the local village, suburb or town, where economic inequalities may be quite modest. Later we may travel further afield, whether for education, employment or enjoyment, and see a broader range of people's living conditions. There is also the internet and television, of course, providing us with images and information about people in distant lands and other regions. By accessing these media, we can widen our horizons without leaving home, but even the information we get through conventional channels often leaves us unaware of how remarkably unequal is the world in which we live. For most of us, the grand parade is quite an eye-opener, isn't it?

Considering inequality: its dimensions and intersections

Each of us is somewhere in that grand parade. We may wonder what determines where we are, whether near the front among the almost imperceptibly tiny figures, somewhere in the middle or at the rear among the towering giants. Is it all a matter of luck, or of how much effort we spend in our lives, studying hard, working hard, being thrifty and generally doing whatever it takes to achieve a higher standard of living? Did the people in the first half of the parade really 'deserve' to be so stunted because they failed to make those efforts? Did the giants at the rear work extraordinarily hard for their rewards; or did they just get lucky, 'choosing their parents wisely' and growing up in wealthy households that gave them enormous advantages from the start? Reflection on these matters can heighten awareness of what gives some people vastly greater opportunities and thereby perpetuates extreme economic inequalities.

We may also come to see economic inequality as multi-dimensional, forming distinctive patterns according to location, class, gender, race, ability and disability. Of these, location is the most obvious initial marker. The countries, regions or towns where people live vary enormously in their average standards of living. The opportunities for economic advancement are so much greater in some places than in others. Geography matters. So too do the intersections between location and the other factors bearing on people's life-chances, determining their economic situation and prospects. In terms of average incomes, the USA is a rich country while Nigeria is poor; but not all people in the USA are rich and not all people in Nigeria are poor. Indeed, some Nigerians are much richer than many people in the USA.

Class position is a key variable shaping who gets what. People who own substantial capital can get large incomes in the form of interest payments, profits or dividends paid on their shareholdings. People owning substantial tracts of land can get rental income and may benefit from capital gains as land values rise, all without expending any physical effort. These capitalists and landowners have a collective advantage over people whose only source of income is the sale of their personal capacity to work, receiving wage payments for their labour. Yet others, having neither income from property nor paid work, must do the best they can with whatever welfare payments or charity is available to help them subsist. Class is a pervasive influence on inequality within both affluent and poor nations.

Race is another dimension of economic inequality, interacting with location and class. The very tall people whom we witnessed during the last few minutes of that grand parade were mostly white-skinned, whereas Africans, Asians and Latinos were disproportionately numerous earlier on. Even when people migrate from poor to affluent countries, the markers of race may still loom large: in most multi-ethnic societies, the different groups vary considerably in their average incomes and living standards.

Likewise, gender is a major seam of economic inequality. In nearly all countries, there is a significant pay gap between the average wages paid to men and women and there are significant obstacles to achieving equal economic opportunities. These gender-based inequalities intersect with the inequalities according to class and race too. Working-class women of colour face much greater obstacles to achieving economic security and prosperity.

Abilities and disabilities also matter. Personal attributes that are greatly prized can lift particular individuals above the ranks of people with otherwise similar characteristics of location, class, race and gender. People with distinctive talents or skills that are highly valued 'in the market' may benefit from handsome remuneration. Not having these attributes can mean consignment to more marginalized positions. People with disabilities almost invariably face restricted economic opportunities.

Our social status, as well as our incomes and wealth, depends substantially upon these inequalities. So too may our personal identity. Status reflects how society sees us, whereas identity is more a matter of how we represent ourselves. These elements introduce a subjective element. Whereas location, class, race and gender are relatively objective attributes, status and identity are more malleable according to social judgements and personal emphasis. You may assert a personal identify according to your sexual preferences, your musical tastes or the sporting team you support, as well as where you live or what work you do. These can be important markers of life-style, sometimes compensating for an economically disadvantaged position by providing local prestige.

Sociologists exploring these features have traditionally distinguished between class, status and power. Class is all about economic position, based on relationships to the means of production – whether as employer or employee. Status relates to social esteem and may involve differentiation between people of the same class position according to whether they are blue- or white-collar workers, for example. Power derives primarily from command over resources, particularly where that involves control over other people, such as the power of business executives to hire and fire or the power of politicians to set the social rules. These three dimensions of inequality – class, status and power – tend to be broadly reinforcing but they are less than completely so. Therein lies considerable social complexity.

Looking primarily at the economic dimension of inequality is a way of cutting through this complexity. It focuses attention on who owns what and who gets what. It also directs attention to the drivers of inequality, such as the processes of globalization, financialization, neoliberalism and technological change that have been significantly re-shaping the economic environment during recent years. Studying inequality also requires analysis of the economic, social, environmental and political implications of these processes. We need to consider whether we are headed towards a more prosperous or a more insecure, inequitable and unsustainable future.

Recognizing competing viewpoints

Describing patterns of inequality – and considering their causes and consequences – almost invariably leads into discussion of what is fair and what is unfair. That, in turn, leads into asking what, if anything, should be done – and by whom? Should governments seek to narrow the gaps? It is at points like these that disagreements are likely to arise. Indeed, controversy is inevitable on a topic where consideration of the facts intertwines with ethical and political judgements. To clarify the principal positions, it is useful to broadly distinguish three competing viewpoints: conservative, liberal and radical.

A conservative view tends to regard whatever inequalities currently exist as 'natural'. Some people taking this view may have never thought seriously about the topic: theirs is a passive conservatism, based on disinterest in – or scepticism about – the possibility of change. Other, more assertive conservatives tend to be explicitly pro-inequality, believing that the current pattern of rewards directly reflects people's productive contributions and that meddling with this meritocratic situation would do more harm than good. This view is characteristic of neoliberal thought in the modern era. Implicitly, it assumes a trade-off between equality and economic growth, believing that attempts at egalitarian policies would reduce overall living standards. From this perspective, any attempt at social levelling would impair incentives, thereby 'killing the goose that lays the golden eggs' (that some people currently enjoy).

A liberal perspective produces a more critical view, inclined to an 'interventionist' politics. This is quite different from the neoliberal perspective, although the terminology is confusingly similar. The liberal view is not anti-capitalist, but it is less complacent than the neoliberal view about the beneficial effects of 'free markets'. Recognizing that monopoly can cause 'market distortions', liberals see a need for public policies to produce more meritocratic outcomes. Government taxes and expenditures that reduce income inequalities are the characteristic focus. Reformist views of this sort have a long lineage, nurtured by liberal and social democratic political philosophies and aspirations. They have received a renewed boost because of the difficult material conditions since the global financial crash of 2008–9. The stagnant wage incomes in the advanced capitalist nations during the last decade loom large in such deliberations.

A third view is more radical, echoing the liberal concerns about the adverse effects of excessive inequality but seeing the need for more fundamental political economic changes. The focus shifts from seeking reduced inequality of opportunity to seeking greater equality of outcomes. A more radical, even revolutionary, agenda beckons, challenging the dominant power of the wealthy. This is a more directly anti-capitalist perspective, emphasizing the embeddedness of existing inequalities in processes of exploitation that are innate to a capitalist economy. This view does not deny the legitimacy of liberal redistributive reforms but regards 'band aids' as insufficient to resolve the systemic injustices arising from extreme inequalities.

As always, when trying to deal with controversial issues, it is important to acknowledge the rival viewpoints. Subsequent chapters will explore and critically examine their theoretical foundations, raising questions about political possibilities for reform and transformation. Is it sufficient to promote equality of opportunity, or do we need to be concerned with greater equality of outcomes? If we actually want a more equal society, do we need to be trying to 'raise the floor' and 'lower the ceiling' as well as creating equality of opportunity in the intervening space? And how might this be done? Looking through a political economic lens can help when considering these controversial issues.

Taking a political economic approach

What does taking a political economic approach to the topic imply? Like any systematic study, it requires observation and analysis, facts and judgements. The modern meaning of the term 'political economy' also signals an alternative to mainstream economic orthodoxy. To see how the world actually works, we can draw from heterodox economic thought to develop a more coherent analysis of markets and states, economic institutions and the factors shaping production, distribution, exchange, accumulation, reproduction, growth and crises. It is a huge agenda (see, for example, Varoufakis, Halevi & Theodorakis 2011; Stilwell 2013; Reardon, Madi & Cato 2018; Tae-Hee, Chester & D'Ipolitti 2018). Four aspects of political economy are most relevant to our current purpose: its focus on inequality, its pluralist method, its transdisciplinary inclination and its ethical orientation.

A political economic approach makes *analysis of inequality* central to understanding the economy. The dominant and most influential school of economic thought – neoclassical economics – has been notably deficient in this respect. Historically, some of its pioneers explicitly sought not only to explain but also to justify the economic inequalities generated in free-market economies. Others developed theories about why economic welfare might be improved by making the distribution of incomes more equal. During recent decades, however, concern with economic inequality has tended to drop out of the picture. The mainstream economic models often simply take the existing distribution as given.

Microeconomics focuses largely on efficiency in the allocation of resources by markets. Macroeconomics has a dominant concern with overall economic performance and growth. Concern with the distribution of incomes or wealth is often said to be 'political' and hence not properly a matter for 'scientific' economic inquiry. Or it is set aside because of a belief that equity could only come at the considerable cost of lowered economic growth. This marginalization of inequality has raised the ire of many critics who see it as indicative of the narrowness and political bias of the orthodoxy. Giving greater prominence to the study of inequality is therefore central to the political economists' alternative.

Second, political economy has a *pluralist* method, recognizing that there are many ways to study economic phenomena. In this respect, modern political economy walks in the footsteps of the great thinkers from the eighteenth century onwards, including Adam Smith, David Ricardo, Karl Marx, John Stuart Mill, Thorstein Veblen and John Maynard Keynes. All of these pioneers of political economic analysis considered inequality an important issue in their attempts to understand how, and for whom, the capitalist economy functions, although they came up with notably different answers. A similar inclination continued during the second half of the twentieth century among leading contributors to the institutional, Marxist and post-Keynesian traditions of political economy: J.K. Galbraith, Michal Kalecki, Gunnar Myrdal and Joan Robinson made the study of economic inequality integral to their political economic analyses. Other modern scholars concerned with the problems of economic development and underdevelopment, such as Samir Amin, Ha-Joon Chang and Amartya Sen, have also placed the issue of inequality at the forefront of their studies. In other words, all the 'big thinkers' about economic issues have seen the study of inequality as an important aspect of economic inquiry. We need to draw on their diverse insights – and on the arguments and evidence of other modern researchers – to develop our political economic analysis. We need to look at heterodox economic perspectives – classical, institutional, Marxist, post-Keynesian, feminist and ecological – to see what is most valuable in understanding how the world actually works. A focus only on neoclassical economic theory and its offshoots cannot suffice.

Third, political economy has a *transdisciplinary* inclination. This is particularly important because of inequality's multi-dimensional character. While its most obvious economic manifestation is in terms of incomes (who gets what) and wealth (who owns what), people's social positions are also involved, as are questions of political power. Which of these aspects gets primary attention usually reflects the choice of social science perspective – geography, history, sociology, anthropology or political science, for example. The personal interests and goals of the investigator may also influence the focus of the inquiry – whether highlighting sources of class exploitation, challenging racism or gender discrimination or planning for less divided cities, for example. The analytical frame that is adopted influences what is regarded as worthy of investigation or simply *what is seen*. A neoclassical economic view, focusing on individuals rewarded according to their personal productivity, needs to be compared with more critical political economic perspectives that highlight the power-plays responsible for exploitation, discrimination and other forms of social injustice.

Fourth, a political economic approach has an *ethical* orientation, putting values, as well as matters of fact, on the agenda. Because the analysis of inequality is a study of winners and losers, it would be difficult, if not impossible, to maintain a completely 'value-free' stance on the topic, especially as discussion shifts from explanation to prescription. Therein lies much of the action in weighing up the pros and cons of conservative, liberal and radical views. Ethical and political judgements are necessary, especially when assessing the capacity of governments to undertake progressive reforms. Analysis of policy prescriptions requires consideration of the goals that those policies are supposed to serve. In practice, values infuse all policy-oriented study: a political economic analysis simply says the values should be explicit rather than implicit – better blatant than latent. As the book progresses, the basis for making judgements of this sort will be carefully considered.

Studying what shapes inequality

Some degree of abstraction from the mind-boggling complexity of the real world is necessarily involved when analysing inequality. We need to develop a framework for identifying and analysing the interrelationships between the key variables. Figure 1.1 on the next page makes a start, providing a foretaste of what is to come. This is the book's 'road map' for studying the political economy of inequality.

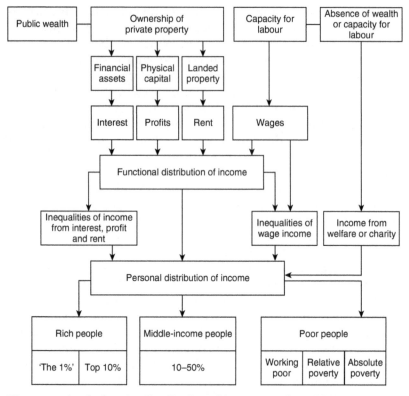

Figure 1.1 Analysing the distribution of incomes and wealth

The top left of Figure 1.1 distinguishes between public wealth and privately owned property. The top right notes the other great economic resource – people's capacity for labour. It also acknowledges the presence of people who have neither wealth nor income from work. The next row indicates the forms in which those who have private wealth hold it (whether as financial assets, physical capital or land) and the types of income that these assets produce (interest, profits and rents). The profit generated by businesses flows partly to (some) households as dividends on shareholdings. Meanwhile, (most) people are primarily reliant on selling their capacity to work for wages. The relative sizes of these different types of income – from wealth and work – is shown a little lower in the diagram as the 'functional distribution of income', so named because it reflects the different economic functions performed by the owners of assets and the suppliers of labour. Looking into this distribution shows what proportion of the total income in the economy goes to the owners of income-generating private wealth and what proportion goes to workers. People having neither income from assets nor the capacity to work do not feature here at all.

Then, moving to the lower parts of the diagram, we see the other main determinants of the 'personal distribution of income' among individuals or households. The key additional influences here are: (a) inequalities among incomes from interest, profits and rent; and (b) inequalities among the wage incomes. Rates of return to asset owners can be highly variable, which is why people and institutions seeking capital accumulation frequently adjust their asset portfolios to get the best rates of return. Wage incomes vary enormously too, ranging from the enormous salaries paid to the chief executive officers (CEOs) in transnational corporations to the more modest payments most workers receive for their efforts, sometimes so modest that their recipients live in poverty. Those workers may not be much better off than people who lack the capacity or opportunity for waged work and are dependent on welfare payments or charity.

The inequalities in the personal distribution of income, as shown at the bottom of the diagram, therefore reflect a multiplicity of interconnecting factors. To categorize the individuals as rich, middle-income or poor is a crude first approximation, of course, but it is an early pointer to where the analysis takes us. It is the relationships between who owns what (in the top half of the diagram) and who gets what (in the lower half) that is crucial.

This depiction of the key variables gets us started on the analysis of inequality. It introduces the four key dimensions:

- the division between public and private wealth;
- inequality of private wealth;
- the division of total income into labour and non-labour shares;
- inequality in the distribution of personal incomes.

The principal focus here is on what economists call 'market incomes': that is, before the effects of any income redistribution by government are considered. Yet governments in practice do play significant roles in distribution and redistribution, and we will have much more to say about this in later chapters: a glance ahead to Figure 10.1 on p. 178 provides a foretaste.

Looking ahead

The following chapters develop the political economic analysis of inequality by looking at patterns, processes, problems, policies and prospects. These 'five P's' raise sequential questions. What *patterns* does economic inequality take around the world today? What *processes* drive those inequalities? What *problems* result? What *policies* might make a difference? What are the *prospects* for future change?

Some *preliminaries* come first. A chapter on methodological issues immediately follows this general introduction. It explores what we mean by inequality and introduces useful concepts for its systematic study. It looks at different interpretations of income, wealth, wellbeing, poverty and development, and at the different ways in which these may be measured. It also considers the bases on which we may make judgements about equity. This chapter is not light reading, and readers impatient to get to see the evidence on patterns of inequality 'out there' in the real world could consider skipping it. Better not to, however, because it is important to be aware of what shapes the political economic lens through which we will be looking.

The bulk of the empirical evidence comes in the next three chapters. This is the most data-rich section of the book. Chapter 3 shows the principal contours of current inequalities – between nations, within nations and globally. Chapter 4 looks at how the shares of income and wealth have shifted during recent years between the world's richest and poorest people and the broad group in-between. Chapter 5 takes a more disaggregated approach to studying inequality, recognizing location, class, gender, race, age, ability and disability as seams along which major socio-economic divisions occur. This shows the social dimensions that structure inequalities and what attributes shape where people stand in unequal societies.

Seeking to make sense of these patterns, the following two chapters begin the process of explaining who gets what. This is not 'theorizing for theory's sake', but a process of trying to understand the forces that shape the nature and extent of inequality. Chapter 6 looks at rival theories that have featured in the development of economic analysis. It explains the conventional economic theories of 'marginal productivity' and 'human capital', liberal economic views that emphasize 'market distortions' and radical views that analyse class power. Then, in chapter 7, we look at processes that cause inequality to increase over time, as has been the case within nearly all nations in recent decades. The focus is on the broad political economic drivers, including globalization, financialization, neoliberalism, technological change and urbanization. This chapter seeks to develop the 'big picture' of income inequality and wealth concentration in a changing world.

The next part of the book poses the 'so what?' question, asking why inequality matters anyway. As already noted, some people see inequality as 'natural', even beneficial for economic prosperity. Chapter 8 reviews evidence and arguments that strongly support a contrary view – that extreme inequality reduces social wellbeing. It discusses the links between inequality and the intensity of economic, social, environmental and political problems. It also raises concerns about peace, prosperity, democracy and human rights. Chapter 9 follows on with a complementary but somewhat different line of inquiry, discussing what makes us happy. Will becoming richer do the trick, as many people surmise? Or does it depend on our relationship to how others are faring? Does the happiness of a society depend, more generally, on how evenly incomes and wealth are distributed? The chapter concludes that the elimination of poverty is necessary but not sufficient. The size of the rich–poor gap is also crucial for our collective wellbeing, perhaps even for our survival. Here is a strong case for pursuing egalitarian policies and strategies.

What could governments do to narrow the gap? The next three chapters examine the policy options. Chapter 10 considers how different forms of taxation and government spending redistribute incomes. Chapter 11 digs deeper, looking at strategies to reshape the 'market' distribution of income and wealth before any such redistributions occur. Chapter 12 then turns attention to the challenge of reducing international inequalities. The capacity of the existing international institutions to promote balanced and sustainable development is necessarily in the spotlight here.

Finally, the book asks about the overall prospects for change. Should we be optimistic or pessimistic about the potential to create equitable societies? Can radical reforms, or even mildly progressive redistribution, be effective? The concluding two chapters weigh the options. Chapter 13 looks on the gloomy side, identifying four big obstacles – ignorance, ideologies, interests and institutions – and discusses how to address them. Then, putting on rather more rose-tinted spectacles, chapter 14 presents a positive assessment, signalling principles and prospects for progress.

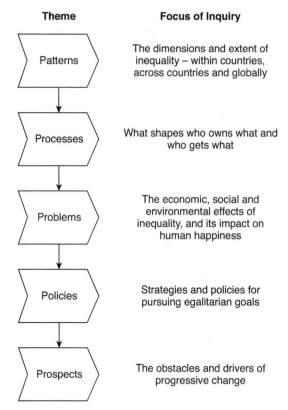

Figure 1.2 Themes in the political economy of inequality

The book's overall structure is summarized in Figure 1.2. Moving from the study of patterns to processes, problems, policies and prospects has a sequential logic, as explained above. It also has a progressive character because it takes us from the study of *what is* and *why* to the study of *what could be* and *how* it might occur.

Treating the topic in this careful, sequential manner is an alternative to remaining in a state of 'blissful ignorance'. Some people evidently prefer the latter, regarding discussion of inequality as a 'turn-off'. Conservatives claim it fosters unnecessary social conflict and call it an 'economics of envy', a 'politics of discord', even fostering 'class warfare'. Liberals also tremble at the last prospect. True, analysis of inequality does put contentious issues in the spotlight. However, as we shall see, the conflicts do not derive from talking about the topic: they reflect the underlying material conditions. Ignorance is not 'blissful' if it leaves the way open for increasing social stresses. Better to seek knowledge of the sources of inequality and the potential remedies. This is the antidote to both ignorance and prejudice, and the prerequisite for purposeful action. By the end of this book, readers should have a clearer understanding of the situation and a better sense of what could be done about it.

Conclusion

Concern with the distribution of income and wealth has a central place in political economic analysis and needs to have a similarly central place in strategies for social progress in the real world. This book seeks to contribute by clarifying the dimensions of economic inequality, analysing its causes and consequences and considering the challenges of reducing it. This introductory chapter has set the scene by:

- presenting a simple but dramatic depiction of how economic inequality looks in the modern world;
- showing why economic inequality matters and what we need to know about it;
- indicating how the necessary knowledge and understanding may be advanced.

'Mind the gap' is a familiar, cautionary warning on trains, ferries and buses. Using the phrase as the title of this introductory chapter sends three pertinent signals – to be mindful, to care and to beware. We need thoughtful awareness of the gap between rich and poor people's material living conditions in modern societies. We need to be mindful of the ramifications for our collective well-being and future prospects. We need to consider actions that could address the challenges posed by inequality and make a difference. For these purposes, our first requirement is clear concepts and effective tools for studying incomes, wealth, poverty and equity.

2

Incomes, Wealth, Poverty and Equity

Complex inquiries like the study of economic inequality need systematic analysis. We need to decide which aspects should receive primary attention, how to frame the issues and what tools are appropriate for the task.

This chapter makes a start by looking at the distinctions between income and wealth and between public and private wealth. It reviews different measures of inequality, considers the nature of poverty and development and discusses the shift from describing inequality to making judgements about equity or fairness. Readers who feel that they already have an adequate knowledge of economic concepts and statistics might consider skipping or skimming this chapter (with the option of returning later). However, we need to be clear about what we are doing when we distinguish between stocks and flows, individuals and households, absolute poverty and relative poverty, capital and labour, equality of opportunity and equality of outcome. We also need to be clear about what we are measuring, how and why. Getting these foundational concerns sorted early enables clearer progress afterwards. Thus, while this is the most 'definitional' of the chapters in the book, it lays important groundwork for subsequent analysis of how the countries of the world look when we view them through a 'political economy of inequality' lens.

Distinguishing between income and wealth

Income is the usual starting point for discussions of economic inequality. Our incomes constrain what we can afford to buy and shape our standards of living. Flows of income may be intermittent or unreliable. Losing your job, for example, can be traumatic because it stops the flow of wage income. If you have some savings or incomes from other sources, however, you may still be able to live comfortably. It is therefore useful to consider the assets that people own as well as their current incomes. We need to look at who owns what as well as who gets what.

Whereas income is a flow, wealth is a stock. This important distinction is conflated in common parlance when people with high incomes are described as wealthy. It is tidier to limit the term 'wealth' to the ownership of assets. These assets may be either physical (such as land, housing, business premises, cars and jewellery) or financial (including cash, bank deposits, shares, bonds, derivatives and foreign currency). They are commonly a mix of both. Owning assets creates a buffer that can be helpful if current incomes stop, for whatever reason. It also provides a source of incomes, usually in the form of interest payments, rent or profits. 'Who gets what' depends substantially on 'who owns what'.

The distribution of wealth is almost invariably more unequal than the distribution of income. In a capitalist economy based on private ownership, a minority of the population usually own most of the income-producing capital assets. Inequalities of income and wealth are also mutually reinforcing. Businesses and households with high incomes can afford to buy capital assets. Having those assets then makes it easier to generate even more income. It is a virtuous cycle that works comfortably well for those enjoying its advantages. Transmitting wealth inter-generationally through inheritance reproduces and reinforces its concentration. Accumulated wealth also conveys economic power, commonly enabling wealth owners to influence the rules of the economic game. Understanding the relationship between wealth and incomes is a key element in the analysis of inequality.

A useful way of thinking about this relationship, for any individual person or household, is in terms of an analogy with water flowing in and out of a bathtub. Income is what flows into the tub from the tap: it may be a gush or it may be a trickle, even just a drip. Wealth is the water in the tub, the volume of which is evident from its surface level. So, if income exceeds spending (because some of the income is saved), wealth increases. The level of the bathwater rises. So far, so good. In the real world of income and wealth, however, the story is more complicated, for four reasons.

First, a substantial volume of wealth almost invariably generates a flow of more income, received in the form of interest payments, profits and rents. In effect, if you are fortunate enough to have a lot of water already in the tub, then the tap will flow faster. This is a hydraulic miracle for those who enjoy soaking in deep bathwater.

Second, having substantial wealth adds to the possibility of benefiting from capital gains. If the market values of capital goods are rising over time, the owners of these goods become wealthier without expending any effort. The reverse may also be true, of course: reductions in capital value erode wealth. Over time, however, inflationary processes are more prevalent, especially for assets like land whose supply is relatively fixed. Thus, even more miraculously, the level of the bathwater tends to rise even without turning on the tap.

Third, a substantial volume of wealth itself creates an alternative form of income. Assets may be sold ('liquidated') if the income flow is interrupted. In terms of the bathwater analogy, this means that there is a feedback loop between the level of the bathwater and the tap. A temporary interruption to the water supply is therefore no problem. In other words, for wealthy people, 'relaxing in a well-filled tub' (or luxury spa) is not particularly threatened by short-term income fluctuations.

Fourth, because wealth is transmitted inter-generationally (through gifts or bequests), its recipients can enjoy the benefits of being wealthy without having to generate their own income. In effect, these recipients of free baths do not need to run their own water. Miraculously, the water quantity remains abundant and its temperature need never go cold ...

Public and private wealth

Private wealth, as just discussed, comprises assets owned by individuals, households or businesses. This is not the full story, however. There is also public wealth, comprising collectively owned assets, often crucial to the functioning of whole economies and societies: roads, railways, bridges, schools and universities, hospitals, public parks, public museums and art galleries, infrastructure for essential services. The quantity and quality of this public wealth vary enormously from country to country, depending on their historical experience and the willingness and ability of their governments to levy sufficient taxes to fund the development of public facilities. Effective management of the assets, including replacement of depreciated assets, is also important in maintaining the public wealth. Working in the opposite direction are policies such as privatization. Governments in many countries, seeking to expand the opportunities for private businesses to make more profits, have sold off former public enterprises, infrastructure and services during recent decades. This has created a substantial shift from public wealth to private wealth, as depicted by Figure 2.1.

For each of the six countries represented in the diagram, the share of public wealth has markedly declined (as a percentage of total national wealth) over the last four decades. These countries range across different continents and different types of government. In China, public ownership was formerly very high, the development of public enterprises having been a key feature of the communist regime established in the 1950s. In recent decades, some have been sold to private interests as the country's economy has been steered along a capitalist road (while retaining an

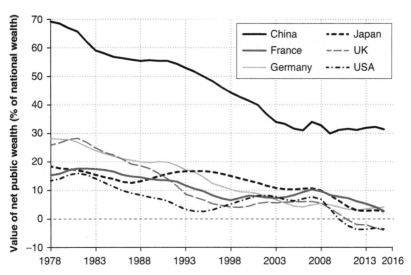

Figure 2.1 The decline of public wealth, 1978–2016

Source: Alvaredo et al. (2018).

authoritarian state). In the other capitalist countries shown in the diagram, privatization policies have produced a similar downward trend in public wealth, albeit starting from a lower base.

The relative sizes of public and private wealth matter. Public wealth directly benefits society as a whole, especially where it takes the form of infrastructure and public facilities. It can also generate income that helps to finance the provision of public services. In addition, public wealth, especially when used to make services freely or cheaply available, creates an important safety net for people who have no private wealth. Privatization has the reverse effect, making people more vulnerable to the vagaries of the market. This is particularly stressful for poor people, whose meagre resources are insufficient to pay for privately provided services. Put simply: if there were abundant public wealth, the inequality of private wealth would be less important. However, because widespread privatizations have shrunk public wealth, the inequalities of access to essential services have tended to be more problematic.

It is important to bear this issue of public/private wealth imbalance in mind as we proceed to examine private wealth inequalities and their determinants. Being a collective asset, public wealth cannot feature in the statistics on wealth distribution. It is nevertheless crucial to the functioning of a productive economy and a healthy society.

Defining and measuring inequality

In studying economic inequality, we need robust measures. Otherwise, we are unable to compare the extent of inequality in different nations or to know whether it is increasing or decreasing over time. This turns out to be quite a complex issue but, for simplicity, we can proceed in three steps.

First, we need to decide exactly what we want to measure. Is it inequality of incomes or wealth? Is it inequalities between individuals or households? If the latter, do we want to compare households according to their total incomes, irrespective of the number and relationship of the people within each household? Alternatively, should we try to standardize for different household compositions (thereby taking account of how variation in household composition affects each household's actual spending power)? Do we want to measure inequality before or after taxes paid to governments are deducted (i.e. gross or net income)? There is no general rule on these matters – it all depends on what is your interest.

Second, we need to have an overall picture of how unevenly the chosen variable (whether wealth or income, before or after tax) is distributed between the chosen units (individuals, households or 'equivalized' households). Figure 2.2 shows this in the form of a Lorenz curve. The population is on the horizontal axis of this graph and the variable in whose inequality we are interested (e.g. income) is on the vertical axis. A 45° diagonal line shows the hypothetical situation of complete equality in the distribution. The actual distribution is always a bowed line, which is the Lorenz curve. The greater the inequality in the distribution, the larger is the area between the Lorenz curve and the 45° line.

The third step is to calculate a statistical measure of the extent of variation in the distribution. Working from the Lorenz curve, this means getting a statistic to show how much the bowed line deviates from the diagonal line. The standard way of doing this is by calculating a *Gini coefficient*. This is the area between the Lorenz curve and the 45° line (i.e. area A in Figure 2.2) expressed as a proportion of the total area below that line (i.e. area A + B). The greater the inequality, the higher the Gini coefficient.

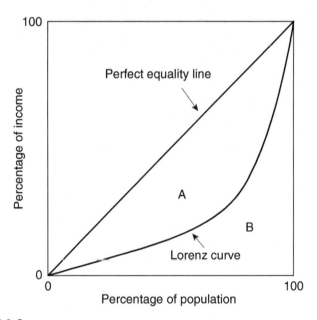

Figure 2.2 Lorenz curve

Although the Gini coefficient is the most widely used measure of inequality, it is subject to some significant limitations. As a statistical artefact, it does not signal the specific dimensions of inequality that exist in society (e.g. what proportion of people get what proportion of the total income). Moreover, different types of deviation from complete equality can produce similar values of the measured Gini. A large increase in the income share of the people in the top 1% of the distribution, for example, may have less impact on the Gini than an increase in the income share of the people in the middle relative to those at the bottom. The Gini tends to be less sensitive to the tails of the distribution than to the middle, which is a particular problem when much of the income or wealth is in the hands of the top 1% of the population (Alvaredo 2011). This bias is greater when household surveys of incomes and wealth under-sample the super-rich, as they commonly do.

For these reasons, some analysts prefer more specifically targeted measures of inequality, such as *decile, quartile and quintile ratios*. The decile ratio is the income (or wealth) of the top 10% of the population divided by the income (or wealth) of the bottom 10%; the quartile ratio compares the top 20% and the bottom 20%; and the quartile ratio the top 25% and the bottom 25%. One useful variation is the *Palma ratio*, which shows the relative size of the incomes (or wealth) of the top 10% and the incomes (or wealth) of the bottom 40%. The former often have more than the latter, in absolute terms, pushing the calculated value of the Palma ratio above unity.

An alternative measure of inequality focuses on the relationship between particular points near the top and bottom ends of the distribution. These are so-called *percentile measures of inequality*. One such measure is the P90:P10 ratio, showing how the income of the household 10% from the top of the distribution compares with the income of the household 10% from the bottom. In effect, this compares the situations of the relatively well off (but not the extremely rich) with the relatively poor (but not the very poor). If, for example, the household 10% from the top had an annual income of $100,000 and the household 10% from the bottom had an annual income of $20,000, the P90:P10 ratio would be 5:1. Comparing different nations according this sort of measure can be useful.

A yet more direct inequality measure is the *share of the total income (or wealth) going to the top percentile* of individuals (or households) in the population. This focus on the top (1%) relative to

Table 2.1 Illustrative measures of inequality for selected countries: latest available data

	Gini coefficient[a,b]	Decile ratio[b]	Top 1% share[c]
South Africa	0.62	25.6	19.2
Sweden	0.28	3.3	8.7
UK	0.36	4.2	13.9
USA	0.39	6.1	20.2

Notes: [a] Gini coefficient based on disposable income, post-taxes and transfers; [b] data for Gini coefficient and GP90:P10 ratio is for 2015; source: *https://stats.oecd.org/Index.aspx?DataSetCode=IDD* (accessed: 15 January 2018); [c] data for top 1% shares relate to share of pre-tax national income: source: *http://wid.world/data/* (accessed: 15 January 2018): South African data for 2012; Swedish data for 2013; US and UK data for 2014.

the rest (99%) reflects the concern with extreme inequality and the extent of its concentration. Variations on this theme include looking at the share of the total held by the top 10% or top 0.1%: the former considers a broad stratum of well-to-do people whereas the latter highlights an elite comprising just the richest one thousandth of the population. Looking at the shares of the 0.01% (as we will do in chapter 4) narrows the focus yet more – to the disproportionate share of the tiny elite-within-an-elite.

Does it matter which of these various measures is used? They are all indicators of inequality, but they have somewhat differing characteristics and emphases. For illustrative purposes, Table 2.1 shows three of them, calculated for household incomes in four countries, chosen because of their very different distributional characteristics. The three indicators are the Gini coefficient, the P90:P10 ratio and the share of national income going to the top 1% of households.

It is obvious from Table 2.1 that, of the four countries, South Africa is the most unequal according to the first two measures. This is hardly surprising because, with its history of dispossession, apartheid and racial inequality, South Africa is well known as a country in which the affluence of an elite contrasts strikingly with the very low incomes of the majority of people. The USA comes in second place, albeit a long way behind, according to the same two indicators. Interestingly, though, the third inequality indicator shows the USA as more unequal: its richest 1% of people have a bigger share of the US national income than the equivalent 1%'s share in South Africa. Evidently, both of the countries have very unequal societies but their inequalities take different forms. At the other extreme, Sweden comes out lowest on all three of the inequality indicators in Table 2.1. This country has a reputation for being one of the most egalitarian societies in the world. The UK has an intermediate position according to each of the indicators.

How do inequalities like these relate to the different types of income received by workers, capitalists and landowners? Exploring this question takes us to the next step in the analysis. It raises some quite different issues, leading towards consideration of class relationships affecting the flows of wages, profits, interest and rent. The relative size of each of these different types of income in the total national income warrants careful consideration.

The functional distribution of income

Disaggregating total income according to the function performed by its recipients – whether supplying labour, capital or land – provides a type of distributional measure that is important in political economic analysis. Looking back to the centre of Figure 1.1, we can see that this is the 'functional distribution of income'. Incomes to labour come primarily as wages and salaries paid for work. Incomes to the owners of capital come in the form of profit (which may be passed on to shareholders as dividend payments) or as interest payments on capital that is loaned. Income to land-owners comes as rental payments for the use of their property. The relative size of these types of income – the 'factor shares' – is what the 'functional distribution' is about. It is a different measure of income distribution from the 'personal distribution', as shown at the bottom of Figure 1.1, although the former certainly influences the latter. Broadly speaking, as one blogger breezily puts it, it shows the relative size of incomes people get from 'doing stuff'' and 'owning stuff' (Roth 2018).

Figure 2.3, compiled by the International Monetary Fund (IMF), shows what has happened to the functional distribution world-wide since the mid-twentieth century, with emphasis on labour's share in the total income (i.e. what proportion goes to workers for 'doing stuff'). It shows a significantly downward trend. In the first half of the last century, economists generally regarded the apparent long-term stability in the functional distribution of income as a 'stylized fact'. We now know differently – stylized, yes, but fact, no. Although subject to some short-term fluctuations, the dominant feature of the last half-century has been a declining share of income

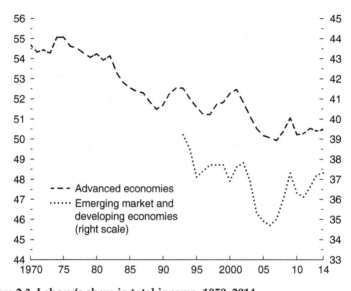

Figure 2.3 Labour's share in total income, 1950–2014

Source: International Monetary Fund, *http://www.imf.org/en/Publications/WEO/ Issues/2017/04/04/world-economic-outlook-april-2017#Chapter 3, p. 122.*

going to labour. This is clearest for the advanced economies, where labour's share has fallen from about 55% in 1970 to below 40%. The trend has not been uniform across all nations, though. In Korea, Greece, Switzerland and Japan, labour's share rose from the 1970s to the 2010s. However, in many more countries, including the USA, the UK, Australia, New Zealand and almost all of Northern and Western Europe, labour's share fell (Stanford 2018: 18). The data series for the poorer nations (bracketed together in Figure 2.3 with Russia and other former communist states designated as 'emerging market economies') has a shorter time-series but points generally downwards over a 20-year period.

Looking at the functional distribution of income can be a window to a class perspective on inequality. In the data shown in Figure 2.3, only two categories are used – labour income and non-labour income – so it is possible to interpret this as the incomes of the working class and the rest (comprising the capitalist class and a landed property class). However, making such inferences requires caution because of technical problems in how incomes are classified (Roth 2018; Stanford 2018). One such problem is that the incomes of managers are treated as labour incomes but, particularly in the case of CEOs of large corporations, that 'labour' is directly working for the interests of capital. Another problem arises because some income-recipients, such as small farmers, self-employed trades-people and owners of family businesses, have both labour and capital components in their economic activities: apportionment of their 'mixed incomes' between payments for capital and labour may be somewhat arbitrary.

Moreover, factor shares do not completely align with class positions, because some households receive some income from ownership of capital or land as well as incomes from labour. Indeed, that is commonly the case among the relatively well-off working-class people in the more affluent nations. Many workers also receive interest payments on their bank deposits (although they invariably pay higher interest rates on their loans). Some households may also receive dividend payments on small shareholdings, giving them a minor stake in the income from capital. This tends to blur the class divisions between households. Fundamentally, these difficulties are intrinsic in looking at class from a purely distributional perspective: class in capitalist society is more fundamentally a matter of who does what rather than size of incomes. Yet, of course, distribution matters.

When looking at the non-labour share of total income (or 'gross operating surplus'), some other complications arise. Rent, for example, counts as part of this surplus, but it goes to landowners rather than capitalists (Collins 2018). Some political economists also argue for distinguishing the share of income going to the finance sector. Indeed, this can have significant implications from a policy perspective in modern capitalist societies when landed property and financial institutions wield considerable economic power (Hein et al. 2007; Peetz 2018). Empirically, however, it is quite difficult to distinguish between these shares because of the interpenetration of the ownership patterns and incomes going to capital, finance and land.

The functional distribution, even in its simplest form as a means of distinguishing between labour incomes and non-labour incomes, is a useful device. It helps to show whether, over time, workers are getting a growing, stable or declining share in the total value of goods and services that their labour helps to create. It is an indicator of how the fruits of economic activity are distributed between those who derive their income from wage labour and those who derive theirs from owning land and capital assets.

Defining and measuring poverty

What about the have-nots? Some people receive no significant income from labour, capital or land. They may be people with physical or mental disabilities who are marginalized from the economic mainstream. They may be people who do have the capacity to work but are unemployed because there are no suitable jobs on offer in their locality. There are also the 'working poor': people who do have jobs but whose wage rates are so low, working hours are so few or employment is so irregular that they barely manage to get by. But what do we really mean when we talk of people living in poverty? Is it just the absence or inadequacy of current income? Or, if poverty implies unmet human needs, what are those needs? Are they purely material – for food, clothing and shelter – or are they also social? Is poverty the inability to achieve standards necessary for living with dignity relative to other people within that society?

Within a large literature on the nature and measurement of poverty (summarized by Serr 2017), one recurrent theme is the distinction between two types of poverty. One is *absolute poverty*, which implies falling below a specified level of income or access to resources. This level may be set at basic human sustenance or, rather more generously, at a standard enabling people to live with dignity and modest material comforts. Having defined that level and collected the relevant data, the proportion of households that fall below the absolute poverty line can be measured. On this basis, one may infer that if, say, one in five households has insufficient means to provide for its basic needs, there is a substantial incidence of poverty.

Relative poverty is different. Its incidence depends on making a judgement about how the economic resources available to poor households relate to the resources of other households in the population. For example, the relative poverty line can be set at half of the median income level in that society. This simple and quite widely used measure implies that any household having less than that amount is living in poverty.

Both types of measure have their limitations. The former ignores the overall income distribution, whereas the latter ignores basic physical need. In the extreme case of a very poor society where even the median-income household has insufficient nutrition, the relative poverty approach would markedly understate the severity of poverty. At the other extreme, the relative poverty measure in a very affluent society may appear rather generous. These are difficult judgements to make. Pragmatically, a compromise is workable, recognizing that humans have both basic material and socially relative needs. Thus, a person may be defined as being poor if s/he lacks sufficient food, clothing or shelter *and* has an income that is less than half the median income in that society. Households that satisfy one or other of the two criteria, but not both, are in an intermediate category, perhaps labelled 'quite poor' or 'near poor'.

Other concepts of poverty emphasize its multi-dimensional character, paying more attention to its causes and consequences and acknowledging that non-economic measures may be as important as economic ones. Social welfare indicators relating to health, education and security may be included, making the identification of a poverty line or a poverty rate more sophisticated, albeit harder to measure. Similarly, a broader consideration of deprivation and social exclusion can illuminate the complex realities of people's lived experience and the interplay of various forms of disadvantage. Deprivation may include a lack of access to services such as public transport, whereas social exclusion draws on the notion of multi-dimensional poverty and the interaction of various factors over time. It can include consideration of how 'causes', such as unemployment and low incomes, and 'outcomes', such as poor health, high crime and family breakdown, manifest as accumulated responses. Applied to areas, not only to individuals, this more multi-dimensional conception of poverty can be useful in understanding problems of community malfunction.

Analysis of poverty can also recognize people's capabilities and whether these are fulfilled. The Indian economist Amartya Sen has been a persistent and influential advocate for seeing poverty as *capability-deprivation* or, in other words, the denial of human possibilities. The requirements for full functioning can range from basic needs, such as being healthy, safe and having good work, to more complex requirements for being fulfilled or happy. The escape from poverty is characterized by having the freedom to achieve these human possibilities (Sen 1980, 1999; Bose 2013; Nussbaum 2000). Because people's characteristics and aspirations differ, however, it is rather difficult to provide across-the-board measures on this basis (Dean 2009). Critics have also pointed out that Sen's approach pays insufficient attention to the contexts in which individual actions occur, reducing its value in studying culturally heterogeneous societies and for cross-cultural comparisons. A structural view sees poverty more as a symptom of the deeper problem of wealth being highly concentrated between and within societies.

Yet Sen's way of seeing poverty as capability-deprivation has been influential, for example, in driving the development of broad-based indicators of human and social progress. The Human Development Index (HDI) is the best known of these measures, regularly featuring in publications by the United Nations (UN) in recent decades. Focusing on nations, rather than on individuals or households, HDI helps to identify the conditions and the countries where poverty is most likely to occur. When combined with data of income inequality, such as the UN's Inequality-Adjusted HDI (which we will be considering shortly), a direct link between poverty and inequality is established.

These deliberations have two implications. First is the recognition that, ultimately, we cannot eliminate poverty without also reducing economic inequality. When looking at relative poverty, this is true by definition because where there is economic inequality there will always be some households with less than half of the median income of the society. It is also generally true when absolute poverty is the concern: ongoing improvement in the material conditions of the poor, including adequacy of food, clothing and shelter, has to be part of a broader change to patterns and processes of distribution. The other implication is that the deeper we delve into questions of poverty and deprivation the greater is the need to consider what constitutes wellbeing and development: one is the inverse of the other.

From poverty to wellbeing and development

Human development implies a notion of wellbeing that is applicable to whole societies, even to generally affluent ones, and includes consideration of whether the members of those societies share the fruits of progress. Escaping from poverty is a necessary but not sufficient condition for achieving this goal.

Creating good measures of progress is a challenge for social scientists. The conventional measure of progress used by mainstream economists is gross domestic product. GDP is the total market value of the goods and services produced within a nation in any one year, regardless of how or where those products go or who gets the incomes created by their production. How sensible is it to treat GDP per capita (i.e. the average income per person) as the principal measure of material wellbeing in a nation? Many senior public figures have expressed scepticism about doing so. US President J.F. Kennedy said in 1961 that 'economic growth without social progress lets the great majority of people remain in poverty, while a privileged few reap the benefits of rising abundance'; and his brother Robert Kennedy subsequently chimed in with the memorable statement that GDP 'measures everything in short except which makes life worthwhile'. GDP is a consistent, economic standard but, when applied as a measure of national wellbeing, it has serious limitations, as critics of this approach regularly note (Stilwell 2000: ch. 22; Stiglitz, Sen & Fitoussi 2009; Fioramonti 2013).

First are the sins of omission. GDP excludes some valuable goods and services that are necessary for economic and social reproduction. Households produce many of these directly for their own consumption, rather than for exchange in the market. Indeed, much household production and voluntary work is of this character. Not counting all this valuable production in GDP is a significant omission if the aim is to get a good guide to actual wellbeing. Similarly, the time spent in producing marketable goods and services is not considered, even though there may be a high 'opportunity cost' of that time in terms of leisure or other pursuits forgone.

A second problem arises because some forms of expenditure counting towards GDP involve only damage repair. If you smash your car in a traffic accident, the cost of the work done by a panel-beater in repairing the damage adds to GDP. A nation may boost its GDP by being at war, especially if there is increased production of armaments, and then post-war reconstruction may extend the boost. The costs of cleaning up environmental damages resulting from production and consumption similarly increase GDP. This all looks like double counting. Indeed, including these 'defensive expenditures' in GDP further strains its credibility as a measure of economic or social wellbeing.

A third problem, most important in the context of this book, is the absence of a distributional dimension in conventional GDP calculations. GDP, as an aggregate, is unaffected by whether the goods and services are consumed by a small group or widely shared among all the people. This makes the link between GDP and social wellbeing look even more tenuous.

Most economists seem to regard this critique of GDP as like water off a duck's back: it does not soak in. They say that the problem is not with GDP but with its misuse for social judgement. Indeed, twentieth-century economists, such as Simon Kuznets, who were prominent in developing GDP-based national income accounting warned against its use as a measure of overall wellbeing. The GDP concept has provided the basis for a consistent international standard of economic measurement, and GDP per capita remains the normal primary indicator of the average material living standard in different countries (Philipsen 2015). On this reasoning, (mis) using it as a measure of social wellbeing or development – or just prioritizing it as a policy goal – is not something for which the economists should be held accountable. Yet the critique of GDP does invite consideration of what would be alternative and better measures of progress.

Famously, the tiny Himalayan kingdom of Bhutan, where a Buddhist way of life prevails, has rejected GDP in favour of the concept of 'gross national happiness'. A more pragmatic 'western' option is to use indicators of welfare that combine measures of consumption with other data on mortality rates, leisure and inequality (e.g. Jones & Clenow 2016). The *genuine progress indicator* (GPI) is a variation on this theme that gives a rounded measure of material wellbeing. It modifies the GDP by adding in values for household production and leisure, subtracting 'defensive expenditures' and adjusting to take account of the extent of inequality (Hamilton 2003: 55–61). Comparing these GPI estimates with the conventional GDP measure commonly reveals a widening gulf between the rates of measured economic growth and 'genuine progress' in economically developed nations (Wilkinson & Pickett 2018: 218). In other words, GDP per capita has a systemic upward bias if what we really want to know is whether people's living standards are actually rising (see also Fioramonti 2013, 2017).

The UN's adoption of the HDI is the most significant institutional response to the demand for a more multi-dimensional measure of wellbeing. Health, education, gender equity and other social societal characteristics are combined when calculating each country's overall HDI score. More recently, the UN has also presented regular data on inequality-adjusted HDI (IAHDI). This involves 'discounting' each dimension of the HDI's value according to the extent of inequality. Thus, hypothetically, if there were no inequality in a country, its HDI and IAHDI would have identical values. Because there is invariably some inequality, however, the IAHDI is always below the HDI: the question is by how much. The next chapter will consider some real-world examples.

All statistical measures of economic and social phenomena need cautious handling. One tricky issue relates to how the constituent elements are added together. To get a composite index of wellbeing such as HDI, it is necessary to decide the weighting of its components (such as education, health, infant mortality or gender empowerment). Similarly, for the IAHDI, it is necessary to decide how much weight to place on inequality in the calculation of these components. Such judgements can have a significant bearing on the calculated values, introducing an inherent element of arbitrariness. Therefore, although HDI has advantages over GDP as a measure of wellbeing – and IAHDI has advantages over the basic HDI – it is sensible to treat all these data as indicative rather than conclusive.

Measuring wellbeing, development and progress raises complex issues that are significant for statisticians but also for any society that needs guidelines for collective action. We tend to act on what we measure. More generally, if what people do depends on what they think, how we evaluate economic and social performance, individually and collectively, can make a big difference. So too can the perception of what is fair or unfair in the distribution of the fruits of these economic efforts.

Equality and equity

Sliding from description of inequalities to talking about unfairness is common in popular discussion. Sometimes the terms 'equality' and 'equity' are used interchangeably. However, it is better to avoid these confusing elisions. Equality and inequality relate to the facts of the matter, whereas equity and inequity involve ethical judgements. Both matter: we must consider what *is* and what *should be* if we are interested in social improvement. For that purpose, we need to be explicit about the basis for making the judgements. Faced with the same facts about economic inequality, different people may regard the situation as fair or unfair, acceptable or unacceptable. Even doing nothing involves an implicit judgement. Some engagement with ethical issues is essential if we are to be active participants in social change.

Mainstream economists sometimes pull back from these concerns, arguing that their task is 'positive economics', leaving normative issues to the sphere of politics. This is unsatisfactory, however, because distributional issues are, by their nature, entwined with ethical judgements. If you were not concerned with equity, you would probably not be interested in inequality. The former motivates concern with the latter, while the latter signals failure to achieve the former. Engagement with ethical issues is integral to the political economy of inequality.

The most initially useful distinction is between *equality of opportunity* and *equality of outcome*. The former is a well-established liberal concept, whereas the latter has a more socialist or social democratic character. Equality of opportunity would require that all members of the society have equal chances to enhance their own economic and social position. Its preconditions are equality before the law, equality of educational access, equality of access to health facilities and the absence of discriminatory practices associated with class, gender, religion, sexual orientation and much else besides. It is a tall order, although it is hard to find people who would argue against its pursuit. Indeed, seeking equality of opportunity is the hallmark of a meritocratic society, although it may never be fully achievable. Equality of outcome is a yet taller order, requiring a more even spread of the distribution of income and wealth.

Equality of opportunity does not necessarily involve reducing the gap between those who succeed and those who fail. Its concern is only with a level playing field on which everyone can compete for the glittering or not-so-glittering prizes. From the liberal viewpoint, the value of the prizes is not the issue. Yet is that really an egalitarian stance? Socialists and social democrats generally say not, although they may disagree significantly about *by how much* narrower the rich–poor gaps should be. However, the practical implication of the commitment to greater equality of outcome is clear: to narrow the gap between rich and poor.

Few people would argue for complete equality of economic outcomes. Even people of a generally egalitarian disposition commonly concede the case for skilled workers getting a premium wage because they have invested time, effort and money into the acquisition of their skills. Making a personal investment like that has opportunity costs. A higher rate of pay is a normal expectation. 'How much more?' then becomes the key question. For society as a whole, is it reasonable to have a ratio of, say, 20:1 between the top and bottom incomes, or should we be aiming for a maximum of, say, 5:1? In practice, the key issue is often not so much the desirable end-point but the direction and rate of change. On such matters, reasonable people may reasonably disagree. Thus, while the call for equality of outcome is always associated with the movement to reduce disparities in remuneration, there is plenty of scope for debate about goals and strategies. In practice, socialists and social democrats have rubbed shoulders with liberals in advocating and developing labour market institutions, regulatory arrangements, taxation structures and welfare state provisions to give practical effect to this quest for more equitable outcomes. And conservatives have resisted.

Applying the conservative/liberal/radical triad introduced in the opening chapter helps to clarify the bases on which judgements can be made about inequality. Michael Schneider, Mike Pottinger and John King (2017: ch. 6) provide a neat summary of the principal positions. For our purpose here, contrasting the views of free-market libertarians, liberals and robust egalitarians is sufficient to show the basic disagreements.

The libertarians, represented by Robert Nozick (1974), put individual freedoms above all else and are sceptical of impediments that they think would result from the state adopting redistributive policies. Interestingly, though, Nozick recognizes the case for reparations paid to people who are poor because of the dispossession they or their predecessors have suffered: a matter to which we will return in chapter 12. Among the liberal political philosophers, John Rawls (1971) is the most renowned for putting a mild case for redistributive justice that increases the living standards of the poorest stratum in society. If a person had to choose the sort of society in which they would live and they did not know whether they would be in the top, middle or lower echelons of that society, it is indeed likely that their preference would be for a relatively egalitarian option. That implies the need for a good society to pay particular attention to the wellbeing of those at the bottom. As Rawls writes: 'Social and economic inequalities ... are just only if they result in compensating benefits for everyone, and in particular for the least disadvantaged members of society' (1971: 15). A stronger egalitarianism derives from observing that substantial social and economic inequality recurrently impedes people's capacity to develop and use their own skills (Tawney 1931). Social democrats and socialists in this more robustly egalitarian tradition argue that having a higher degree of equality and social cohesion creates a more cooperative and less 'dog eat dog' world in which personal and community development can flourish.

Blending equality of opportunity with greater equality of outcome is the hallmark of an egalitarian approach. This is because creating equality of opportunity tomorrow requires, as a precondition, more equality of outcome today. It is only by closing rich–poor gaps that the advantages and disadvantages impeding equality of opportunity can be reduced over time. A level playing field requires that successive generations start from a similar position. Thus, although the two aspects of inequality are conceptually distinct, they are bound in practice.

These considerations raise profound questions about how and why we engage with issues of equality. Essentially normative issues cause us to reflect on the big question we all face: in what sort of economy and society do we want to live? One in which high incomes and wealth are relentlessly sought and celebrated? One in which incomes and wealth are more evenly distributed? Or one which starts to question material affluence as the primary indicator of success? As we move in this book from the description of economic inequality to the discussion of its implications and possible responses, these questions come increasingly clearly into view.

Conclusion

This chapter has reviewed preliminary issues that need consideration in any analysis of economic inequality. Having clear concepts and appropriate analytical tools is important in avoiding ambiguity, whether about purpose, method or values. As we have seen, what initially appear to be technical concerns in the study of income and wealth turn out to require quite complex judgements about what matters and why. Interim conclusions arising from these preliminary deliberations include the following:

- Both incomes and wealth – and the relationship between these flows and stocks – matter when considering economic inequality.
- Developing an understanding of inequality needs attention to notions of poverty, development and wellbeing.
- Making judgements about what inequalities are acceptable requires engagement with normative issues. The key issue is whether, as a society, we should try to narrow the rich–poor gaps.

The ultimate test of our theories, concepts and measures is how well they illuminate the real world and guide intelligent, purposeful action. We therefore need to put the concepts introduced in this chapter to work in studying the evolving situation 'out there'. It is to this examination of the actually existing inequalities between nations, within nations and worldwide that we next turn.

Patterns

3

Scales and Shapes of Inequality

Having clarified the issues involved in analysing income and wealth, we now take a more directly empirical turn: studying what the inequalities actually look like in the world today. In general terms, of course, we know there are 'rich' and 'poor' countries, based on average material living standards. We also know that, within each country, there are 'rich' and 'poor' households. We have already glimpsed the broad dimensions of global inequality in the grand parade. It is now time to look more carefully at the data and at the patterns they reveal.

This chapter takes a three-step approach to considering the distributions of incomes and wealth. First, an international analysis contrasts the average incomes or wealth of a selection of rich and poor countries, looking at how wide are the intervening gaps. Second, an intra-national analysis considers the extent of economic inequality within individual countries. Finally, a global analysis considers inequality among the world's people as a whole, irrespective of the countries in which they live. Not surprisingly, when both international and intra-national inequalities are huge, global inequality tends to be even greater.

International inequalities

Comparing the rich and poor nations is the most familiar of the three scales of economic inequality shown overleaf in Figure 3.1.

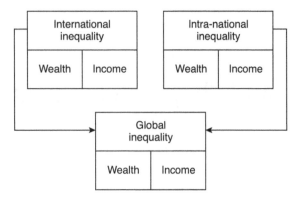

Figure 3.1 The scales of economic inequality

The *international* inequalities appear in the standard 'league tables' that are regularly compiled and paraded by the UN and the Organization for Economic Cooperation and Development (OECD). Taking each country as a single unit, they are compared according to their average levels of income or wealth. It is on this basis that the distinction between developing and developed nations has normally been made. The primary economic measure for this purpose is GDP per capita, although the HDI is a more comprehensive summary of the diverse factors affecting people's living standards.

Table 3.1 provides illustrative data for 20 countries, based on the latest available information at the time of writing. To try to consider all 195 countries of the world would be a daunting prospect, but this selectivity helps to keep the comparative process manageable. It also highlights some significant contrasts. Our selection here involves a wide geographical coverage and illustrates the dramatic diversity that exists internationally in material living standards. It comprises four groups, each of five countries. The first is the 'Anglos', a cluster of generally affluent English-speaking nations: Australia, Canada, New Zealand, the UK and the USA. The second comprises countries in Europe: France, Germany, Italy, Spain and Sweden. The third group of nations is the BRICS – the standard acronym for Brazil, Russia, India, China and South Africa – five nations all having significantly lower average material living standards than the Anglos and the Euros, but each containing a stratum of extremely wealthy people. The last group – identified here as the JINKS – has been included to ensure overall coverage of diverse nations on all five continents, rich and poor, relatively egalitarian and highly unequal: it comprises Japan, Indonesia, Nigeria, the Republic of Korea (i.e. South Korea) and Saudi Arabia. Although the selection is somewhat arbitrary, these 20 nations provide a fine basis for cross-country comparisons.

Three measures of living standards for each of the nations are shown in Table 3.1, based on data provided by their national governments and incorporated into the standard UN databases. The preceding chapter considered the advantages and disadvantages of each of these indicators. GDP per capita appears first in the table because, for better or worse, it is still the most widely used comparator: it is robust and consistent, however flawed as a measure of wellbeing. The GDP measure used here is calculated

Table 3.1 International inequalities, selected countries

Country	GDP per capita, 2017 (PPP) ($ international)[a]	HDI, 2015[b]	IAHDI, 2015[b]
Anglos			
Australia	47,047	0.94	0.86
Canada	46,378	0.92	0.84
New Zealand	40,917	0.92	n/a
UK	43,877	0.91	0.84
USA	59,532	0.92	0.80
Euros			
France	42,779	0.90	0.81
Germany	50,716	0.93	0.86
Italy	39,817	0.88	0.78
Spain	38,091	0.88	0.79
Sweden	50,070	0.91	0.85
BRICS			
Brazil	15,484	0.75	0.56
Russian Federation	25,533	0.80	0.73
India	7,056	0.62	0.45
China	16,807	0.74	n/a
South Africa	13,498	0.67	0.44
JINKS			
Japan	43,878	0.90	0.79
Indonesia	12,284	0.69	0.56
Nigeria	5,861	0.53	0.33
Republic of Korea	38,260	0.90	0.75
Saudi Arabia	53,845	0.85	n/a

Sources: [a] *https://data.worldbank.org/indicator/NY.GDP.PCAP.PP.CD;* [b] *http://hdr.undp.org/en/composite/IHDI.*

in terms of purchasing power parity (PPP), taking account of the different costs of living in each country. The other two measures, HDI and IAHDI, are more sensitive to the complex factors shaping actual living standards. The latter explicitly takes account of intra-national inequality too. We can look column by column at the numbers and their significance.

According to the economists' standard measure of GDP per capita, adjusted for PPP as shown in the first column, the USA comes out top with over $59,000 annual income per person, followed by Saudi Arabia with over $53,000. Then come all the other Anglo nations and all the Euros, ranging from Germany and Sweden on $50,000 to Spain on $38,000. Two of the JINKS – Japan, and South Korea – are also in the same range. Then there is a big gap in average incomes until we get to Russia at $25,000 and the rest of the BRICS (except India) and Indonesia in the $17,000 to $12,000 range. Nigeria and India bring up the rear of the countries shown in the table, although some countries in Africa are poorer. While these general rankings would probably not be a surprise to most readers of this book, the extent of the inequalities is startling. The average purchasing power of people in the USA is about 10 times higher than in Nigeria.

The second column in Table 3.1 shows the HDI scores for the same range of countries. Although broadly correlated with the ranking according to GDP per capita, there are significant differences. The HDI for the USA is a little below that for Australia and Germany, for example, while Japan and Spain also look significantly better than they do in terms of GDP. Saudi Arabia's second-place ranking for GDP per capita drops to thirteenth place for HDI.

Then, in the final column of the table, we see the 'inequality-adjusted HDI' figures calculated by the UN, taking account of how inequality affects the overall wellbeing of the people in each nation. This is a trigger for thinking about the relationships between average incomes, inequality and human development. Among the richer nations, for example, the USA's performance looks significantly less impressive when inequality is considered. Among the mid-ranking nations, the impacts of differences in inequality are even more striking. The high inequality in Brazil reduces its IAHDI by a quarter of its general HDI score; the even greater inequality in South Africa causes its IAHDI to plunge by a third. In contrast, Sweden's IAHDI is only about about 6% below its HDI score. These are indications of how economic inequality may influence national wellbeing.

Generalizing across the four groups identified in Table 3.1 is hazardous because each country is unique, but some broad patterns are worthy of comment. The first two clusters (the Anglos and the Euros) have the least diversity in material living standards: these are representative of the world's most prosperous nations. The third and fourth clusters (the BRICS and JINKS) exhibit much more heterogeneity, not surprisingly in the latter case because the countries were chosen for that purpose. Nigeria and Indonesia are populous and generally poor, whereas Japan and South Korea have mid-sized populations with material living standards comparable with some of the Anglo and Euro nations. Saudi Arabia, the largest of the oil-rich Middle Eastern states, has high per capita incomes but its mid-range HDI points to a significantly lower general standard of living for most of the people, as is also the case in Brazil and China. Among the BRICS, there is great diversity. Russia is the only one having middle-income status, while India is much the poorest in per capita incomes. As in South Africa, its low HDI and IAHDI scores signal that most of the people continue to have a very poor standard of living.

Looking at these data, although based on national aggregates, hints at the relevance of inequality when examining international 'league tables' of economic and social performance. Huge gaps in material prosperity are evident on a world scale. The countries with per capita incomes over $30,000, with few exceptions, are in Europe, North America, East Asia and Australasia. Meanwhile, most of the world's people – in Africa, Asia and South America – live in countries with per capita incomes less than half of that level. Among the BRICS, only Russia is clearly a 'middle-income' country. There is little to suggest a general escape from the 'middle-income trap' that has impeded efforts of low-income countries to achieve per capita income levels comparable to the Anglo and Euro nations (Felipe, Abdon & Kumar 2012; Bulman, Eden & Nguyen 2014; Elsenhans & Babones 2017; Gore 2017). China's remarkable economic growth during the last three decades has put it on track to do so, but it has a long way to go, while India's impressive growth still leaves the people of the country predominantly poor. The common characteristic of the otherwise very diverse BRICS is their high degree of inequality.

To understand these countries more fully requires study of how their international inequalities are entwined with intra-national inequalities.

Intra-national inequalities

All nations have uneven distribution of income and wealth but they vary enormously in its extent. Table 3.2 uses an array of measures to show some of the more vivid contrasts.

What are the salient features that stand out from this table? First, looking at the values of the Gini coefficient, we can see that

Table 3.2 Intra-national inequalities, selected countries

Country	Gini coefficient[a]	Top 1% share of income (%)[b]	Quintile ratio[c]	Palma ratio[c]
Anglos				
Australia	0.34	9.1	6.0	1.4
Canada	0.32	13.6	5.8	1.3
New Zealand	0.30	8.1	n/a	n/a
UK	0.36	14.5	5.3	1.3
USA	0.39	19.6	9.1	2.0
Euros				
France	0.30	11.1	5.3	1.3
Germany	0.39	13.0	4.6	1.1
Italy	0.33	9.4	6.7	1.4
Spain	0.35	8.6	7.3	1.5
Sweden	0.28	8.7	4.2	0.9
BRICS				
Brazil	0.47	23.6	15.5	3.5
Russian Federation	0.38	20.2	8.2	2.0
India	0.50	21.7	5.3	1.5
China	0.51	13.9	9.2	2.1
South Africa	0.62	19.2	27.9	7.1
JINKS				
Japan	0.33	10.4	5.4	1.2
Indonesia[d]	0.39	8.5	6.6	1.8
Nigeria[d]	0.43	n/a	9.1	2.2
Republic of Korea	0.35	12.2	n/a	n/a
Saudi Arabia[e]	0.61	20.0	n/a	n/a

Sources: [a] *http://stats.oecd.org/Index.aspx?DataSetCode=IDD*, data for latest available year in each country; [b] data for top 1% shares relate to share of pre-tax national income for latest available years, and are from *http://wid.world/data/*; [c] quintile ratio and Palma ratio data for years 2010–15, and from *http://hdr.undp.org/en/composite/IHDI*; [d] Gini data for Indonesia and Nigeria from *http://hdr.undp.org/en/indicators/67106#*; [e] all data for Saudi Arabia from *http://wid.world/document/alvaredoassouadpiketty-middleeast-widworldwp201715/*.

Sweden has the least inequality while the USA is the most unequal of the Anglo and Euro nations. The clustering of the Gini scores in the 0.28 to 0.39 range is indicative of the tendency for this indicator to show only small variations despite significant differences in the form that inequality takes in different countries. There are some notable outliers, however, especially among the BRICS and JINKS. Six of the nations exceed the 0.40 level: Brazil, China, India, South Africa, Nigeria and Saudi Arabia. South Africa, at 0.62, is clearly the most unequal. Brazil's very high inequality is notable too, typical of Latin American countries, with striking contrasts between the living conditions of their very rich and very poor people. Japan, South Korea, Russia and Indonesia have inequalities in the same range as the Anglos and Euros.

The second column of the same table, showing the concentration of income within the top 1% in each country, indicates a somewhat different picture. Brazil takes top spot, closely followed by India, Russia, Saudi Arabia, the USA and then South Africa: these are all countries with fabulously wealthy elites. At the other end of the scale, New Zealand comes just ahead of Indonesia, Spain and Sweden as the least unequal on this measure.

Then, in the final two columns of the table, we see the results according to broader indicators of comparative income shares. The quintile ratio compares the incomes of the top 20% and bottom 20%, while the Palma ratio compares the top 10% with the bottom 40%. South Africa is clearly the most unequal nation on both of these inequality indicators, while the USA is clearly the most unequal of the Anglo nations. On both indicators, Sweden is the most equal. There are some interesting variations among other countries, though. China looks notably more unequal than India on both the quartile and Palma indicators, for example, although the two countries have a similar Gini score and India has the higher concentration of incomes in the top 1%.

Evidently, these different indicators reveal different types of inequality. The concentrated elite inequality of Brazil, India, Russia and the USA shows up more in the top 1% measure than in the broader indicators of income shares or even the Gini coefficient. Notwithstanding these variations, however, the striking feature of all these data is how varied are the differences between nations.

Turning from incomes to wealth, we can look at the same countries to see the concentration of asset holdings in each. The financial institution Credit Suisse produces regular compilations of private wealth that are helpful for this purpose. Its estimates

Table 3.3 Intra-national wealth inequalities, selected countries, 2017

Country	Gini coefficient	Top 1% share of wealth (%)
Anglos		
Australia	0.65	22.9
Canada	0.74	26.1
New Zealand	0.72	23.8
UK	0.74	24.3
USA	0.86	38.3
Euros		
France	0.70	21.6
Germany	0.79	32.3
Italy	0.66	21.5
Spain	0.66	25.1
Sweden	0.83	41.9
BRICS		
Brazil	0.83	43.5
Russian Federation	0.83	56.0
India	0.83	45.1
China	0.79	47.0
South Africa	0.87	41.2
JINKS		
Japan	0.61	14.6
Indonesia	0.84	45.4
Nigeria	0.70	n/a
Republic of Korea	0.70	26.8
Saudi Arabia	0.79	n/a

Source: Credit Suisse (2017a).

are drawn from sources such as national accounts, national-based surveys and 'rich lists', augmented by statistical analysis. Table 3.3 shows the latest available information for the same array of countries. Two features are immediately evident. First, inequality of wealth is much greater than inequality of incomes in each country. Second, the two wealth inequality indicators show markedly different patterns. The values of the Gini coefficient lie in a quite narrow range: from 0.61 (Japan) to 0.86 (USA). The concentration of wealth in the top 1% shows much wider variation: from 14.6% (Japan) to 56% (Russia).

The BRICS feature conspicuously in the top rank of nations, according to both of these measures of wealth inequality. Indonesia also looks highly unequal in terms of the top 1% share. Sweden, a country renowned for the relative equality of post-tax incomes, has notably high inequality of wealth (with a Gini score of 0.83). Overall, the concentration of wealth appears more fundamentally entrenched than income inequalities across nations with otherwise widely varying characteristics. These are important findings: the interdependence between wealth and incomes, as discussed in the preceding chapter, is central to the process of reproducing inequalities within nations. Over time, wealth inequalities tend to increase income inequalities unless public policies have a strong and persistent redistributive effect.

Global inequality

Global inequality is the third and broadest scale at which we can view economic inequality, showing the inequality among all the people of the world, irrespective of the country or region in which they live. It combines the two scales of inequality that we have already considered. Constructing global income inequality data is not easy, however, because there is no global survey nor are there taxation arrangements that might generate the information. Branko Milanovic (2016: 12–18) provides a careful guide to how it can be aggregated from nationally based sources.

Using the most up-to-date information on global income inequality, Table 3.4 shows the incomes of people at various points in the distribution. The person at the 50th percentile is at exactly the mid-point of the global income distribution, getting the equivalent

Table 3.4 Global pre-tax annual income of adults, by percentile, euros, 2016

Percentile	Income
5th	853
10th	1,467
30th	3,530
50th	6,757
70th	13,374
90th	35,035
98th	102,671
99.8th	388,996
99.991th	2,443,536
99.999th	30,738,073

Source: World Inequality Database: *https://wid.world/data/*.

of 6,757 euros per annum. Below that average income, the numbers fall away markedly, down to a mere 853 euros for people at the fifth percentile. Above the average, the incomes climb increasingly sharply, reaching 102,671 at the 98th percentile and a stupendous 30,738,073 at the 99.999th percentile. These are the data informing the grand parade with which this book began.

Turning from income to *wealth*, we can assess global inequality in terms of the concentration of asset ownership. For this purpose, we can return to the database of Credit-Suisse. Table 3.5 shows its summary of the global distribution. This information is initially rather hard to interpret but, once understood, the greater problem is in coming to terms with the truly amazing inequality that it reveals. Almost half of the total private wealth in the world is owned by 36 million people. These comprise just 0.7% of the global population of just under 5 billion adults. The other half is almost wholly in the hands of 1.5 billion people, leaving 3.5 billion people with a mere 2.7% of the total. Drilling down even further into the wealth holdings of the super-rich, Table 3.5(b) shows that 3 million people each have assets worth between $5 million and $10 million, while just under 150,000 households each have over $50 million.

Table 3.5(a) Distribution of global wealth, 2017

Wealth range ($)	No. of adults (million)	% of global adults	Total wealth ($ trillion)	% of global wealth
Over 1 million	36	0.7	128.7	45.9
100,000–1 million	391	7.9	111.4	39.7
10,000–100,000	1,054	21.3	32.5	11.6
Under 10,000	3,474	70.1	7.6	2.7

Source: Credit Suisse (2017b).

Table 3.5(b) Distribution of the top tier in Table 3.5(a)

Wealth range ($)	No. of adults
Over 50 million	148,200
10–50 million	1,527,600
5–10 million	3,009,800
1–5 million	31,365,100

Note: The data from different countries are aggregated on an exchange rate basis, not adjusted PPP.

Source: Credit Suisse (2017b).

If the heights of the people in the grand parade with which this book began had been proportional to their wealth, rather than to their annual incomes, the picture would have looked even more startling than it did. Making the height of each marcher equivalent to one centimetre per $1,000 of wealth, two-thirds of the hour would have elapsed before the appearance of people only 10 centimetres tall. People 1 metre tall would not have appeared until after 55 minutes. Then, during the last minute, the height of the marchers would have risen from about 10 metres to over 10,000 metres, which is over 1,000 metres taller than Mount Everest, the world's highest peak. Wealth inequalities like this make our earlier grand parade of income inequalities look almost egalitarian by comparison.

Billionaires

Who are the people at the very top of the wealth distribution? Left-wing political organizations used to publish pamphlets about the richest people in each county, revealing the who's who of the capitalist or ruling class. Now that role is played by business magazines celebrating the success of these top 'wealth-creators'. Either way, the information is interesting for researchers into economic inequality. Branko Milanovic, drawing on data in the *Forbes* list of billionaires, noted that, in 2013, there were 1,426 individuals in the world whose net worth was equal to or greater than $1 billion. He calculated that this small and select group, together with their family members, comprised only one-hundredth of one-hundredth of the global 1% and valued their total assets at $5.4 trillion, adding that these rich billionaires 'own twice as much wealth as exists in all of Africa' (Milanovic 2016: 41–2).

The Bloomberg Billionaires Index of the wealthiest 500 people in the world gives us the most up-to-date information on the very biggest of the wealth holders. According to this source, Jeff Bezos, the founder of Amazon, was the wealthiest person in the world in July 2018, with a total net worth of just over $150 billion, surpassing Microsoft co-founder Bill Gates on $95.5 billion and investor 'folk hero' Warren Buffett on $83 billion. Bezos's wealth in late January 2018 had been $114 billion, which means that in six months it had risen at an average of $200 million per day.

The global distribution of the top 500 wealth holders is shown in Table 3.6 on the following page. Three continents dominate: North America with 35%, Asia with 24.6% and Europe with 24.2%.

A further 5.8% are from Russia and former countries of the Soviet Union, 4.4% from Central and South America, 2.6% from Oceania, 2.4% from the Middle East and 1.4% from Africa (comprising five people in South Africa and Nigeria). The dominant position of the USA is the table's most striking feature, but the Asian nations represented there have significantly gained in prominence. Four of the five BRICS nations are well up the league table, while South

Table 3.6 Locations of world's top 500 billionaires, by nation, 2018

Country	No. of billionaires
USA	155
China	39
Germany	39
Russian Federation	27
India	25
Hong Kong	17
Brazil	15
UK	15
Canada	13
France	13
Sweden	13
Thailand	8
Japan	7
Mexico	7
Switzerland	7
Australia	6
Austria	6
Denmark	6
Indonesia	6
Italy	6
Republic of Korea	6
Singapore	6
Taiwan	6
Malaysia	5
Philippines	4
Saudi Arabia	4

Note: In addition, Colombia, Israel, Norway, South Africa, Spain and the United Arab Emirates each have three billionaires; Chile, the Czech Republic, Egypt, Ireland, the Netherlands and Nigeria each have two; and Belgium, the Cayman Islands, Cyprus, Finland, Georgia, Monaco, New Zealand, Ukraine and Venezuela each have one.

Source: Bloomberg (2018).

Africa is among other countries that do not appear in the main body of the table because they have fewer than four representatives among the top 500 billionaires (see table note).

Conclusion

The information introduced in this chapter shows the dimensions of economic inequality at three geographical scales: international, intra-national and global. These are snapshots of the situation taken through different lenses. They enable us to see the following:

- International economic inequalities are huge, notwithstanding substantial material economic progress during recent decades in previously very poor countries like India and China.
- Internal inequalities vary considerably between countries, ranging from modest in Europe and Japan, to middling in the USA, Russia and China, and to huge in Brazil and South Africa.
- Global inequality, as the combined effect of the preceding two factors, is also huge. While this is not surprising, its dimensions are startling, even more so when viewed in terms of wealth rather than incomes.

Powerful evidence like this invites further consideration of how the patterns of income and wealth shares have shifted over time. Are the inequalities growing or declining? Is there evidence of shifting shares between the super-rich, people living in poverty and those in-between? Getting a glimpse of these dynamics is our next concern.

4

Shifting Shares

We have seen the big picture: the three scales at which inequality can be studied and the enormous variations at each. We now need to see how the situation is changing over time. Are inequalities at the three scales increasing or diminishing? Which social groups have been improving their position – and which have not benefited from economic changes – during the last few decades? Addressing these questions, we transition from looking at snapshots to watching a movie, albeit one that we need to pause occasionally to peruse particular frames.

This chapter reveals significant shifts in how unequally incomes and wealth are distributed. It pays particular attention to the relative economic positions of the top 1% of the population, the top 10%, the bottom 50% and the intermediate 40%. While this is not, strictly speaking, a class analysis (Rasch 2017), it is indicative of which groups have gained and which have lost ground in the 'race for riches'. A combination of data from three sources already introduced – Milanovic (2016), the *World Inequality Report 2018* (Alvaredo et al. 2018) and Credit Suisse (2017a, 2017b) – provides a good basis from which to assess what has been happening. The chapter also shines a spotlight on the incomes of the CEOs of large corporations, an occupational group that has been faring spectacularly well. The shifting relationships between the winners and losers form a key part of the ongoing global political economic drama.

Changing national patterns

Let's look first at the changing pattern of income inequality in a sample of nations. Table 4.1 considers three illustrative cases – China, the USA and France – and shows data on how the income distribution in each has changed over a 37-year period. The way in which income shares are 'sliced' here is primarily 10:40:50, providing a general view of how the top, middle and bottom groups have been faring. It is supplemented by more detailed disaggregation at the top end to show the shares of the top 1% and even the top 0.001%.

As you can see, China is the most dramatic case, having experienced a more than eight-fold increase in per capita incomes between 1978 and 2015. The poorest half of the people had a four-fold increase, the middle 40% nearly eight-fold and the richest 10% nearly 13-fold. Whether these numbers reflect how much materially better off the people have become is a moot point, however. The Chinese government used to provide goods and services at little or no cost; now people have higher incomes but face higher costs for housing, transport, education, health care and food (Hart-Landsberg 2018). While the net impact on wellbeing is hard to identify, there is no doubt that the fruits of economic growth have skewed to the top end.

Table 4.1 Income growth and inequality: China, USA and France, 1978–2015

Income group (distribution of per adult pre-tax national income)	Total cumulated real growth, 1978–2015 (%)		
	China	USA	France
Full population	811	59	39
Bottom 50%	401	–1	39
Middle 40%	779	42	35
Top 10%	1,294	115	44
Inc. top 1%	1,898	198	67
Inc. top 0.1%	2,261	321	84
Inc. top 0.01%	2,685	453	93
Inc. top 0.001%	3,111	685	158

Note: The data show the distribution of pre-tax national income (before taxes and transfers, except pensions and unemployment benefits) among adults. They are corrected estimates combining survey, fiscal, wealth and national accounts data, and for married couples the household income is apportioned on an equal-split basis.

Source: Alvaredo et al. (2018).

The experience with inequality in the USA over the same period is similar in some respects but very different in others, as can be seen from the middle column in Table 4.1. The overall economic gains have been quite modest and the bottom half of the population experienced no income growth at all, indeed had a slight decline. Meanwhile the richest 10% of people more than doubled their incomes. Those in the middle 40% had middling gains.

The data for France show a much more even sharing of the income growth. Overall, income growth was rather slower than in the USA: a 39% increase on the income levels of the base year (1978), compared with 59% in the USA. However, the rate of income growth was broadly similar for the different segments of the population. The poorest half of people had 39% income growth, exactly matching the national average. The richest 10%, with income growth of 44%, did rather better than middle-income group. The broad picture is of a relatively egalitarian distribution of modest gains. Indeed, it looks like a case where a slowly rising tide did lift all boats.

The bottom four rows of Table 4.1 show more detail of who, among the top 10%, did best of all. In each of the three countries, the top 1% had a much higher income growth rate than the top 10%. Even more striking, a tiny elite comprising the top 0.001% of the population (i.e. the richest one in a 100,000 households) fared much the best in each case. Thus, although the three country cases show remarkable contrasts in the overall distributional gains of the people, they also reveal one common and consistent element: in each case, the super-rich had much faster rates of income growth than any other group. While these were not necessarily all the same individuals (because, over time, there are deaths and there is a turnover in each income group), it is clear that the people at the top of the income distribution in each country did extraordinarily well. One may infer that those who started the race at the front of the pack finished streets ahead.

Figure 4.1 casts the net wider by looking at the experience of the top 10% of income recipients across a broader range of countries for approximately same period (1980–2016). It shows evidence of significant between-country variations in the timing of the gains made by this top decile. Russia is the most remarkable case because of the strong surge in rich people's incomes that took place when, following the collapse of the former USSR, the 'oligarchs' effectively helped themselves to the assets of the former communist state. China had a somewhat similar surge at

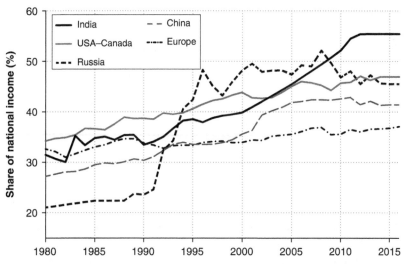

Figure 4.1 Top 10% income shares, selected countries and regions, 1980–2016

Source: Alvaredo et al. (2018).

the start of the 1990s, with income growth of the top 10% continuing more slowly until a further surge in the next decade. India shows the most consistently increasing share of income going to the top 10%, rising to be the top of the group, surpassing North America – combining the USA and Canada – which had started highest. In Europe, the share of incomes going to the top 10% rose too but much more slowly. These differences are significant but the general conclusion is clear: rich people generally got much richer.

The top, bottom and middle

The ability of a small elite to increase its share of total incomes and wealth during these recent decades has attracted considerable attention. The now widespread use of the term 'the 1%' owes much to the 'Occupy' movement, which grew rapidly in response to the global financial crash of 2008–9. Demonstrations were held in about 900 cities in over 80 countries, protesting the adverse consequences of extreme concentration of incomes, wealth and power. Oxfam, the international non-governmental organization

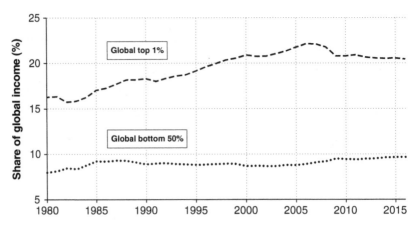

Figure 4.2 Shares of global income going to the global top 1% and the global bottom 50%, 1980–2016

Source: Alvaredo et al. (2018).

(NGO), has maintained the momentum by publishing a series of reports, drawing on the Credit Suisse data and other sources, to show the extreme concentration of income gains in the years following the crash. Taking a longer view, the *World Inequality Report 2018* has also pointed out that the global top 1% captured 27% of the world's total income growth between 1980 and 2016 (Alvaredo et al. 2018).

So who has been missing out? In general, it has not been the poorest half of the world's people, whose share has been quite stable, as Figure 4.2 shows. Rather, the squeeze has been mainly on the working-class and middle-income people living in the relatively affluent nations, particularly in North America, Europe and Australasia.

Equally interesting are the regional differences in the pattern of shifting shares. Consider Figure 4.3. Here you see the contrast between the evolving situations in the USA and Western Europe. In the USA the share of income going to the top 1% has been soaring, doubling within 36 years, while the bottom 50% experienced no overall income gains at all (as previously shown in Table 4.1) and has a shrinking share of the total income – down from over 20% to about 13%. As shown in the lower part of Figure 4.5, Western Europe, taken as a whole, has been more stable: the bottom 50% still has a much higher share of total income than the top 1%, which has not been the case on the USA since the mid-1990s.

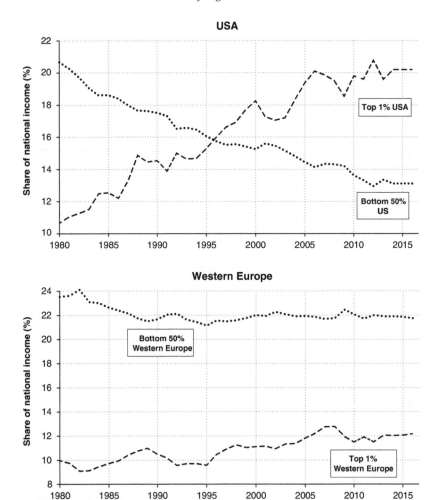

Figure 4.3 The top 1% and bottom 50% income shares in the USA and Western Europe, 1980–2016

Note: The vertical axes of these two diagrams are truncated, cutting in at 10% and 8%, respectively. This is how the diagrams appeared in the original source, having the effect of magnifying the contrasts in the trends pictured.

Source: Alvaredo et al. (2018).

These two contrasting cases illustrate two different models within the affluent nations: one in which there is little restraint on increasing inequality and the other capable of modestly egalitarian redistributions.

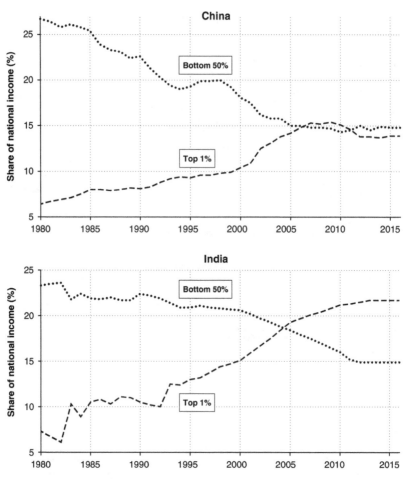

Figure 4.4 The top 1% and bottom 50% income shares in China and India, 1980–2016

Source: Alvaredo et al. (2018).

Turning to the two most populous developing nations, China and India, Figure 4.4 shows their comparable experiences. China's plunging share of income going to the poorest 50% mirrors the US pattern, as does India's surging share going to the top 1%. In terms of distributional shares, both countries are much more like the USA than Western Europe. Rapidly growing income inequalities are the common feature. Their economic transformations have been remarkable, but in terms of their patterns of economic inequality, they are on the US track rather than a road to widely shared prosperity.

Changing global patterns

Worldwide, has income inequality risen or fallen in recent times? A general answer is surprisingly difficult because it depends on the net effect of the changes in international and intra-national inequalities, which are pulling in opposite directions (Bourgignon 2015). On the one hand, there has been a narrowing of international economic inequalities because of the positive economic growth experience in India, China and some other developing nations, whereas economic growth has been relatively weak in the richer countries, especially since the global financial crisis of 2008–9. On the other hand, there has been rising inequality in almost all nations. This is most strikingly clear in the USA, albeit less pronounced in the other Anglo nations and in the Eurozone. It has also been strongly evident in the BRICS. In China and India, as we have seen, for example, many millions of people have risen out of absolute poverty, but economic inequalities have become much greater. Other poor nations have had varied experiences, but many of them, particularly in sub-Saharan Africa, have languished, notwithstanding claims about 'Africa on the rise' (Obeng-Odoom 2015a; see also Jerven 2015). In South America, there have been attempts to establish more egalitarian policy regimes and institutions for regional cooperation, but with only modest effect in stemming the global tide (Gasparini & Lustig 2011; Tsounta & Osueke 2014). Almost every country in the world has had a greater concentration of incomes at the top end, making this a defining feature of the current era of global capitalism (Kaur & Wahlberg 2014).

How are these shifts showing up statistically in measurements of the global distribution of income? Pioneering research by Milanovic (2016) sought to answer this by comparing global income inequality in 2011 with the situation 23 years earlier. His summary diagram is reproduced as Figure 4.5 on the following page. Its interpretation is somewhat complicated because the horizontal axis of Figure 4.5 has a logarithmic scale, the effect of which is to stretch the distributions when moving towards the upper income levels. This gives most visual prominence to the lower- and middle-income ranges (up to about $10,000 p.a.).

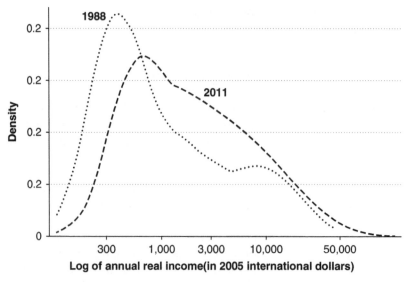

Figure 4.5 Distribution of world population by real per capita income, 1988 and 2011

Source: Milanovic (2016: 33). Reproduced with permission.

Looked at in this way, it is clear that the two 'bell curves' for 1988 and 2011 have significantly different characteristics. Most obviously, the 2011 distribution is less sharply peaked than the 1988 distribution. It is also significantly further to the right, reflecting the reduction in the proportion of the world's people on annual incomes of less than $1,000 (which is less than $3 per day), and a roughly corresponding increase in the proportion of people getting between $1,000 and $10,000 p.a. Indeed, a significant 'fattening in the middle' is evident: put simply, millions of previously poor people got more to eat. Over the 23 years studied by Milanovic, many very poor people became rather less poor, albeit still mainly within a still modest average annual income below $10,000 and still mostly below $3,000. As Milanovic points out, at the end of this period, 'the global middle class is still relatively poor by western standards' (2016: 33).

To see how the rich have been faring requires more scrutiny of the 'upper tail' at the right of the distributions shown in Figure 4.5. This is not easy to interpret because the number of people at the far end of the distribution is relatively small in comparison with the masses of people having low to middling

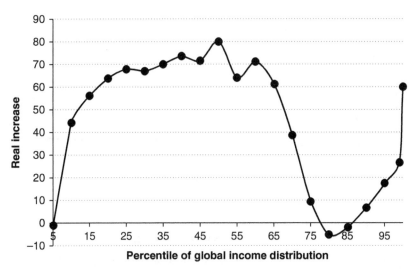

Figure 4.6 Relative gain in real per capita income by percentiles of global income, 1988–2008

Note: The vertical axis shows the percentage change in real income, measured in constant international dollars. The horizontal axis shows the percentile position in the global income distribution. The percentile positions run from 5 to 95, in increments of five, while the top 5% are divided into two groups: the top 1%, and those between the 95th and 99th percentiles. All figures calculated in 2005 international dollars.

Source: Milanovic (2012).

incomes. To investigate this situation more fully, it is useful to construct a different diagram that shows the percentage change for each global income percentile. This is Figure 4.6, again taken from Milanovic's pioneering study. It provides a different way of showing the rate at which people's incomes rose during the two decades 1988–2008. It is what has come to be called the 'elephant curve', so named because of its distinctive shape. The curve has a big bulge in the middle (because so many poor people, especially in Asia, got increased incomes), a drooping head (because people in an upper-middle-income group, especially in North America, Europe and Australasia, had little income growth) and then an upright trunk (because of the rapidly rising incomes of the world's richest people).

A newer version of the elephant curve has been produced by the compilers of the *World Inequality Report* (Alvaredo et al. 2018), reproduced here as Figure 4.7 and including the authors' annotations on its salient features. The differences from

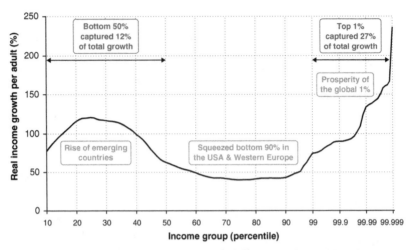

Figure 4.7 Total income growth by percentile across all world regions, 1980–2016

Note: On the horizontal axis, the world population is divided into 100 groups of equal population size and sorted into ascending order from left to right, according to each group's income level. The top 1% group is divided into 10 groups, the richest of these groups is also divided into 10 groups, and the very top group is again divided into 10 groups of equal population size. The vertical axis shows the total income growth for an average individual in each group between 1980 and 2016, taking account for differences in the cost of living between countries.

Source: Alvaredo et al. (2018).

Milanovic's original elephant curve diagram are three-fold: (a) it covers a longer time-period, starting eight years earlier and coming forward eight years to bring it more up to date; (b) it uses improved data, according to the authors; and (c) its horizontal scale is stretched at the right end (making a more elongated 'trunk'). This latter feature enables us to see that the top 1% has increased its income faster than the top 10%, that the top 0.1% has done even better, the top 0.01 better still and the top 0.001 best of all. The result is not so clearly 'elephant' shaped, as you can see by comparing the two figures. However, the newer version reveals that the percentage income gains made by people in the lower-middle part of the distribution (the 'elephant's body') have been quite modest in comparison to the tremendous gains made by the people right at the top (towards the 'tip of the trunk'). It is the increased oncentration of incomes at the top end that is the most striking feature.

Table 4.2 Distribution of global wealth, 2010 and 2017

Wealth range ($)	No. of adults (million)		% of global adults		Total wealth ($ trillion)		% of global wealth	
	2010	2017	2010	2017	2010	2017	2010	2017
Over 1 million	24.2	36	0.5	0.7	69.2	128.7	35.6	45.9
100,000–1 million	334	391	7.5	7.9	85.0	111.4	43.7	39.7
10,000–100,000	1,045	1,054	23.5	21.3	32.1	32.5	16.5	11.6
Under 10,000	3,038	3,474	68.4	70.1	8.2	7.6	4.2	2.7

Source: Credit-Suisse (2017a, 2017b).

The changing shares of wealth

What about wealth inequalities: have there been similar shifts in who owns what? We noted in chapter 2 that strong interconnections usually exist between incomes and wealth over time: remember the bathwater analogy? Having wealth generates easy income, while having high income facilitates the accumulation of wealth. It is a two-way process, although there can be significant time lags between changes in the flow of income and stocks of wealth.

Table 4.2, drawn from Credit Suisse data, shows recent shifts, focusing on the seven years to 2017. It gives an indication of whose wealth has 'rebounded' well from the global financial crisis. Evidently, there has been a substantial jump in the percentage of the global population with wealth over $1 million. These people comprised a tiny proportion of the world's population in 2017, just 0.7% of the total, which is up 0.2% since seven years earlier. As well as being somewhat more numerous, this elite group has markedly increased its share of total world wealth: from 35.6% to 45.9%. In other words, the dominant feature of global inequality since the global financial crisis has been that some already very wealthy people have become much wealthier. Perhaps calling it an 'elite' might strike a discordant note for some readers, because wealth of $1 million may seem a rather modest entry ticket. Indeed, the median market price of houses, even apartments, in modern global cities is usually above that now, so wealth of $1 million or more does not necessarily make the owners of houses and flats feel part of the elite. On a world scale, however, it is sobering to note that anyone who owns real estate in such places is in the top 1% of wealth holders worldwide.

At the other extreme, the percentage of people with wealth less than $10,000 also went up between 2010 and 2017, and their share of the total wealth has gone down: from 4.2% to a mere 2.7%. It may sound like a cliché to say 'the rich get richer and the poor get poorer' – and I have steadfastly refrained from saying it in this book until now – but that is what happened, in terms of relative wealth shares, in this decade.

There is also evidence of a significant squeeze in the middle. According to the data in Table 4.2, people with wealth between $10,000 and $1 million have become a smaller proportion of the world's population and hold a significantly smaller proportion of the total wealth: down from 60.2% to 51.3%. Thus, the income squeeze affecting the middle-income groups in the affluent nations has been accompanied by a similar squeeze in the distribution of global wealth.

What has been happening to the distribution of private wealth in individual countries? Figure 4.8 presents wealth data for three nations: France, the USA and the UK. It looks over a whole century, enabling us to interpret the recent trends in long-term context. The striking feature is that, for the first three-quarters of the twentieth century, the share of total wealth held by the top 1% had been steadily falling in each of the three countries. However, this trend sharply reversed in the last quarter of the century as the fortunes of the 1% had a renewed uplift. The surge in the last two decades has been strongest in the USA. Having experienced declining wealth

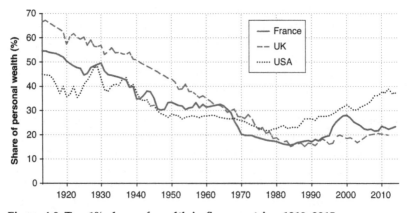

Figure 4.8 Top 1% share of wealth in five countries, 1913–2015

Source: Alvaredo et al. (2018).

shares for much of the twentieth century, the top 1% is now again in the ascendancy.

CEOs

Finally in this chapter, it is useful to turn a spotlight briefly onto CEOs within large corporations because they are commonly said to be the group that has been doing best of all. Indeed, they have fared spectacularly well in recent decades. While they are formally employees of the businesses for which they work, their principal role is the management of capital and the development of corporate strategies. They are effectively 'agents of capital'. Notwithstanding their standard rhetoric about giving priority to shareholder value, CEOs have also been extraordinarily successful in securing their own interests, individually and collectively.

The relative income of CEOs, compared with the average wages paid to workers employed in the same corporations, has risen dramatically during recent decades. This is partly because of increases in CEO base salaries, but, equally importantly, because of the changing forms of remuneration that emphasize payment of bonuses and share options.

A useful source of evidence on trends in CEO-to-worker income relativities in the USA is the report by the Economic Policy Institute (Mishel & Schieder 2017), reproduced on the following page in Table 4.3. The two columns in the table provide different measures of CEO remuneration (sometimes called 'compensation'), expressed as a multiple of workers' median incomes. The first measure includes the realized total value of their stock options as well as their salary, bonuses, restricted stock grants and long-term incentive pay-outs. By this measure, the CEOs received in 2016, on average, 271 times the annual average worker's wage. This compares with the 59:1 ratio that had been typical in 1989 and the even lower 20:1 ratio back in 1965. The average remuneration in 2016 was $15.6 million per CEO.

The second column in the same table shows a different calculation of CEO incomes, based on the original value of the stock options granted to CEOs. By this measure, the total income was generally a little lower. This is not surprising, because CEOs holding these stock options can watch the fluctuating stock market trends and choose the best times to cash in their options. One would hardly expect less from the 'agents of capital' when strategically managing their own assets and incomes.

Table 4.3 Trends in CEO-to-worker income ratio, USA, 1965–2016

Year	CEO-to-worker remuneration ratio[a]	
	Based on options realized	Based on options granted
1965	20.2	18.4
1973	22.5	20.5
1978	30.1	27.4
1989	58.9	53.7
1995	122.6	136.8
2000	376.1	411.3
2007	347.5	240.8
2009	196.6	183.9
2010	230.3	206.3
2011	232.7	213.2
2012	281.5	209.8
2013	291.8	214.5
2014	298.7	224.5
2015	286.1	219.7
2016[b]	270.5	223.8

Notes: [a] Data values based on averaging specific firm ratios and not the ratio of averages of CEO and worker remuneration; [b] projected value for 2016 is based on the change in CEO pay as measured from June 2015 to June 2016 applied to the full-year 2015 value – projections for remuneration based on options granted and options realized are calculated separately.

Source: Mishel & Schieder (2017: 6).

Countries vary significantly in the ratio of CEO incomes to median wages but the relativities have widened everywhere. The USA is at the top end, internationally, in terms of the levels to which extra CEO remuneration has risen. This is not surprising, given the broadly positive correlation between countries according to the inequality of incomes, measured by the Gini coefficient, and the ratios of CEO incomes to average workers' incomes (Block 2016: 5).

Are CEOs worth it? If their expertise boosts the profits of the businesses they manage, some might say that they 'earn' their incomes many times over. However, empirical studies show little evidence of any direct connection between the performance of the businesses and the level of these rewards (Shields 2005; Schofield-Georgeson 2018). One study of 429 large companies in the USA even found that returns to shareholders were lower over a 10-year period in companies where the CEO got a higher than average payment (Wilkinson & Pickett 2018: 245). In other words, there seems to be little justification in terms of increased business efficiency or long-term company performance. This is despite the ostensible connection often built in when part of the remuneration takes the form of incentive payments and bonuses based on movements in the company's share price. Indeed, as has been commonly noted in the business press, such arrangements can have perverse effects because they encourage a short-term focus on share prices that is not conducive to long-term business success.

We may reasonably infer that it is not efficiency but the behaviour of a self-rewarding oligarchy that explains the spectacular growth of CEO remuneration. As Lars Syll writes (2014: 39), 'It is indeed difficult to see the takeoff of the top executives as anything else but a reward for being a member of the same illustrious club.' Some political economic analysts regard it as just the apex of a more pervasive hierarchical process operating throughout modern business (Fix 2018). There is a broader stratum of top managers having distinct interests that diverge from those of shareholders, notwithstanding recurrent assertions about shareholders' interests being the top priority. The divergence of their interests from the interests of other *stake*holders (including customers and workers) is yet more evident (Schofield-Georgeson 2018).

Conclusion

When a spotlight shines onto the extremes in any distribution, quite striking differences usually appear. When looking at economic inequality – in comparison with, say, people's height or weight – this is particularly apparent. At the top end of the distribution of income and wealth, the extreme affluence is hard for most people to imagine. The top 1% are faring extraordinarily well, getting a rapidly growing share of income and wealth, in both developed and developing countries. The situation of the low-income groups and people living in poverty is comparatively stable in both. However, while the middle-income people are becoming more numerous in many, but not all, of the poorer nations, the middle-income groups in the richer countries are not getting the gains that had been their normal experience for much of the twentieth century. These shifts in the global pattern of income and wealth have potentially enormous economic, social, environmental and political implications that will be discussed in later chapters.

In summary, the evidence in this chapter shows the following:

- Worldwide, the top 1% of households has become much richer during recent decades, both in absolute incomes and relative to a broad middle-income group.
- The total income of the poorest half of the world's population is growing but comprises a stable share of the total.
- Countries vary considerably in how their inequalities are changing. Among the poorer nations, there are huge contrasts between those in which many people have risen from poverty and those where few people have experienced significant gains. Among the affluent nations, the USA is the prime example of where economic inequality is high and growing.

This evidence provokes – and leads directly into – a more detailed consideration of what characteristics shape people's economic positions in a highly unequal world.

5

Multi-dimensional Inequalities

To what extent are personal attributes relevant to inequality? The preceding two chapters have looked at broad economic aggregates. Their focus has been on the principal patterns of inequalities in incomes and wealth, internationally, within nations and globally. Probing who gets what also requires study of the structural elements shaping people's personal positions in the pecking order. If we are not 'all in the same boat', what determines who floats and who sinks? We need analysis of the socio-economic characteristics of distribution.

This chapter looks at location, class, gender and race as four primary influences. Beginning with location provides a bridge with the international differences discussed in the preceding two chapters, but also introduces consideration of urban and regional differences. Attention then turns to how class, gender and race relate to the social structure of capitalist economies. Consideration of age comes next, reflecting current concerns about stressful inter-generational economic inequalities. Looking at the effects of ability and disability then leads into concluding reflections on whether luck or effort is the bigger influence on personal economic outcomes. This is a step-by-step exploration of some complex territory, traversing geography and sociology as well as political economy. It leads to a view of inequality as multi-dimensional and multiplicative, creating cumulative advantages for some and cumulative disadvantages for others. Figure 5.1 on the next page provides a general guide to the journey.

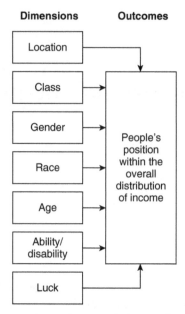

Figure 5.1 Social intersections of economic inequality

Location

Geography matters. Its fundamental importance should already be evident from the preceding two chapters. The probability of being poor or rich depends on the country you inhabit but also on where in those countries you are located: within cities or rural areas, in rich suburbs or slums.

The country in which you were born is the foundational influence. As Branko Milanovic says: 'Our world today is still a world in which the place where we were born or where we live matters enormously, determining perhaps as much as two-thirds of our lifetime income' (2016: 5). He goes on to call this the 'citizenship rent' of being in a generally affluent nation. It signals a strong reason to consider the locational 'luck of the draw'. It also signals the importance of international inequalities as a driver of economically motivated migration flows.

A second spatial scale of economic inequality involves regions within nations. Although often less dramatic than international inequalities, regional inequalities can be substantial and are to be found in most nations. In the USA, for example, the prosperous cities and regions in which economic growth is buoyant contrast with 'rust-belt' areas facing the problems of de-industrialization and persistent unemployment; think Seattle versus Cleveland. In Italy, there is a long-standing difference between the circumstances of the north and south, with the economic conditions in the latter (*il mezzogiorno*) remaining more problematic despite decades of government assistance. In the UK, there is a similarly long-standing north–south inequality problem. Indeed, it is hard to think of countries other than small city-states like Singapore where there is not some degree of regional economic inequality. Like international economic inequalities, these intra-national spatial inequalities are also a big influence on migratory processes and pressures.

The third geographical scale relates to the urban–rural differences within nations. Imbalances between city and country are usually evident in the range of economic opportunities they offer. Historically, the growth of towns resulted in part from the creation of economic surpluses in agriculture within the countryside (Jacobs 1969). The larger cities, then, tend to have the economic edge because it is there that modern industries are more developed, economic opportunities more diverse and services more readily available. Average incomes also generally tend to be higher. Rural regions can be prosperous, too, of course, especially where they have fertile soil and efficient agricultural practices. Alternatively, they may have valuable mineral resources, the extraction of which boosts local incomes (although commonly those incomes flow substantially to urban elites) (Østby 2016). Nevertheless, rural–urban migration, propelled by the perception of better economic opportunities in the cities, continues to be one of the main drivers of urban growth, nowhere more so today than in China.

Structural economic and social inequalities are also etched into the landscape at the 'micro' level of localities and communities. There are big differences between the more affluent and poorer neighbourhoods in most cities, where housing markets act as harsh 'sorting mechanisms' dividing rich and poor people according to their ability to pay. Discriminatory practices, too, may intensify ghetto formations by marginalized groups. Mobility at this intra-urban scale is notably hard: even though the physical distances are relatively small, the economic and social barriers are often formidable. Wealthy households congregate in elite areas while poorer households inhabit whatever places they can afford with their lower incomes. As urban political economist David

Harvey (1989: 265) aptly observed, the rich command space, while the poor are trapped in it.

Does this matter? Some say not, arguing that the spatial inequalities are simply the outcome of where people are born and where they choose to live, taking account of job opportunities, housing costs and transport facilities. Seen from this perspective, markets for land, labour and capital facilitate choices that lead to the most efficient geographical outcomes, allowing people to locate where they can afford, given the prevailing distribution of income and wealth. By contrast, a spatial political economic viewpoint draws our attention to the systemic factors that reproduce and amplify the spatial inequalities. Spatial inertia is pervasive because mobility is constrained by border restrictions, economic resources, familial connections, personal networks and loyalties. Vicious circles commonly intensify spatial inequalities too, tending to compound the inequalities that originate from people's different socio-economic positions.

Class

Class is the second major dimension of inequality. It shapes people's economic and social relationships, whether as waged workers, self-employed contractors, small business owners or 'captains of industry'. Like location, it can also affect the entrenched character of inequality. However, class, as a concept, requires careful handling (Wright 2005). Used in popular discourse, it can have quite different interpretations and meanings. Many people are uncomfortable about even using the word, perhaps because of its association with the politics of Marxism and the encouragement of class struggle. Some conservatives think that even talking about class is a source of unnecessary social division. Seriously considering the relevance of class as an analytical tool must acknowledge but also challenge these discomforts and misconceptions (Das 2017).

David Harvey makes the point strongly when he writes that 'inequality is foundational for capital. The inequality derives from the simple fact that capital is socially and historically constructed as a class dominance over labour. The distribution of income and wealth has to be lopsided if capital is reproduced. Distributional equality and capital are incompatible' (2014: 171–2). Why is this so? The key point is the identification of capitalism as an economic system based on class relationships. To produce goods and services requires cooperation between capital and labour. There is also a fundamental tension, however, because capital and labour have differential power and receive different types of material reward.

As a class, capital owns the means of production; labour in general does not. Capital hires labour, not vice versa. Workers get wages; employers get profits. It is therefore not surprising that class conflicts recurrently arise over questions of distribution. If the productivity of a capitalist business is rising, for example, how should the fruits be shared? How much should go to the employees and how much to the employer? Class relations are crucial in shaping the outcomes. As in any power struggle, these outcomes depend upon relative bargaining power. For example, the power of labour relative to capital is weaker when there is a 'reserve army of labour' comprising unemployed people and newly arrived migrants willing to work for lower wages. Capitalist employers may also enhance their power if they fragment the workforce to inhibit the possibilities for labour's collective organization.

Similar tensions relate to landowners and tenants (whether tenant farmers, small businesses or residential users). As humans, we need physical space. Land is necessary for most forms of economic activity. To produce food, extract minerals, manufacture goods and provide services entails the use of land to greater or lesser degrees. Who owns or controls access to these 'gifts of nature' is therefore crucial. Thus, landed property is a distinct class, even though in the modern economy there are significant crossovers with the ownership of capital. Still, the interests of businesspeople who want to lease land on which to situate their business activities commonly conflict with landowners' interests, even if only in haggling over the rent payable. Landowners' interests are also commonly at odds with the interests of dispossessed indigenous peoples and with workers whose economic opportunities depend on access to the land.

Certain things follow from this way of conceptualizing class in terms of relationships to the means of production. Perhaps the most challenging notion is that the size of a person's income class does not define their class. Capitalists, landowners and workers may all be either rich or poor. Within classes, too, there can be enormous differences of incomes and wealth. Nor do people's different consumption patterns define their class: capitalists may ride bicycles or drive expensive cars, while workers may go to work in overalls or suits. Of course, income levels and patterns of consumption often correlate with their ownership or non-ownership of the means of production – and they may therefore be useful secondary indicators of class position – but they are not themselves defining features. Class positions depend primarily on the source and nature, not the size, of incomes.

The question of 'class consciousness' then arises. Individual workers sometimes perceive themselves to have a common interest with other workers in the same firm, in other firms or in distant lands. Alternatively, they may think they have more interests in common with their employers and, if so, that will usually have a significant bearing on their behaviour, including their political inclinations. Only when people are class conscious are they likely to act collectively to address their common circumstances.

Class structures, interests and actions are also in continual flux. As shown in Figure 2.3, there has been a worldwide shift of income shares from labour to the owners of capital and land during the last half-century. This is *prima facie* evidence of a shift in relative class power. As US multi-billionaire Warren Buffett famously said, 'There's class war all right, but it is my class, the rich class, that's making war, and we're winning.' This refreshingly frank statement shows both capitalist class consciousness and recognition of the trends in income shares. Indeed, the class to which Buffett belongs has been gaining, making class position increasingly important in shaping political economic outcomes.

Gender

Gender divisions in society are also pervasive. Indeed, they are more directly visible than class divisions because there is less ambiguity about the basis of classification. Importantly, though, gender is not the same as sex: it refers specifically to socially constructed, rather than biologically determined, roles for men and women. Labour market segmentation, often with men dominating in the better-paid occupations, is usually unrelated to physical capabilities. The result is that women consistently show up less well on indicators of economic position and reward. A political economic analysis of inequality needs to take account of this pervasive gender dimension of who does what and who gets what.

The 'gender wage gap' is the clearest numerical expression of the inequality between average male and female incomes from paid employment. It is normally calculated as the difference between the two averages when this is expressed as a percentage of the male

Table 5.1 Gender wage gap: difference between wages of full-time female and male employees as percentage of male median wage, 2000–15[a]

Country	Wage gap (%)	
	2000	**2015**
Republic of Korea	39.6	37.2
Estonia[b]	25.0	28.3
Japan	28.7	25.7
Chile	6.1	21.1
Latvia[b]	18.9	21.1
Israel[c]	28.1	19.3
Portugal	13.5	18.9
USA	18.8	18.9
Canada	19.0	18.6
Finland	18.9	18.1
UK	19.2	17.1
Austria	19.2	17.0
Switzerland[d]	23.8	16.9
Mexico	11.6	16.7
Czech Republic	15.8	16.5
Germany	16.6	15.7
Ireland	12.8	14.5
OECD	17.8	14.3
Netherlands[b]	16.1	14.1
Slovak Republic[e]	20.4	13.4
Sweden[f]	15.5	13.4
Australia	14.0	13.0
Spain[b]	17.2	11.5
Poland[g]	14.3	11.1
France[b]	13.3	9.9
Iceland[h]	19.2	9.9
Hungary	14.1	9.5
New Zealand	7.2	7.9
Norway	8.1	7.1
Turkey[d]	n/a	6.9
Greece	n/a	6.3
Denmark	8.9	5.8
Italy[i]	8.5	5.6
Slovenia[b]	9.4	5.0
Belgium	13.6	4.7
Luxembourg[b]	15.1	3.4

Notes: [a] Includes full-time and self-employed workers; [b] data for Estonia, France, Latvia, Luxembourg, the Netherlands, Slovenia and Spain are for 2002 and 2014, respectively; [c] data for Israel in the left column are for 2001; [d] data for Switzerland and Turkey in the right column are for 2014; [e] data for the Slovak Republic in the left column are for 2002; [f] data for Sweden in the right column are for 2013; [g] data for Poland are for 2001 and 2014, respectively; [h] data for Iceland in the left column are for 2004; [i] data for Italy in the right column are for 2014.
Source: https://data.oecd.org/earnwage/gender-wage-gap.htm.

wage. Table 5.1 on the preceding page shows the gender wage gap for full-time workers and self-employed workers in OECD countries in 2015, ranked from those with the biggest gap to those with the smallest. Evidently, most European countries are streets ahead of countries like Japan and South Korea in nearing gender wage equality. Closing the gap is proving to be painfully slow in most nations, despite the influence of equal-pay policies and attempts to prohibit discrimination. As Table 5.1 shows, some countries have even slipped backwards since 2000. Because waged part-time work is normally more common among women workers, the gaps are yet wider when wages of part-time workers are included.

Opinions vary as to why these gender wage inequalities persist. Does the higher proportion of women generally in lower-paid occupations reflect a genuine choice or does it reflect processes of socialization and the cultural value attached to different types of work? If, as mainstream economists tend to argue, women's educational and career paths are based on objective choices, influenced by their expectations of more interrupted working lives, the persistence of gender wage gaps does not seem to be such a problem. That is, if women anticipate shorter and more discontinuous work lives than men because of their child-bearing roles, they have less incentive to invest in training or in education designed for long-term employment in a particular occupation. On this reasoning, the general wage relativities reflect gender differences in 'human capital' – differences in how much investment the workers have been prepared to make in themselves (for a survey, see Blau & Kahn 2017).

Political economists, particularly those of feminist inclination (both female and male), present more critical perspectives. They are more inclined to see the problem arising from processes of socialization originating during childhood and from discriminatory practices that operate in labour markets and workplaces, notwithstanding the frequent presence of regulations formally requiring gender equity (e.g. Folbre 2012). Occupational aspirations are often formed early in life as young girls tend to express a preference for work that involves creative expression or helping others – and these occupations often have low wages from the outset (England 2005). Thus, it is the typically lower wage rates for occupations in which women are concentrated that is the more fundamental issue. Public policies may add to this tendency if they are based on assumptions about women's child-bearing roles reducing their labour-force participation. Then once an occupation becomes characteristically female, it tends to incur a wage penalty. This observation supports the 'devaluation' thesis: that, culturally, women are commonly deprecated and thus, by association, the work that they typically do is undervalued (Folbre 2018).

Women's under-representation among the higher echelons in many occupations is indicative of these deep-seated influences on gender inequalities. Most notorious is the 'glass ceiling' that results in under-representation of women in senior professional and managerial positions and on companies' boards of directors, with few country exceptions. The problem is not just located at the top, though: it reflects a relatively pervasive bias throughout promotion and career advancement processes. The introduction of quotas to deal with all such ongoing problems can make a difference, although attempts at affirmative action (or 'reverse discrimination', as its opponents call it) frequently encounter entrenched resistance.

How gender inequalities relate to the structures and interests within capitalism has long been controversial (Hewitson 1999). Gender inequalities preceded capitalism, of course, but they continue to serve important purposes for capital. Feminist theorist Sylvia Federici (2004, 2012) argues that the inequalities facilitate the capital accumulation process, not primarily because of pay inequalities in capitalist workplaces but because of the more fundamental divisions between paid and unpaid work. The latter is a disproportionately female sphere, shaping the relationship of the household to the needs of capital and underpinning gender division within the working class. Such considerations have more transformative political implications, emphasizing everyday life, communities and new forms of solidarity.

Gendered differences in wealth are yet more significant than gendered inequalities of income. This wealth–income distinction is central throughout the political economy of inequality, as we have seen in earlier chapters, and it is not surprising that it has a gender dimension. Over centuries, women have been put at a disadvantage by patrimonial influences on rights to hold property and get bank loans, and, particularly, by patterns of inheritance. Because the household is the basic unit of analysis in many official statistics, gendered wealth inequality is less easy to track than gender pay gaps. Yet it is arguably more fundamental for those seeking a genuinely level playing field.

Gendered inequalities are pervasive and multi-layered. Their origins and manifestations include household composition, unpaid work and socialization, differences in job opportunities, wages and promotion possibilities, together with social factors and public policies compounding inequalities of wealth. These gendered inequalities also intersect with other socio-economic differences, such as class and ethnicity. Women from lower class positions, indigenous communities, disadvantaged ethnic groups and marginalized social groups, such as single parents, are often doubly or trebly disadvantaged, faring worse than men in similar social positions and ranking closer to the bottom of the economic scale.

Race

Economic inequalities based on ethnicity or race are similar to gender inequality in some respects but fundamentally different in others. Both involve differences in economic rewards arising from personal characteristics rather than from ability or productivity. Both are violations of equality of opportunity. Race-based inequality also relates closely to class. As David Harvey writes: 'Racial issues in many parts of the world (such as the United States) have long been so intertwined with questions of class as to make the two mutually reinforcing if not sometimes indistinguishable categories' (2014: 166). Yet both analytically and socially, race *is* different. Current scientific knowledge shows no clear physical basis for classifying people according to race (showing the fundamental fallacy of the so-called 'science of eugenics' that was formerly used to provide legitimacy for the differential treatment of ethnic groups). Yet *racism* certainly persists and it has a major bearing on who does what and who gets what. It results in people of different ethnic origin being concentrated in different types of occupations or having different degrees of difficulty in getting paid work. Minorities may face a smaller array of economic opportunities and have average incomes well below more favoured groups.

Analysis of how racism, as a socially constructed process, impacts on economic inequality is controversial. One view is that it is quite independent of the economic system. From this perspective, racism, and the associated processes of discrimination and socio-economic disadvantage, is not attributable to capitalism and equally likely to characterize any other socio-economic system. Mainstream economists have sometimes taken this position. Gary Becker (1971) developed an influential theory to explain why capitalism should actually reduce racism. He posited that, if racially discriminating employers prefer white employees to black employees, for example, they have to pay a wage premium. Employers who are willing to hire ethnic minorities will therefore have a lower wage bill and lower overall costs of production. In a competitive market economy, the higher-cost firms will go out of business; only the non-discriminating employers will remain. The renowned conservative economist Milton Friedman had previously expressed a similar view to that of his Chicago colleague, saying that 'a businessman or entrepreneur who expressed his preferences in his business activity that are not related to productive efficiency is in effect imposing higher costs on himself than other individuals who do not have such preferences. Hence, in a free market they will tend to drive him out' (Friedman 1962: 108). On similar neoclassical economic reasoning, it would be best for the government to refrain from trying to prohibit discrimination because any such regulations would tend to create unemployment among the less favoured ethnic groups. In other words, enforced wage parity would tend to benefit those fortunate to get jobs, but at the expense of those who would then find it harder to get work at all.

Political economists generally regard the problem of racial discrimination quite differently. They criticize neoclassical theorizing like Becker's and Friedman's on grounds that you, the reader, may already be anticipating. They point out that it is unrealistic to assume that both labour and commodity markets operate in a competitive manner and that racist 'preferences' are purely personal rather than institutionally embedded. Looking from a broader political economic perspective, racism needs to be analysed as systemic. Seen in this way, the reproduction of race-based economic inequalities arises from the normal functioning of institutions and the economic interests that have a stake in their perpetuation. If, for example, racism results in divisions among workers that undermine their ability to achieve higher wages through collective action, one may judge that to be in the general interests of capitalists, irrespective of whether individual employers have racist or non-racist hiring practices. Moreover, enacting a 'divide and rule' strategy that fragments the working class, while not causing the racism, may perpetuate it to the advantage of capitalist employers (Leiman 2010).

A vicious circle of discrimination and material disadvantage also pervades processes of exclusion created by racism, leading to its perpetuation. The members of a marginalized minority group, being relatively poor, are likely to be less well educated, more poorly dressed and more prone to anti-social behaviour such as crimes against property. That fuels widespread belief that the minority group is inherently different, unworthy of a helping hand and probably to be shunned or suppressed. In effect, the legacy of past discrimination thereby serves as a justification for further discrimination. Spatial concentration of disadvantaged ethnic groups may compound the problem, as in ghettos where minority groups are concentrated. The possibility of an individual achieving upward economic and social mobility becomes more remote in these circumstances.

The nature and extent of the resulting economic inequalities vary from country to country. South Africa is a particularly problematic case: a legacy of racism and nearly half a century of apartheid left the country with deep scars that persist after more than two decades of democratic government by black African political leaders. According to the 2017 *Living Conditions of Households in South Africa* survey, while the gap between the average incomes of white and non-white citizens had narrowed since the previous survey results released in 2011, a huge disparity remains. The survey revealed that white South Africans receive the highest average incomes, over one and a half times greater than Indian and Asian South Africans, more than double the income of mixed race (what in the local context have been called 'coloured' people) and almost five times more than black South Africans.

In the USA, the relative economic advantage of African-Americans is also notorious. Even after a century and a half of freedom from slavery – and the symbolic value of having had an African-American as President – their economic disadvantage remains entrenched. Contrary to national narratives about progress towards racial equality, the country remains deeply divided along racial lines. One study showed that, in 2016, the median household income of African-Americans was $39,500, compared with $65,000 for non-Hispanic white Americans (Chetty et al. 2018). Another, looking at the dimensions of inequality in terms of household wealth, showed that median white household wealth in 2011 was $111,146, while the median wealth of African-American and Latino households was only $7,113 and $8,348, respectively. Thus, black and Latino households had an average of only around 7% of the wealth of white households. Race evidently trumps education too, judging by the financial returns to higher education: the same study also found that there was an average return of over $55,000 wealth for people in white families completing a four-year college degree, but the corresponding figures for black and Latino families were under $5,000 (Sullivan et al. 2015). In 2013, the wealthiest 100 people on the *Forbes* list of the richest Americans had wealth roughly equal to the entire African-American population, while the wealthiest 186 people on the same list owned as much wealth as the entire Latino population (Collins et al. 2016).

Popular perceptions are quite different. As Michael Kraus, Julian Rucker and Jennifer Richeson (2017) demonstrated in their study of the divergence between the perception and reality of racial inequality in the USA, 'Americans, on average, systematically over-estimate the extent to which society has progressed toward racial economic equality, driven largely by overestimates of current racial equality.' The same study also showed, not surprisingly, that the race of respondents had a significant effect on their perception of the ongoing problem of racial inequality. High-income white respondents were more likely to overestimate advancement towards racial equality than low-income white participants or black participants of either income group.

Meanwhile in the UK, immigrants from India, Pakistan and the Caribbean have been the major groups experiencing economic disadvantage. These ethnic minorities continue to experience significantly worse than average living standards. A report by the Resolution Foundation (Corlett 2017) demonstrates the continuing dominance of white British households relative to many minorities. The median equivalized disposable income (before housing costs) for white British families was calculated as £25,300. For British Bangladeshis and Pakistanis, it was less than £17,000 and just under £20,000 on average for black African households. British Indian households had average incomes significantly higher than other minority groups and closer to their white counterparts at £25,000. On the other hand, British Bangladeshis were worse off than any other community with average household disposable incomes of around £8,900 (35%) less than white households, while Pakistani households earned £8,700 (34%) less. All groups had an upward trend in disposable incomes over the decade, as shown in Figure 5.2 on the next page, but the race-based inequalities have persisted. These inequalities loom even larger if housing costs are considered, because the immigrant groups tend to be in towns and cities where rents and housing prices are generally more expensive.

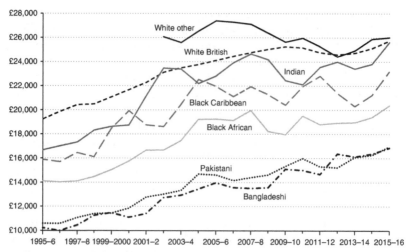

Figure 5.2 Median equivalized disposable income, by ethnicity of household, UK, before housing costs (2016–17 prices), two-year average

Source: Corlett (2017).

The racial dimension of inequality is not only an intra-national phenomenon. Migrants and refugees who come from other countries, especially when they do not speak the language of the country in which they now live, face particular problems in establishing anything resembling socio-economic equality. Where racism is pervasive, this is a further impediment. The disadvantage faced by Indigenous peoples is yet more deep-seated. When their dispossession from their land is compounded by ongoing racial discrimination, this adds insult to the injury of social injustice. The situations faced by Indigeous peoples in many settler and post-colonial societies, such as Canada, New Zealand and Australia, are illustrative. The failure of successive governments (especially in the last of these three cases) to provide much more than token recognitions of the problems is a clear illustration of how entrenched is this racial dimension of inequality.

Age

Is age another basis on which economic inequality is structured? This has become a hot topic recently because many young people are feeling more than usually disadvantaged by the difficult economic conditions that an older generation has bequeathed to them. You have probably heard the complaint: that the 'baby boomer generation' had an easy run but has left generations 'X' and 'Y' and 'Millennials' facing a much tougher situation. Soaring housing costs in many nations feature prominently among such concerns, making home ownership or even rental more unaffordable for younger generations than it was for their parents. Thus, the rising land and housing values that have added to the wealth of owner-occupiers have, as their flip-side, the housing unaffordability problem facing younger first-home buyers. Concurrently, labour market conditions are now commonly insecure, making it difficult for young people to plan and develop careers with predictable income streams.

The existence of age-based inequalities is not novel, of course. A distinctive life-cycle pattern in incomes and wealth is normal. Income is nearly always non-existent or tiny when people are very young, grows as they move into adulthood and employment, usually peaks during middle age and often falls after retirement and into the senior years. Wealth has a characteristically different pattern over the life-cycle, starting at zero, typically growing during middle age and continuing to increase after retirement as personal living expenses diminish, while the accumulated wealth produces ongoing income. At that later life-stage, declining independence may be associated with care in an extended household or in an elderly persons' nursing home. These are typical 'Western middle-class' life-cycle patterns of income and wealth. If that were all that is at issue, one might well say: so what's new? Moreover, compared with inequalities based on class, gender or race, those based on age seem less contentious, since each of us can reasonably expect to pass through the different stages.

A more nuanced view is that *intra*-generational inequalities interact with the inter-generational inequalities, causing distinctively different degrees of stress. People with different class, gender and racial characteristics seldom experience the life-cycle in similar ways. For working-class households, especially those in poverty, the difficulty of accumulating assets dominates the life-cycle income and wealth pattern. This means that old age, if reached at all, is typically much tougher: dependency on younger family members, charity or the state (if any such policy exists) is often unavoidable in those circumstances. At the other extreme, young people born into families with rich parents normally enjoy a much easier and steadier economic trajectory through each of the life-stages.

A careful analysis by Brett Christophers (2018) indicates that these 'within-generation' inequalities are important drivers of what appear to be inter-generational inequalities. First, the broad temporal shift in national (or global) income shares from labour to capital has generally added to the relative economic advantage of older people. This is because it is usually older people who have more capital, having had a longer opportunity to accumulate wealth. Second, there is the effect of growing disparities in economic opportunities and reward for different types of labour. Those well-educated young people getting the best-paid jobs surge ahead of their peers, and are therefore in a better position to save and buy assets as they get older. Their relative advantage is accentuated if they inherit wealth from parents or grandparents. Even if they do not directly inherit a family home, children in the more wealthy families are the main beneficiaries of inter-generational transfers to assist them with their purchase of housing. As a study of changing housing arrangements in OECD countries put it: 'In the millennial cohort, exit from the parental home increasingly requires supplementing own wages with parental resources' (Flynn & Schwartz 2017: 472). At a time when the median price of a house or apartment is many multiples of the average annual wage, young people receiving parental support like that can avoid the problem of exclusion from home ownership that so many other young people experience.

Christophers concludes that 'within-generation housing inequality ... begets between-generation housing inequality' (2018: 115). None of this, he emphasizes, is to downplay the difficulties many young people currently experience in both labour and housing markets. Rather, those problems need to be understood in relation to more long-standing class inequalities and the advantages and disadvantages that tend to compound over time.

In the end, we are all gone (although, hopefully, not all at the same time). Death and inheritance is then the issue. On average, the rich live longer than the poor; but when they die, their wills nearly always transfer the bulk of their estates to spouses and children (and sometimes grandchildren). Gifts may also precede these legacies, especially where that helps avoid any taxation of inherited wealth. Thus, the inter-generational transfer of wealth reproduces in succeeding generations the wealth inequalities of the previous generations.

Ability, disability, effort and luck

What about personal abilities and efforts? That this consideration comes towards the end of this chapter may seem surprising to some readers because, in a truly meritocratic society, one would expect ability and effort to be the primary influences on material rewards. Isn't being especially good at something the key to economic success? Isn't ability, combined with effort and perhaps a slice of luck, the principal basis for differential rewards?

People's ability does have a significant bearing on their prospects of receiving above-average incomes and therefore having the possibility to accumulate wealth. Ability is sometimes a matter of innate talent but, more typically, it is an outcome of human capacities that have been nurtured by education and training. Those born into privileged circumstances are more likely to have their talents developed in ways that add to future incomes and wealth. Inheritance is not just a matter of what you get when older family members 'drop off the twig'. It is a broader array of environmental benefits (or deprivations) that shape people's life-chances. 'Choosing your parents wisely' is a tongue-in-cheek phrase, of course, because none of us makes any such choice. Yet our parents and their wealth (or lack thereof) crucially shape our life-chances, quite apart from the possibilities of getting gifts or material inheritance when they pass on. Home environments and schooling shape networks of social contacts that may be crucial for jobs, developing careers, opening up investment opportunities and much more. Or not.

Effort matters too. Exceptional ability may flourish even in the absence of a privileged environment. Combined with effort, it can lead to significant upward mobility. Indeed, effort is the necessary corollary of ability in many fields of human endeavour, particularly for people 'from the wrong side of the tracks'. Effort spent on acquiring and developing skills is particularly important. Economists often posit a quite straightforward relationship between skill and rewards, saying that skilled people tend to be less numerous, have higher productivity and can always command a premium wage. Thus, skill affects the conditions of both demand and supply in ways that are conducive to higher market rewards. But what really is 'skill' and how high is the premium it commands? There can be a tendency to circular reasoning here: in effect, identifying the value of the skill as whatever is the wage premium. Take, for example, payments to professional sportspeople or movie actors. International superstars earn multiple millions of dollars annually. They are great to watch but so too are many other players and performers who get only a small fraction of their incomes. What determines the relativity? Some say that a winner-takes-all (or at least winner-takes-most) tendency swamps payment differentials in fields such as this (Frank & Cook 1995; Frank 2016). In other words, to the extent that skill affects incomes, it does not do so in a linear manner; rather, it is part of a broader set of polarizing political economic influences that determine market power and rewards.

Chance is the most enigmatic element in this story. It has diverse forms. One is betting. A big lottery win can certainly make a life-changing difference to the lucky winner, although the more likely effect of habitual gambling is to cause poverty rather than riches (Rooke 2018). Other forms of chance are as pervasive as life itself. Think about just 'being in the right place at the right time' to take advantage of particular economic opportunities. Getting a job in the finance industry in the late twentieth century just before it took off into spectacular growth would be a case in point. Or, conversely, getting a job with the financial institution Lehman Brothers in 2008 just before it went out of business, precipitating the global financial crash. There is often, if not always, an element of randomness bearing on personal outcomes in the real world (Leigh 2015). For individuals, not everything is explicable in terms of political economic structures. Many things over which we have little control can make a difference, for better or worse, throughout our lives. Even whether you are physically pretty or handsome, as commonly understood, tends to bear systematically on personal economic outcomes (Hamermesh 2011).

For people with disabilities the situation is different. The presence of personal disability correlates strongly with the incidence of poverty. A number of factors contribute to this close association. They include problems of workplace participation, the extra costs that people with disabilities may incur and inadequate government assistance. On average, people with disabilities have lower workforce participation rates and higher unemployment rates than most other groups in society. Combined with the higher cost of living – such as the costs of medication, special equipment and appropriate housing – this leads to an increased risk of poverty. Inadequate government assistance in various policy areas, such as education, health, transport and housing, frequently exacerbates the situation (Soldatic & Sykes 2017). The dominant representation of disability only as a medical phenomenon also tends to shift the focus away from the responsibility of society to accommodate people with a disability, labelling the impairment, rather than society's response to it, as the problem. What constitutes a disability is indeed, to an extent, socially and subjectively defined (Gibilisco 2014).

Conclusion

This chapter has taken a disaggregated approach to considering inequality, acknowledging a more variegated pattern than revealed in the preceding two chapters. It shows the systemic influences of location, class, gender, race, age, ability and disability, both in structuring the extent of inequality and in determining individually who gets what. Being born a white male in a capitalist class household in an affluent society reliably produces more economic and social opportunities than are normally available to, say, a girl of colour in a poor household in a less developed nation. The inequalities start early and tend to cumulate over lifetimes.

We may conclude the following:

- People's positions in the overall distribution of income or wealth depends substantially on differences of location, class, race, gender, age, ability and disability.
- These factors shaping advantage and disadvantage are not merely additive: they tend to be multiplicative, creating cumulative advantage and disadvantage.
- Skills, effort and luck also shape economic rewards and social positions; personal disposition and chance thereby add greater complexity to the structural aspects of inequality.

Studying these socio-economic dimensions of inequality reveals the patterns of advantage and disadvantage. Yet some big issues remain unresolved. What determines the overall extent of inequality? What makes inequalities increase or decrease over time? Seeking answers to these questions requires engagement with competing political economic theories.

Processes

6

Explaining Who Gets What

What shapes the patterns of inequality described in the three preceding chapters? Do markets provide 'level playing fields' on which the prices of labour, capital and land are equitably determined? Or is it the capacity to extract 'rents' above market prices that leads to the highest rewards? Is analysis of class power a useful prism through which inequality may be viewed?

This chapter explores questions like these by looking at the theories that mainstream economists and their political economic critics have developed to explain the determinants of income and wealth. Identifying three clusters of theory helps to clarify the competing perspectives. The first emphasizes productivity, seeing the value of people's economic contributions reflected in their incomes. The second emphasizes 'market distortions' that enable some people to extract more than their productive contributions while others get less. The third view emphasizes the processes of exploitation and oppression in more deeply embedded inequalities. Finally, we look at Thomas Piketty's influential book *Capital in the Twenty-First Century*, seeing what is significant about its message and where its sits in relation to these theories.

Attributing inequality to productivity

There is a 'folksy' view that, in general, people get what they deserve. Modern mainstream economists would normally distance themselves from such an explicitly normative interpretation of inequality. Yet some economic theories give it legitimacy and support by representing income inequalities as the outcome of an economic system that rewards people according to their productive contribution. The most obvious example is *marginal productivity theory*, a standard part of neoclassical economics taught to university economics students, usually in their introductory course. The textbooks present the theory with varying degrees of elaboration and qualification. Simply, it explains that labour, capital and land are 'factors of production' that are rewarded at the margin according to their contribution to the aggregate product. The phrase 'at the margin' denotes that the income attributed to each factor of production (or component thereof) depends on the addition to total output that results from employing an extra unit. It is the marginal productivity of the different factors of production, relative to their market prices, that determines employers' demand for them. More broadly, variations in productivity between labour, land and capital shape the income shares.

This reasoning rests on a theoretical logic of profit-maximizing behaviour and pays little attention paid to actual business practices. Its focus on the demand for factors of production also tends to neglect their supply, even though (according to standard neoclassical principles) demand and supply jointly determine the market price. Neoclassical economists developed *human capital theory* (Becker 1964) to address the latter concern. This theory focuses on how the market prices of different types of labour relate to human attributes: an amalgam of intelligence, training and experience that may affect productivity. This is a step forward in two respects. First, it emphasizes the heterogeneity of labour as a factor of production, ranging from relatively unskilled to highly skilled. Second, it recognizes that investment in the acquisition of skills can pay off, sometimes handsomely. It is useful to see how education, for example, can enhance skills and what incentive structures are conducive to that investment, whether by individuals or by whole societies. What is the private return on investment in education? What is its social return? Indeed, it is interesting to explore to what extent inequality results from different amounts of investment in 'human capital'.

It may be said, however, that calling labour 'capital' is a rather uncomfortable elision of human and physical elements. Indeed, the concept of human capital is controversial, like using the terms 'natural capital' and 'social capital' to analyse issues of environmental quality and social cohesion (Fine 2010; Gleeson-White 2014; Hodgson 2014). The commodification of the human person is implied. Moreover, the basic message conveyed by human capital theory remains fundamentally similar to the more long-standing marginal productivity theory. Both emphasize market determination of rewards according to productivity. The main difference is that, instead of taking productivity as given, human capital theory directs attention towards how individual and societal investments may raise it. In both cases, there is the presumption that productivity, not power, fundamentally determines market rewards. Joseph Stiglitz describes marginal productivity theory as providing the theoretical underpinning for the 'trickle-down' notion in economics: the view that that increased rewards for the rich will produce higher incomes for all, according to their productive contributions (2016: 2)

The normative dimension of marginal productivity theory was explicit in the writing of some of its pioneers. The American economist J.B. Clark was quite candid about his concern to justify the existing pattern of income distribution and to show that markets produce equitable as well as efficient outcomes. According to Clark, 'the distribution of income of society is controlled by a natural law' (1965 [1899]: v) which assigns to each person what they have specifically created. In a similar vein, the Italian economist and social theorist Vilfredo Pareto claimed in 1906 that 'the constancy of inequality in the distribution of income reflects inequality of human ability, which is a natural and universal category' (cited in Roll 1973: 453). These views created a basis not only for the neoclassical economic analysis of distribution, but also for justifying the status quo of inequality under capitalism.

Although neoclassical economists nowadays usually eschew such explicitly normative propositions, the nature of their analysis and its social influence has not fundamentally changed. Marginal productivity theory implies a symmetry between the reward for capital, land and labour, seeing each factor of production rewarded in proportion to its marginal productivity, which is both efficient and preferable to any other arrangement. On this basis, one may infer that the falling share of labour in the functional distribution of income during recent decades (as shown in Figure 2.3) reflects labour's declining productivity relative to capital's (Stanford 2018). Better not to 'intervene' to raise labour incomes because this would 'distort' or damage the natural state of economic affairs. The Austrian economist Friedrich Hayek (1944), doyen of subsequent right-wing politicians, famously took this view. So did the Chicago economist Milton Friedman, arguing 'against the attempt to separate this function of the price system – distributing income – from each of its other functions – transmitting information and providing incentives', because 'if prices are prevented from affecting the distribution of income, they cannot be used for other purposes' (Friedman & Friedman 2011 [1980]: 124). This implies that we must accept substantial economic inequalities as a natural and necessary feature of a capitalist market economy.

Do these arguments stand up to critical scrutiny? Political economic critics think not, arguing that marginal productivity theory cannot comprehensively explain the distribution of income because it omits a key variable: the ownership of the factors of production. The neoclassical analysis focuses on trying to explain how the demand for the different factors of production relates to the factor prices but pays no attention to who owns them nor to the concentration of that ownership. This is a significant omission because any pattern of factor prices is consistent with an infinite array of income distributions. If land, labour and capital resources are widely dispersed among the population, the distribution of income is likely to be more equal than if the ownership is concentrated in the hands of a few. Thus, even if marginal productivity theory, together with a human capital theory and analysis of the supply of land, labour and capital, were able to explain factor prices, it would be incomplete as a theory of economic inequality. To neglect who owns what prevents a full understanding of who gets what.

A second problem is the difficulty of measuring each factor of production. The neoclassical theory asserts that wages reflect the productivity of labour; that profits reflect the productivity of capital; and that rental payments reflect the productivity of land. However, it is hard to disentangle and measure the productivity of these factors of production when combined to produce goods and services. Neoclassical theorists say that this problem can be dealt with, in principle, by seeing what happens to the total product when the amount of one factor is varied, while holding the amount of other factors constant. In practice, however, the identification of the marginal product of each factor is difficult, usually impossible, to achieve. The conventional measure of labour productivity, for example, is the total output divided by the total hours worked; but this is a measure of average rather than marginal productivity. Moreover, the total output used in this calculation reflects the contributions of land and capital as well as the contribution of labour to producing it.

A yet more troubling concern is an element of incoherence in the neoclassical theory that results from the way in which 'capital' is defined. Marginal productivity theory seeks to treat labour, land and capital in an analytically symmetrical manner. For that purpose, the physical quantity of each factor must be calculable, so that its contribution to production can be compared with its monetary reward. This is feasible in relation to labour because measuring labour according to the number of person hours of work done allows the reward to labour to be expressed as a wage rate per hour and related to the productivity of each hour's labour. Similarly, land can be measured in hectares, so its reward can be expressed as the rent per hectare and related to the land's productivity. However, for capital, no common physical measure exists. Capital goods comprises diverse items – buildings, tools, machinery, computers, robots – so how can we add them up to identify the total amount of capital being used? The only common measure of the diverse capital goods is their market value. That value, however, depends on the profitability of the firms using those capital goods. When the firms are profitable, capital goods will have a higher market value; when they are unprofitable, capital will have a lower market value. Thus, the denominator in the measure of the rate of return on capital depends on the market prices of the capital goods. This means that the theory cannot explain the rate of payment to capital because that profit rate must be known already when calculating the value of the capital goods.

This last point may seem esoteric, but its significance is considerable. It means that the neoclassical attempt to establish a theory of distribution by treating land, labour and capital symmetrically is ultimately unsuccessful. The conceptual problem arises because, in reality, profit is quite different from wages and rents. It is not a payment for the productivity of capital; rather, it is an economic surplus. For an individual firm, profit is what remains after deduction of costs (wages, rent, etc.) from revenue. At the macroeconomic scale, the profit share in the national income reflects the capacity of capitalists, as a class, to appropriate part of the value created in the production process. The attempt by neoclassical economists to explain profits as a reward for productivity is therefore fundamentally flawed.

These problems in neoclassical economic theory created a flurry of theoretical debate between economists on both sides of the

Atlantic half a century ago (the significance of which is discussed in Cohen & Harcourt 2003). The debate came to be known as the 'Cambridge capital controversies' because the principal participants on either side came from Cambridge, Massachusetts (the neoclassicals), and Cambridge, UK (the post-Keynesians). The arguments of the latter were stronger and won the day, leading one commentator to say: 'All this is especially embarrassing to the mainstream of the [economics] profession since it now turns out that it has been making increasingly complex and elegant mathematical models in which, however, a key term is not, and cannot be defined' (Harrington 1976: 142). Yet this did not lead to the acceptance of defeat and the demise of marginal productivity theory. Revealingly, one prominent neoclassical theorist defended his continued acceptance of the theory by saying that it was 'a matter of faith' (Ferguson 1969) – hardly a satisfactory position for a subject claiming to be a science.

Neoclassical economists have moved on more recently to debating the causes of changes in the functional distribution of income, for example (Karabarbounis & Neiman 2013; Abdih & Danninger 2017). However, they are still implicitly using the same conceptual tools, presuming that aggregate capital is measurable and that changes in the relative returns to factors of production reflect changes in the amounts of them that are used and their productivity at the margin. It is an example of how a discredited theory can survive when it serves a useful purpose – but useful for what and to whom? A growing number of economists are saying that theorizing about inequality should shift focus from productivity to power.

Attributing inequality to 'market distortions'

Alternatives to marginal productivity theory that deal with real-world 'market imperfections' have been widely voiced in recent years. Some of the exponents, such as Joseph Stiglitz, Paul Krugman and Jeffrey Sachs, are among the best-known economists of the era: Stiglitz and Krugman have been prolific and influential contributors to debates about macroeconomic and microeconomic policies, while Sachs has been a significant contributor to discussions of world poverty, its causes and possible remedies. These are economists with backgrounds in neoclassical and Keynesian economics who have taken their analyses in a different direction.

The alternatives they proffer differ from the conservative view, being much more critical of the status quo and supportive of 'interventionist' policies to achieve greater equality of opportunity. While favouring a market-based economic system, the new liberal orthodoxy is also much less tolerant of the 'market distortions', 'market imperfections' and 'market failures' that pervade capitalist economies.

However, the continuing influence of neoclassical theory shows in how the liberal theorists analyse inequalities because 'perfect competition' is still taken, implicitly, as the ideal market structure. From the liberal perspective, the problem is that the real world does not match up to this ideal. Thus, to get closer to the ideal, the 'market imperfections' of the real world have to be acknowledged and addressed. The most commonly identified are monopoly, asymmetric information, rents and externalities.

The most fundamental of these 'market imperfections' is *monopoly*. Indeed, this has always been a bugbear among economists, from Adam Smith to the present day. Smith famously wrote that 'people of the same trade seldom meet together, even for merriment and diversion, but that the conversation ends in a conspiracy against the public, or in some contrivance to raise prices' (1976 [1776]: 144). Similarly, neoclassical economists concede that when monopoly power exists, prices are usually higher and outputs restricted, so that the monopolists can make excess profits. Hence their tendency to rail against the 'evils of monopoly'. Monopoly need not imply only a single seller: it can result from collusion or other actions that concentrate power over market processes. Other market structures, such as oligopoly, in which big firms can exercise market power, attract similar criticism because they also tend to push product prices above the level that would prevail (theoretically) under perfect competition. The argument is not consistently persuasive. If oligopoly is more conducive to innovation, thereby creating dynamic effects that expand the production possibilities, we cannot know whether prices will be above or below the perfect competition level, and the criticism therefore tends to fall away. Putting this awkward complication aside, however, the dominant view is that monopoly power is a problem because it produces a misallocation of resources relative to the competitive ideal. Seen in this light, it is thoroughly consistent with the neoclassical view.

What more clearly differentiates the liberal school of thought from the more conservative neoclassical tradition from which it emerged is the concern that monopoly power can amplify economic inequality. A report from some OECD researchers explains how this comes about:

> The existence of market power has a dual effect on the income distribution, not only generating higher economic profits for business owners, but also imposing higher prices on consumers. The increased margins charged to customers because of market power will disproportionately harm the poor who will pay more for goods without receiving a counter-balancing share of increased profits. The wealthy, while paying more for goods, will at the same time receive higher profits from market power, due to their generally higher ownership of the stream of corporate profits and capital gains. (Ennis, Gonzaga & Pike 2017: 7)

Links like these between monopoly power and inequality reflect the inadequacy of market competition. If inequality is a problem, more competition is therefore the solution. As one critic of unjustifiably high incomes puts it, 'to bring the elite down to size, we need to make them compete' (Rothwell 2016: 2).

A second, more narrowly focused, aspect of market imperfection arises from *asymmetric information*. This may also tend to increase inequalities. The textbook case is where sellers of a product know more than the buyers know about the nature of the product and the prevailing market conditions. The neoclassical presumption that buyers and sellers meet on equal terms to determine a mutually advantageous price is not applicable in these circumstances. Rather, one may expect that sellers will get the better of the process. Thus, it is not their monopoly power per se (i.e. the absence of market competition) but their advantageous position regarding information that produces the 'market distortion'. This has distributional implications. If, in general, the sellers are large corporations and the buyers are dispersed customers, the consequence of information asymmetry will be greater economic inequality than would otherwise prevail. Of course, the roles can be reversed: in principle, buyers can have more information than sellers. However, if those buyers are large corporations with deep knowledge of market conditions (as is commonly the case, for example, in international markets for labour), the distributional effect will also be to increase economic inequality.

A third market distortion recognized in the new liberal orthodoxy is *'rent'*. The use of the term 'rent' here is quite different to its use in common discourse (as in 'I've rented an apartment'). It also gives a quite a different meaning to 'rent' than is found in the long tradition of economic thought associating rent with payment for the use of land. Instead, rent refers to income over and above what would be necessary to ensure the continued supply of any factor of production. People with the capacity to get any such surplus payment are 'rentiers'. They receive higher incomes than necessary to get them to do the job. Rent is therefore unrelated to productivity: on the contrary, it reflects the power to extract payment without additional effort. In a 'neoclassical world', competition is supposed to prevent such over-payments. That it does not do so in the real world, and that the consequences include greater inequality, has become a distinctive theme in the new liberal orthodoxy. Indeed, for Stiglitz, 'rent seeking' recurs as the key driver of inequality. He says that '[a] closer look at the successes of those at the top of the wealth distribution shows that more than a small part of their genius resides in devising better ways of exploiting market power and market imperfections – and, in many cases, finding better ways of ensuring that politics works for them rather than for society more generally' (Stiglitz 2013: 50).

The relationship between the market and the state is crucial in this reasoning. To quote Stiglitz again: 'Rent seeking takes many forms: hidden and open transfers and subsidies from the government, laws that make the marketplace less competitive, lax enforcement of existing competition laws, and statutes to allow corporations to take advantage of others to pass costs on to the rest of society' (Stiglitz 2013: 48). Where mixed market and state arrangements are present (as they nearly always are), problems of 'regulatory capture' are pervasive, allowing businesses to effectively shape the regulatory processes in their own interests. The likelihood of corruption occurring is significantly greater in these circumstances. As Stiglitz says, rent seeking is ultimately about 'getting to set the rules of the game and pick the referee' (2013: 59), thereby enhancing your prospects of gaining advantage over competitors. Evidently, the presence of government is at the heart of the problem: it causes 'political distortions' that interact with and amplify 'market distortions'. In this respect, as Roger McCain notes, 'Stiglitz's position sounds remarkably close to that of some free-market, small-government conservative economists. ... But, in context, Stiglitz's position is quite opposite. He regards the free market as a myth' (2017: 18). The chain of reasoning sees the problem as the inadequacy of the design, implementation and enforcement of laws and regulations, rather than the presence of government per se. Thus, the liberal position requires the very institution that created the opportunities for rent seeking to eradicate them.

A similar tension is evident in the fourth of the market imperfections identified in the liberal analysis of inequality. This involves *externalities*, widely acknowledged by neoclassical economists as sources of 'market failure'. Externalities arise wherever and whenever people who are engaged in economic activities, whether producing or consuming, pay prices that do not align with the social costs and benefits that those activities produce. The effects can be either positive or harmful. Education is a common example of a positive externality because it usually produces benefits for the wider society over and above the benefits going to the educated individuals themselves. Environmental degradation is the classic example of a harmful externality, arising because the use of nature is under-priced. Neoclassical economists, recognizing the pervasive presence of externalities, look to enlightened governments for market interventions, such as taxes and subsidies, to better align the market prices with the full social costs and benefits. This would 'internalize the externalities' and thereby produce a more efficient allocation of resources.

Like the concern with the other market imperfections, this concern with externalities as a source of 'market failure' is not radical. It retains a market ideal at its core, simply adding on policy prescriptions for market 'fine tuning'. However, it has a stronger political economic character when the focus on allocative efficiency shifts to distributional equity. If, for example, negative externalities, such as pollution or other forms of environmental degradation, impact most harshly on poor and vulnerable sections of society, then inequity as well as inefficiency result. Costas Panayotakis (2011), pursuing this more radical interpretation of the externalities problem, argues that, under capitalism, the tendency to cost shifting is systemic rather than incidental. Externalities, when seen from this perspective, are a means whereby capitalists shift some of their costs to labour and, more generally, to those in society with little power and least ability to resist. This imparts a class dimension of the analysis that is lacking in the milder 'market distortions' versions of neoclassical theory.

These four strands of concern with market distortions – focusing on monopoly, asymmetric information, rent seeking and externalities – have similar policy implications. They indicate the need to rectify the market imperfections, not to fundamentally change the political economic system. The posited reforms include anti-monopoly legislation, improved product information, regulations to limit the appropriation of rents through premium payments and policies to internalize externalities through taxation. Making modifications to markets is the characteristic approach. Notably, how vigorously these reforms are advocated depends on the implicit weights given to problems of 'market failure' and 'government failure'. That latter concept is an offshoot of neoclassical reasoning normally associated with public choice theory. It sees governments as the source of problems, not solutions, especially where 'regulatory capture' arises from the interaction of self-interested governments with self-interested market participants. There is a symmetry of sorts: market failure justifies 'intervention' but government failure suggests it is best to leave things to the market. This is the modern liberal dilemma: how to balance market and state, knowing the pitfalls of each.

Explaining inequality in terms of 'market distortions' is central to modern reformist politics. It has been enthusiastically embraced by popular writers who sense that there is something profoundly wrong with modern capitalism but who think that an assault on 'rent seeking' and 'market distortions' will fix it (e.g. Bregman 2016; Mineau 2016; Lind 2017). There is a veneer of radicalism in this approach, especially where a prominent economist like Stiglitz brings a critical view of the state into the picture (on which more in chapter 8), yet the analysis remains within a capitalist market paradigm. Power is certainly part of this 'liberal' story but, for the most part, it is power within markets; individual power, not systemic class power.

Attributing inequality to class power and exploitation

There is a well-known joke about a person in the street being asked how to get to a particular place and replying: 'If I wanted to get there, I wouldn't start from here.' Political economists tend to see mainstream economics in this way, arguing that, if we want to understand inequality, perhaps we should not start from neoclassical economic theory. Liberal economists like Stiglitz have made significant departures from the neoclassical base of perfect competition, perfect information and perfect mobility, as discussed above. However, proponents of radical political economy contend that more progress may result from a different starting point. They begin the study of economic inequalities by considering the structural characteristics of capital, class and exploitation.

The importance of dominant class power is not difficult to appreciate when looking at different modes of economic organization. In slave-owning societies, the relationship between slave-owners and slaves is the main structural inequality: the power that the former have over the latter shapes the economic and social order. Under feudalism, control over land becomes the central issue: here, the main seam of inequality is between those who own and control the land and those who work on the landowners' property. Under capitalism, it is the owners and managers of capital who are in the driving seat, making profit-seeking decisions that shape the availability of jobs, the nature of work, the level of wages, the patterns of surplus generation and capital accumulation. Whether capitalist firms are competitive or monopolistic in particular markets does matter, but more important is the overall power of capital as a class to exert the dominant influence over inequalities and the social order.

On this reasoning, the key to studying the modern economy lies not in the study of 'market imperfections' and 'market failures' on which Stiglitz and other economic liberals focus, but in the study of capital and class. This more radical approach shifts attention to the relative shares of capital and labour in the national income and to explanations of capital's increasing share during recent decades (Peetz 2018). Yet more profoundly, it shifts attention to the production relations that underpin the distributional patterns.

In chapter 5, we looked at how people's class positions interact with gender and race to shape who gets what. Marxist political economy seeks to present a more developed analysis of how class operates, not in terms of social positions but as a matter of economic functions and power. This analysis of class relations in capitalist economies illuminates how the ownership (or non-ownership) of economic property shapes market positions and power. As Marx and Engels emphasized, in every form of society a dominant class has been able to organize the extraction of surplus labour from another class. The process continues under capitalism, despite the existence of 'free markets' for labour and capital. The key is the non-symmetrical relationship between capital and wage labour. Capital hires labour in the expectation of paying wages that are less than the full value of the commodities that labour creates. This is the systemic source of exploitation. It is not primarily a matter of employers behaving badly, as the term is popularly used. Rather, it is a systemic feature without which capitalism could not function, because exploitation creates the economic surplus from which capitalists derive their profits. Notwithstanding all the changes to capitalism that have occurred since Marx's time, as long as profits are generated in this way, class and exploitation remain central to the system's normal functioning. The greater the imbalance of class power, the higher is the rate of exploitation and the greater are the economic inequalities.

The process is not free of contradictions. The capital–labour relationship involves both cooperation and conflict. Cooperation between capital and labour is necessary to keep the wheels of industry turning, whether in transnational corporations or small businesses and irrespective of whether labour is unionized or not. Without this cooperation, both workers and the owners of capital lose income: employers do not make profits and workers are not paid. Simultaneously, however, there is a conflict of interest, manifest in the continual contest over the distribution of income, managerial prerogatives and other aspects of industrial and workplace relations. This contradictory nexus between cooperation and conflict is the essence of the capital–labour class relationship. It is rather like some marriages in which there is recurrent tension: the couple can neither live comfortably together nor agree to part.

Systematic analysis of capitalism is therefore at the centre of radical political economy. Seen from this perspective, capitalism is not synonymous with 'the market economy'. For sure, capitalist economies have markets – for capital, labour, land and goods and services – but the more fundamental characteristics are the private ownership of property in the means of production and the corresponding structures of class power. Complicating the picture somewhat, not all economic activities in modern societies are capitalist. In both rich and poor countries, much useful work is done by households, cooperatives and communities, while exchange is not always monetized and focused on profit seeking. Such productive but non-capitalist economic activities may give rise to inequalities: to the extent that they rest on a racialized or gendered division of labour, for example. However, capitalist economic and social relations are most pervasive because capitalism is the dominant mode of production, exchange and distribution worldwide at this stage of human history. Even China, an avowedly 'communist state', has taken a capitalist road to expanding its economy and engaging with global capitalism. Its internal economic inequalities reflect this (with its number of fabulously wealthy billionaires now nudging the nation into joint second place, as shown in Table 3.5). Any economic system geared to the accumulation of capital through the extraction of a surplus product from labour creates class inequality as an integral feature of its normal functioning, reproduction and growth. Thus, economic inequality is a systemic condition rather than a regrettable aberration.

Organizing economic activity on capitalist principles has its pros and cons, as do all types of political economic organization. In the case of capitalism, its great strength is also its Achilles' heel: that is, the quest for profit, the essential dynamic of the capitalist system driving the process of capital accumulation. The resulting process of wealth generation depends on firms continually seeking to minimize their production costs, putting downward pressure on the incomes of the working class. The periodic regeneration of a pool of unemployed people within this class – what Marxists call a 'reserve army of labour' – simultaneously facilitates capital accumulation while further polarizing the income distribution. Meanwhile, environmental stresses multiply. A growth-oriented economic system, driven by the quest for profits and capital accumulation, recurrently butts up against environmental limits in a world where many physical resources are finite and where the capacity to deal with waste products is restricted. These features of capitalist production and distribution, somewhat baldly stated here, have been characteristic of the system since its inception and have been a central concern in studies in political economy for over two centuries.

In the current era, the integration of capital's owners and senior managers accentuates the imbalance of class power. Interlocking directorates involve many of them sitting on the boards of directors of multiple companies. The concentration and centralization of capital enhance their capacity to shape the business environment in their own interests. It gives managers of large corporations greater power to administer prices and wages, and thus greater power over consumers and employees. Influence on – even power over – government policies also becomes possible. These features of corporate power have been particularly evident as mergers and takeovers have swept through many sectors of the world economy. The exercise of class power, as the dominant influence on inequality, has an increasingly global 'logic'.

The Marxian political economic perspective, as outlined here, has its advantages and disadvantages. Its emphasis on the structural characteristics of capitalism as an economic system gives analytical strength. Some critics of Marxian analysis, however, challenge its underpinnings in the labour theory of value (e.g. Keen 2001), arguing that this is not supportable. Moreover, because national economies are so varied in their extent of inequality, a broad class analysis needs supplementation with more detailed study of who gets what, going beyond generalizations about capital–labour relations. The differential pay rates of occupational groups of workers needs to be explained in terms of a more disaggregated analysis. Marxian approaches also need to focus on the state, showing how governments are constrained on the one flank by the interests of capital and on the other flank by the need to provide social legitimacy by 'civilizing' capitalism. These conflicting demands make the state an arena of perpetual struggle (as explained in Stilwell 2013: ch. 38). Attention to historical and geographical contexts is necessary when analysing how these capital–labour–state tensions play out in varied and evolving situations (e.g. Harvey 1982; Ruccio 2011; Burgmann 2016).

Table 6.1 compares the three explanatory approaches discussed in this chapter, noting their different views of how, in a capitalist economy, the market and state shape economic inequality. As a simple summary table, it sets aside the details of market forces, class interests and state actions which need fuller consideration when seeking practical guides to action. Moreover, not all the conceptual approaches fit neatly into these three categories. One that does not is Thomas Piketty's, the controversial character of which warrants the following special consideration.

Table 6.1 Theorizing inequality: alternative perspectives

Viewpoint	View of markets	View of the state
Conservative	Markets cause incomes to be determined by productivity	State prone to 'government failure'
Liberal	Market imperfections cause incomes to be distorted	State needs to implement policies to rectify 'market failures'
Radical	Markets allow incomes to be shaped by exploitation and class-based power	State currently serves the interests of capital, so needs to be transformed

The Piketty phenomenon

Do books change the world? Probably not, but if the world is already changing, timely books can have significant impact and influence. Thomas Piketty's *Capital in the Twenty-First Century* is a case in point. Originally published in French in 2013, then published in English in 2014, it has been a phenomenal publishing success, occupying high places in bestseller lists – a truly remarkable feat for a huge book full of economic statistics and charts. It established Piketty's reputation as a 'rock-star economist', constantly in demand in the media and drawing huge attendances to his public lectures. It has stimulated numerous responses, some laudatory and some deeply critical (see, e.g., Galbraith 2014a, 2014b; Sheil 2014/15; Morgan 2015; Pressman 2015; King 2017). We need to consider its nature and significance.

Piketty's purpose is ambitious: to document the extent of wealth inequalities in many countries and to account for the factors that have caused variations in inequality over a very long sweep of time. He makes a powerful case for focusing political economic analysis on the ownership of wealth (although he provides lots of information on incomes too) and has compiled a hitherto unprecedented amount of data about wealth on a consistent basis.

Piketty's analysis adopts the widest possible definition of wealth, including all kinds of assets held by households. These include both financial assets, such as shares, bonds and cash, and physical assets, such as housing and land. Rather confusingly, he calls it all capital, perhaps partly because he wanted a cute title for his book that would echo Marx's *Capital*. Political economists of a Marxist inclination have been duly irritated (e.g. Galbraith 2014a; Morgan 2015). Calling it 'wealth' would be simpler and fit better with popular understandings.

Piketty's focus is on distribution, not on the production relations on which Marxian political economy focuses when studying class relations and contradictions. This means that Piketty is right on the money for studying inequalities between rich and poor people, rather than the structural relations between capitalist and working classes.

Piketty's work is also distinctive because of its claim to theoretical innovation. This centres on the equation $r > g$, representing the relationship between the rate of return on capital (r) and the rate of growth in gross national income (g). According to Piketty,

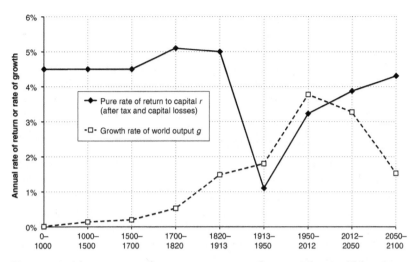

Figure 6.1 After-tax rate of return versus growth rate at the world level, from Antiquity until 2100

Source: Piketty (2014a: 356). Reproduced with permission.

the former generally exceeds the latter. Yet, it ain't necessarily so, as he has clarified in his subsequent writing (Piketty 2014b, 2015). Figure 6.1, extracted from his book, provides a summary of his evidence and argument, showing that the rate of return to capital (after tax and capital losses) was below the growth rate of national income during a large part of the twentieth century. Moreover, there is nothing inherent in *capitalism* about the relationship between r and g. It could apply equally to any socio-economic system in which the accumulation of wealth proceeds faster than the general growth of incomes. r being greater than g produces greater income inequality wherever incomes from the ownership of capital are more concentrated than incomes from other sources (such as wage incomes). Indeed, it is hard to imagine any society in which incomes from profits, interest and rent would be more widely dispersed than wage incomes. Thus, the crucial variable is the extent of concentration of capital incomes. That is what determines inequality in practice, and it varies in both time and space.

The greatest contribution that Piketty makes is empirical: providing an enormously impressive compilation of data to show the evolving patterns of inequality in a range of different countries over a remarkably long time. It reveals cyclical swings rather than the relentless move towards greater inequality that a simple

$r > g$ theory would predict. Broadly speaking, three phases are identifiable across the leading capitalist nations in the modern era. The first is up to about 1915, featuring steady wealth accumulation and a tendency to growing inequality. The second runs from 1915 to the 1970s, which was a period of reduced inequality. In the first three decades, two world wars and an intervening great depression destroyed much of the capital, resulting in considerable narrowing of wealth and income inequalities. Then came the three decades after the Second World War when welfare states were developed, income taxes were more progressive and organized labour was relatively strong. This was the time of the 'great compression'. Since then, a third phase, running from the 1980s to the present, has featured renewed concentration of wealth. Organized labour has been weakened, privatization has reduced states' commitments to welfare, business taxes have been cut and flatter income taxes have been in vogue.

Figure 6.2, reproduced from Piketty, shows the growing share of capital income (relative to total national income) in this most recent phase since the 1980s. For all the eight nations shown, capital's share was higher at the end of the period than at the start. In effect, this is another way of illustrating the declining share of labour in the functional distribution of income (as shown in Figure 2.3 of this book). Some minor cyclical features may be discerned, including temporary setbacks experienced by wealth holders

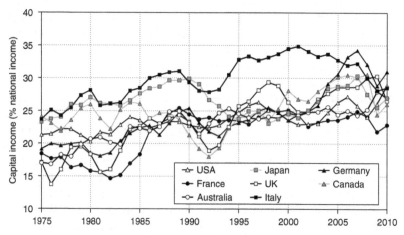

Figure 6.2 Capital's share of income, eight OECD countries, 1975–2010
Source: Piketty (2014a: 222). Reproduced with permission.

occurring during recessionary periods such as 1980–3, 1990–3, 2000–3 and after the global crash of 2008–9, but the general trend is clearly upwards.

A double-whammy is evident when the evidence on wage inequalities is also introduced. Looking back to Figure 1.1 reminds us that inequalities of wage income are a key element, alongside the functional distribution of income, in shaping the overall extent of inequality. Piketty shows how this operated in practice in the twentieth century. Taking the case of the USA, the relevant diagram is reproduced here as Figure 6.3. It shows that growing wage inequalities have worked in tandem with growing capital incomes to return overall income inequalities to historically high levels.

The top two lines in Figure 6.3 show the share of the top income decile in total income (with the lower of the two lines excluding incomes from realized capital gains, but still including all other capital incomes). Clearly, there was a big plunge in the share of total income going to the top decile of the population around the time of the Second World War – from over 45% to below 35%. After continuing at that lowered level through to the 1970s, the share has fully recovered since then – rising to nearly 50%. The lower line in Figure 6.3 shows what happened during the same period to wage inequality, again taking the share of the top

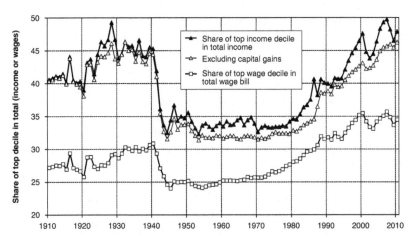

Figure 6.3 Shares of the top decile in wage incomes and total incomes in the United States, 1910–2010

Source: Piketty (2014a: 299). Reproduced with permission.

decile as the measure of concentration. The pattern is remarkably similar: a sharp fall in wage inequality at the time of the Second World War, stability for a quarter of a century and then a strong increase that made wage inequality even more pronounced than it had been during the first half of the twentieth century. One may surmise that the tremendous surge of managerial incomes, especially for CEOs, during the last few decades is a key component in this process.

These data are illuminating because, notwithstanding Piketty's primary focus on capital incomes, here we see evidence of inequality driven by labour market processes too. One may infer that the increasing 'rents' (which liberal scholars like Stiglitz blame) can play a parallel role to the increasing capital incomes on which Piketty's theoretical construction puts primary emphasis. Indeed, this may reflect some blurring of the capital–labour distinction when it comes to real-world experience. As noted in chapter 4, to count CEO salaries as income to labour may seems somewhat bizarre when the primary task of those managers is to operate as agents of capital.

In view of these observations, it is pertinent to reflect on how Piketty's analysis fits into the three approaches summarized in Table 6.1. The short answer has to be 'not neatly'. Although Piketty's treatment of mainstream economics is generally critical, he toys with marginal productivity theory when explaining the shifting shares of capital and labour. He also sides with the neoclassicals when referring to the Cambridge capital controversies, saying that 'Solow's so-called neoclassical growth model definitively carried the day' (Piketty 2014a: 231), but he criticizes both sides in the debate for their post-colonial rivalries and insufficient concern with empirical data. It is therefore tempting to regard Piketty's contribution as being in the liberal camp, but he explicitly says his analysis does not depend on 'market imperfections', which is a significant difference from the approach to inequality taken by Stiglitz and other liberals, as described earlier in this chapter. What, then, about the radical camp? At first sight, Piketty's focus on capital seems to put his analysis there, but his conflation of capital with wealth limits the possibility of class analysis based on relations of production. Jamie Morgan writes of Piketty's book that 'it lacks a theorisation of capitalism, of power, of the state, of social movements and social transformations', creating 'calibration economics' rather than radical political economy (Morgan 2015: 803). The separation of distribution from production differentiates it from the Marxian tradition in political economy.

Perhaps we might conclude that Piketty's work is at the radical edge of liberal analysis or at the liberal end of radical analysis. Perhaps its categorization is of no great matter anyway. Piketty describes his own approach as pragmatic. Indeed, it has all the hallmarks of a data-driven, rather than theory-driven, analysis, notwithstanding his own emphasis on the structuring role of the $r > g$ relationship. There is extensive discussion about economic theory in his book, perhaps largely intended to engage the interest of the economics profession. However, its ultimately outstanding contribution is great data, showing the underlying tendency to inequality, the drivers that propel it and the historically specific forces that have interrupted it. It is surely worthy of the phenomenal attention it has received. Equally importantly, Piketty's more recent work, in conjunction with other international inequality scholars, to develop the *World Inequality* database is a prodigious contribution. Ignorance of inequality, its character and its changing dimensions can no longer be an excuse for inaction.

Conclusion

The differing viewpoints about inequality in a large and rapidly expanding political economic literature put varied emphasis on a range of causal factors: productivity, human capital, monopoly, rent seeking, class, exploitation and power. Formal theoretical propositions and normative judgements intermingle throughout. In summary:

- A conservative view of inequality, drawing on neoclassical theories, generally emphasizes market-determined rewards based on people's productive contributions.
- Liberal analyses take a more critical view of how market distortions create unjustifiable inequalities, leading to positive support for government 'interventions' intended to create a more equitable distribution.
- A more radical approach puts emphasis on the power of capital and the systemic basis of class inequalities, indicating the need for fundamental challenge to capitalist economic arrangements.

Thomas Piketty's analysis is a further important contribution. As one reviewer has said: 'Piketty et al. have mainly measured inequality in various ways: the point now is to explain its origins and grapple with its consequences' (Godechot 2017: 5). The next chapter seeks to do so by studying how capitalism is evolving in the modern era.

7

Driving the Disparities

The theories reviewed in the preceding chapter provide lenses through which the causes of inequality can be seen. Comparing the lenses shows quite a lot about the contested character of economic theories. We need now to broaden our gaze to the political economic features of the real world that are currently driving economic disparities.

This chapter probes factors commonly held responsible for the increasing income and wealth inequalities occurring in almost every nation. It begins by considering the general tendencies of 'circular and cumulative causation' before turning to influences that are more specific to modern capitalism, such as corporate globalization, financialization and neoliberalism. Then, looking at processes like urbanization and technological change, it explores other factors creating winners and losers. We thereby seek to develop an understanding of the complex, interacting elements and processes involved in shaping our world.

Circular and cumulative causation

Vicious and virtuous circles pervade our lives. A run of bad luck can create a downward spiral; a lucky break can create a springboard for further success. Similar processes operate in relation to economic inequality. Capital makes capital and poverty reproduces poverty. If you already have wealth, your capacity to generate future income – even without working – is usually greater than for a person who has no wealth. Meanwhile, poor people commonly find themselves trapped within conditions of further marginality and deprivation.

Understanding these processes has been central to the thinking of a school of institutional economists who describe it as a process of circular and cumulative causation. This contrasts sharply with the emphasis on equilibrium tendencies in the dominant neoclassical economic theory. If there is any equilibrium at all, institutional economists are wont to say that it is the equilibrium of a pencil standing on its end, rather than the equilibrium of a ball in a bowl (Myrdal 1957: 153). Divergence rather than convergence is the norm. This way of understanding economic and social processes was pioneered by Thorstein Veblen in the USA more than a century ago (Argyrous 2011). It was simply expressed by economic historian Ragnar Nurske when he said:

> A poor man may not have enough to eat; being undernourished his health may be weak; being physically weak, his working capacity may be low, which means he is poor, which in turn means he will not have enough to eat; and so on. A situation of this sort, applying to a country as a whole, can be described by the trite proposition: 'a country is poor because it is poor'. (1952: 1)

The Swedish political economist Gunnar Myrdal developed this way of understanding socio-economic processes in his wide-ranging studies of regional inequality, racial discrimination and the obstacles to development (Myrdal 1944, 1957, 1968), while post-Keynesian economist Nicholas Kaldor applied it to understanding productivity and industry development (Holt & Pressman 2009).

Circular and cumulative causation is a particularly useful concept for understanding the processes that reproduce patterns of unequal opportunity. The wealthiest individuals have the most options. Through running businesses, through leasing their land or simply through getting interest on their financial capital, they can expand their initial wealth. They may also be able to use their wealth to exert powerful pressure on governments to cut tax rates on high incomes, thereby facilitating yet more wealth accumulation. Meanwhile, the options for people without capital are usually restricted to working for wages (if jobs are available), doing informal work or seeking whatever charity or welfare payments are available. Thus, processes of circular and cumulative causation tend to create polarizing cycles of advantage and disadvantage.

This is not to deny the possibilities of escape routes or turning points. A trend can bend. Myrdal (1957) pointed out that economic growth processes usually have both 'backwash' and 'spread' effects. The former create cumulative inequality. Simply having the advantage of an early start may give a person, institution or place an initial advantage that cumulates over time. Late starters, on the other hand, have difficulty ever catching up because of the 'backwash' effects of being behind. In some circumstances, however, 'spread' effects may also occur. As a city grows, for example, rising land values mainly benefit the owners of existing land; but people working in the peri-urban areas may also benefit from growth in job opportunities in market gardening or other industries that serve the demands of the city-dwellers. In a 'trickle-down' situation, to cite a familiar phrase, the minimal spread effects are usually swamped by the backwash effects. It is the relative magnitudes of the backwash and spread effects that shape the distributional consequences of any economic action.

The process of *inheritance* is a clear case in point, having obvious importance for the evolution of wealth inequalities over time. People in wealthy families have a normal expectation of benefiting from the inheritance of the wealth of parents and grandparents, whereas people in poor families only rarely receive substantial legacies. The spread effects of inheritance are therefore modest or negligible relative to the backwash effects that concentrate wealth transfers in ways that perpetuate economic inequality inter-generationally. Three elements operate to perpetuate the inequalities across the generations. First are the material benefits that young people in high-wealth families typically get during their upbringing (including expensive private schooling, extra tuition, access to resources, contact with future employers, and so forth). Second are gifts from wealthy parents (helping their children to purchase a first home, for example). Third is inherited wealth when parents (and grandparents) die. Combined, the circular and cumulative character of these processes is clear. Economic disparities widen as inheritance interacts with capitalism's class-based relations of production and inequalities of distribution. Owning capital – whether acquired through capitalistic endeavours, inherited or received as gifts – expands possibilities for generating income without personally undertaking wage labour: the more income from profit, rent or interest payments, the more capital can then be reinvested.

More than two decades ago, the liberal US economist Lester Thurow opined that '[c]apitalistic economies are essentially like Alice in Wonderland, where one must run very fast to stand still – just stopping inequality from growing requires constant effort' (1996: 245). It is important to ask why. Is there something beyond the general processes of circular and cumulative causation that is specific to the current era of capitalist economic development on a world scale? Globalization is an obvious something. But in what sense and why?

Corporate globalization

Politicians, business leaders and media commentators commonly herald globalization as inevitable and desirable, representing it as a process driven by the progressive forces of technological change and economic liberalization, overcoming the tyranny of distance and political parochialism. We are encouraged to treat globalization as inexorable, turning political choice mainly into a question of how best to respond to this positive external imperative. Yet a careful consideration of what is actually happening makes us aware of globalization's major stresses, its polarizing processes, particularly when its principal driver is corporate interests.

Globalization universalizes the processes of circular and cumulative causation. As interconnectedness in production, trade, investment and financial arrangements increases, globalization's spread effects extend the growth impulses to areas previously not fully integrated into world markets. US-based businesses still dominate the 'rich list' of global corporations, although there has been a notable 'rise of the rest', including corporate rivals based in China, India, Brazil, Mexico, Turkey and South Korea (Drache, Rioux & Longhurst 2016). Other nations, experiencing the backwash effects of corporate globalization, remain stranded as bystanders in an increasingly integrated world economy. There are dramatic winners and losers not only among nations but within nations too. Regional and class inequalities are growing in almost all countries, most strikingly in India and China.

Increased global competition for investment, jobs and customers tends to create a race to the bottom. Workers in different locations are pitted against each other, vying for jobs in an economic environment in which capitalist businesses can quickly relocate their segmented production processes according to the variations in prevailing wage rates, both within and between countries. Low-paid workers face pressures for wage reduction, especially when trying to negotiate in labour markets where the global reserve army of labour limits their bargaining power. Increased flows of migrants and refugees may also compound the difficulties of achieving the solidarity of labour that is necessary when bargaining for wage increases. Globalization thereby increases the power of capitalists, enabling them to maximize profits by relocating their investments around the globe. Workers are more 'on the back foot' as their relative bargaining position weakens. Downward pressure on wage rates is a predictable consequence. Concurrently, national governments, adjusting tax rates on businesses in order to attract capital to their jurisdictions, create a different type of race to the bottom. If they also try to attract internationally mobile capital with the lure of lax environmental regulations, that imparts potentially disastrous consequences for global ecological sustainability.

Meanwhile, there is a race to the top for others. Most obviously, this has applied to the corporate executives enjoying the rapidly rising salaries and remuneration packages described in chapter 4. They have become more integrated as a class, managing rivalries in inter-corporate competition while capturing a growing share of the economic surplus for themselves. The famous rallying call by Marx and Engels, you may recall, was 'Workers of the world, unite!' In practice, it seems that the main response has been from the managers of capital. 'CEOs of the world, unite!' does not have quite the same ring, although it is a reminder of the power – and probably greater perception of common interests – of an increasingly integrated transnational capitalist class. The British sociologist Leslie Sklair (2001) was among the first to identify this phenomenon, and it has become a major theme in subsequent social research (e.g. Carroll 2010; Murray 2012). Sklair pointed to the four main fractions forming the global capitalist class:

- the corporate fraction, comprising executives of transnational corporations and their local affiliates;
- the state fraction, comprising politicians and bureaucrats pushing the globalization process;
- the technical fraction, comprising professionals, such as academics, who legitimize and endorse globalization;
- the consumerist fraction, including the media and merchants who promote the culture and practices of global consumerism.

Inequality is integral to this story. Sklair argued that 'the transnational capitalist class is working consciously to resolve two central crises, namely: (i) the simultaneous creation of increasing poverty and increasing wealth within and between communities and societies (the class polarization crisis); and (ii) the unsustainability of the system (the ecological crisis)' (2001: 6). With the benefit of greater hindsight, we can see that, far from 'working to resolve these problems', the transnational capitalist institutions have significantly exacerbated them. The plutocrats have rapidly increased their incomes and their wealth, but Sklair's two crisis tendencies have intensified. As recent books like Graham Dunkley's *One World Mania* (2016) and John Mikler's *The Political Power of Global Corporations* (2018) show, the rhetoric of universally beneficial globalization sits awkwardly with the harsher realities of corporate globalization in practice. A particularly troubling dimension of these tensions results from the interaction of globalization with financialization.

Financialization

Financialization refers not only to the increasing influence of financial markets in corporate activities, but also to the growing infusion of financial calculation and criteria throughout social, economic and political life. This has important implications for the distributions of incomes and wealth. Directly, a larger share of the economic surplus goes to financial institutions and intermediaries. Indirectly, financialization constrains government policies, favouring short-term market-oriented initiatives over other policies with more long-term nation-building and egalitarian intentions.

The financial markets exercise a distinctive discipline on investment behaviour, prioritizing a short-term focus on maximizing shareholder value. As Geoff Dow notes, 'This finance-led capitalism disadvantages firms that need long run rather than short run criteria in the provision of finance (that is, most manufacturing operations), but also the economy as a whole by increasing the volatility of "hot money" flows and investment generally' (2002: 67). Moreover, as Dick Bryan and Mike Rafferty argue, '[A]llong with rising inequality, there are widespread changes in people's experiences of finance and social risk that are generating ... vulnerability and insecurity' (2018: 2). It is financial risks, not incomes, that become more widely spread.

Looking at the several bouts of financialization in the history of capitalism, David Harvey notes: 'What makes the current phase special is the phenomenal acceleration in the speed of circulation of money capital and the reduction in financial transaction costs. The mobility of money capital relative to that of other forms of capital (commodities and production in particular) has dramatically increased' (2014: 178). Significantly, this increases the share of income going to the financial institutions rather than the productive enterprises of industrial capitalism. It also increases inequality to the extent that the economic surplus becomes more concentrated, even within the capitalist class. Harvey notes a deep irony in this process, pointing out that industrial capital, historically, had to free itself from the power of the landlords, usurious financiers and merchants. Now, evidently, 'the merchants, the media and communications moguls' (Harvey 2014: 179) are in the ascendancy with industrial capital on the back foot. It is the most volatile and least productive form of capital that has become the best remunerated. It is to this feature that Harvey attributes much of the explanation for the emergence of a plutocracy comprising financiers and rentiers (2014: 180).

While Harvey's analysis explicitly links financialization and inequality, other political economic analyses point to increased tendencies towards macroeconomic instability and crises (Foster 2008; van Treek 2009; Bezemer & Hudson 2016). Some point in particular to the hazards associated with the growth of the FIRE (finance, insurance and real estate) sector (e.g. Kelsey 2015; Schroeder 2018), comprising a range of institutions whose common interest is in capturing an increasing share of the economic surplus. As a 'fraction' of capital, it has a stake in asset price inflation that leads directly to capital gains and greater income flows from commissions based on current market values. Inflationary processes in real estate markets have attracted 'investors' seeking capital gains from trading in housing who compete with (and usually outbid) people simply wanting to own a house to live in. A high and growing volume of mortgage debt for the purchase of housing is a predictable result, creating other stresses and anxieties. Some of these stresses are personal; others are systemic and macroeconomic. The low interest rates on loans in most capitalist nations in recent years have made the borrowing process appear attractive but presage widespread difficulties of servicing the debts. The banks do not usually worry much about defaults because they ultimately own the property. However, a situation where house prices are rising faster than wages, creating speculative real estate bubbles in the context of inadequate financial regulation, looks eerily like the conditions preceding the global financial crash of 2008–9.

Governments in many nations have been complicit in these processes, urged on by international institutions like the IMF. Policies of financial deregulation have been widespread, leading to soaring bank profits and similarly soaring salaries for senior management. As David Ruccio (2016) notes, '[E]pisodes of capital account liberalization are associated with a persistent increase in the share of incomes going to those at the top.'

Are these conditions sustainable? There are growing doubts about the compatibility of financialization and the long-term viability of capitalism. The structure of incentives has shifted away from productive investment (with the attendant need for expanding markets and for cooperative industrial relations) towards more short-term gain from speculation on the value of financial assets. The financiers have become the ascendant fraction of capital, relegating industrial capital – formerly the engine of long-run capitalist development – to subordinate influence. At least equally problematic is the prospect of financial institutions taking charge of climate change policy by becoming 'market makers' and risk managers for emissions trading schemes. Access to liveable environments is already often dependent on ability to pay. Financializing nature looks like capital's conquest of the final frontier (Smith 2007). Indeed, these are deeply unsettling effects of financialization when seen from both liberal and radical perspectives. The likelihood of systemic change, however, is constrained by financialization's close association with neoliberalism.

Neoliberalism

As Paul Mason writes, 'Among the 1 per cent, neoliberalism has the power of a religion: the more you practise it, the better you feel – and the richer you become' (2016: ix). However, one might add, the more you look at neoliberalism, the more confused you can become. Even after decades of use, the term's interpretation remains contested, as an ever-growing literature debates the meaning and usefulness of the concept (e.g. Cahill 2014; Cahill & Konings 2018; Cahill et al. 2018; Rodgers 2018).

Yet some (not altogether consistent) elements are evident. First, the neoliberal rhetoric about 'market freedoms' is powerful ideology, code for prioritizing the economic over the social and the market over planning. Second, the emphasis on the individual, incentives, markets and competition sits comfortably with neo-classical economic theory, which provides it with some academic legitimacy. Third, the political economic practice relates to a class agenda: commodifying, privatizing and changing regulations to suit the interests of capital. Thus, neoliberalism works hand in hand with globalization to shift power from public to private, thereby expanding the capacity for further private wealth accu-mulation. As James Ferguson says, neoliberalism 'has become the name for a set of highly interested public policies that have vastly enriched the holders of capital while leading to increased inequal-ity, insecurity, loss of public services, and a general deterioration in the quality of life for the poor and working classes' (2009: 170). It changes the relationships between states and markets through multiple means: deregulation, privatization, market proxies in the public sector, internationalization and cuts in direct taxation (Jessop 2016: 412). Overall, as an ideology, a class project and a political practice, it has been integral to the process of increasing intra-national inequalities. Therein lies the political economic sig-nificance of neoliberalism as a means of legitimizing regressive redistribution.

One important thrust has been international. The so-called 'Washington consensus' – and even the post-Washington consensus – imparted a neoliberal character to policies of the IMF and World Bank by imposing more market economic discipline on nation states in the developing world. Structural adjustment processes and other characteristically neoliberal 'reforms' paved the way for more rapid trade liberalization and the removal of controls on the international movement of capital during the last quarter of the twentieth century. Yet, as Jonathan Ostry and his research colleagues from the IMF have noted, '[F]inancial open-ness has distributional effects, appreciably raising inequality.' The same authors note other additional risks 'in terms of increased eco-nomic volatility and crisis frequency' (Ostry, Loungani & Furceri 2016: 39). Apparently undaunted, the international credit rating agencies continue working off a neoliberal scorecard to determine what risk premium will be added to the interest rate applicable to government borrowings (Schroeder 2015).

Within the domestic policies of individual countries are other channels of anti-egalitarian neoliberal influence. From a class perspective, the most obvious of these are government policies affecting the capacity of the institutions of organized labour in the advanced capitalist countries to bargain affectively on behalf of the workforce. The attempt to undermine what little economic power is still in the hands of trade unions is actually somewhat inconsistent with neoclassical economics. The latter is formally even-handed between capital and labour, emphasizing the benefits of competition in all markets. To single out trade unions for special attention shows the class-based rather than market-based priorities of neoliberalism that dominate in practice. Indeed, the concern to secure and deepen the inequality of class power has emerged as perhaps neoliberalism's most distinctive feature.

'Fiscal consolidation' is a further element of neoliberalism with strong implications for inequality. Formally, the technical term relates to reduction of budget deficits, but it has come to be associated more generally with the policies of 'austerity'. Balancing government budgets and reducing public debt have become entrenched in economic policy orthodoxy – although more practised in the breach than the observance, as William Shakespeare might have said. Cutting social welfare and the size of the public sector are the hallmarks in practice. Neoliberalism morphing into the politics of austerity has been for many people a thoroughly unwelcome process. Moreover, the results of austerity programmes have often been disappointing even by mainstream economic standards. As Ostry and his IMF colleagues note: '[E]pisodes of fiscal consolidation have been followed, on average, by drops rather than expansions in output' (Ostry, Lougari & Furceri 2016: 40). Keynesian economists would find this no surprise, of course, having consistently warned of the depressing effects of spending cuts on aggregate demand. To the extent that austerity policies also increase income inequalities (as they usually do when they reduce state spending on social welfare rather than corporate welfare), the economically depressing effects compound.

The neoliberal push for privatization of public enterprises also tends to intensify inequality, notwithstanding claims about privatizations fostering 'people's capitalism'. Institutional shareholders and wealthy players in the markets, being best placed to take advantage of the opportunities for further capital accumulation, usually feature prominently among the buyers of shares in newly privatized businesses. Moreover, following privatization, the public interest criteria that used to apply to the practices of the former public enterprises have less traction. Privatized businesses need not be so sensitive to the situation of their poorer customers.

Monopoly or collusive oligopoly pricing by privatized entities is also likely to be more prevalent unless increased regulation prevents it.

After more than three decades of neoliberal 'reforms', a broad pattern in these processes is evident when seen from a 'political economy of inequality' perspective. First, neoliberalism 'works' as a means of rolling back public sector practices that restrict private capital accumulation and as a precursor to rolling out a more stridently anti-egalitarian alternative, usually following a real or confected crisis of some sort (Peck & Tickell 2007). Second, neoliberalism works to compress labour's share in national income. Because the spread of capital incomes across households is invariably more concentrated than labour incomes, this tends to lead to yet greater concentration of wealth. Third, neoliberalism works much less well in creating conditions for overall prosperity. The increased inequalities intensify the problem of macroeconomic demand deficiency. This is problematic, even from a capitalist perspective, leading numerous central bankers to bemoan how stagnation of wage incomes during the last decade has impeded economic growth.

That is not to say that neoliberalism is a project nearing exhaustion. Its influence has not been notably less since the global financial crash, reports and predictions of its demise notwithstanding. Nor have academic analyses pointing to its incoherence and/or anti-social character derailed it. The resilience is explicable partly by 'the flexibility of neoliberalism – its amenity to reinvention in particular contexts' (Redden 2017: 2). Processes of circular and cumulative causation also have strong relevance because the increased inequality caused by neoliberalism generates class-based pressure for more of the same. The privatization of public assets, for example, leads major shareholders to oppose any change of policy that might threaten the value of their assets. Weakened governments facing strengthened corporate interests are more inclined to accede to such demands. This points to a two-way connection between neoliberal 'reforms' and inequality. The appetite of a wealthy elite grows the more it is fed. Indeed, it would be surprising, from a political economic perspective, if there were not mutually reinforcing processes operating during decades when neoliberal reforms and increasing inequality have been occurring in tandem.

Urbanization

Urbanization is perhaps a more surprising inclusion in this otherwise rather standard political economic catalogue of factors driving inequality. Yet it is crucially important. The FIRE sector, discussed earlier in relation to financialization, skews modern capitalist interests – and the associated economic inequalities – distinctively to the cities. It is in the cities that the process of surplus capture by these financial institutions is most evident. It is also in the cities that residential and commercial development offers the greatest opportunities for property owners to get capital gains and for all manner of agents, intermediaries and consultants to cream off fees and commissions. More generally, the processes of urban expansion create multiple opportunities for capital accumulation.

The growth of cities, historically, pre-dated (and in some ways pre-figured) capitalism. It is perhaps the most obvious physical manifestation of development and modernity. The last few decades have seen a spectacular surge, particularly in developing countries and most phenomenally in China. The proportion of the world's population officially classified as urban is now passing the 50% mark. Few would doubt urbanization's impact on where and how people live. Yet mainstream economists have paid it relatively little heed. Generally, their analytical approach is based either on decision-making by individuals, whether firms or households (microeconomics), or the performance of nations (macroeconomics). Spatial considerations, such as those relating to cities and regions, tend to be overlooked, despite (or perhaps partly because of) Paul Krugman and others carving out a small sub-field of geographical economics a couple of decades ago. Some economists might say that spatial analysis is for geographers, but the lack of attention to the analysis of land in mainstream economics is a deeper part of the story. A concerted attempt to marginalize the influence of Henry George diverted attention from the economic surplus arising from land ownership (Gaffney & Harrison 1994). Urban and regional development does not feature analytically in Piketty's story either, other than in his brief commentary on historical shifts in the dominant forms of wealth (Piketty 2014a: 113–20), largely because his broad definition of wealth does not differentiate between capital and land. This is unfortunate.

Complex socio-economic processes are involved in the connection between urbanization and economic inequality. Some relate to rural–urban migration processes that fuel urban growth. The inflow of people from country to city is partly a response to rural poverty, but selectivity in who migrates can have adverse consequences for spatial inequalities. It is the younger and more entrepreneurial people who usually have the higher social and geographical mobility; and their exodus tends to deplete the human and social capital of the rural regions. Even though they may send remittances home to parents and other family members, those spread effects are often swamped by the backwash effects of rural–urban migration. The processes of circular and cumulative causation thereby operate to increase inequalities.

The capture of increased real estate values is another important element in capital accumulation and the complex redistributions that occur in and around the expanding cities. Conversion of land uses at the urban fringe from rural to residential and commercial creates massive windfall gains for landowners or institutions who have anticipated the coming bonanza of rising land values. Inner-city values rise yet further, particularly in the global cities, where central business district land values soar even more spectacularly than the lofty buildings. The prestige of downtown locations and the premium price put on accessibility to the urban core in increasingly crowded and congested cities increases the land price–distance gradient. The share of the economic surplus going to people speculating and profiting from these urban land market processes rises. If elites who benefit from this surplus capture dominate political processes, an 'urban bias' becomes further accentuated, as Michael Lipton (1977) argued in a pioneering work, while more recent studies, such as Charles Gore's analysis of the 'middle-income trap' (2017), have also shown how particular aspects of urbanization may tend to inhibit development in late industrializing nations. Spatial inequality in cities stratified by class and race is so normal that it almost ceases to be noteworthy.

Urbanization in itself does not account for growing inequality. Indeed, the fact that urbanization is effectively a continuous process means that it cannot explain the long waves of growth, decline and regrowth in wealth inequality that Piketty, for example, identifies. The period of 'great compression' in economic inequality during the decades after the Second World War was also an era of rapid urbanization. Yet the longer trend, strikingly evident during recent decades, is for urban land values to rise relentlessly and create correspondingly greater problems of housing affordability for low- and middle-income earners (see Piketty 2014a: 79). Indeed, it is hard to think of political economic processes where the interests of winners and losers are so sharply polarized. The influence of landed property interests and their interconnections with the more general interests of capital and the institutions of the state are key features of modern urbanization. Some consideration of spatial political economy is therefore pertinent to the economic inequality story.

Technological change

Are technological change and structural shifts between industries a yet more fundamental driver of economic inequality? Substantial changes, particularly in transport and communications technologies, have facilitated the processes of globalization, financialization, neoliberalism and urbanization. In agriculture, mining and manufacturing, technological changes have had transformative effects on the patterns of industry development, jobs, productivity and much else besides. The shifts between agriculture, mining, manufacturing and service industries has created opportunities and dislocations, winners and losers.

The threats, opportunities and challenges arising from technological change and structural shifts in the current era are much discussed (e.g. Mason 2016). One widely cited study posited that 47% of all US jobs and an even higher proportion of jobs in developing countries could be susceptible to automation due to computerization (Frey & Osborne 2013: 38); if so, the employment and income distribution implications would be enormous. The current wave of changes affecting transport, logistics, administrative and service jobs, as well as manufacturing industries, is undoubtedly very powerful. Artificial intelligence (AI) is a coming wave of change, offering further potential for eliminating unnecessary labour while also tending to undermine the basis for full employment unless new jobs evolve in comparable numbers to the positions displaced. We can anticipate growing inequality between those in control of, and benefiting from, these technologies and those who bear the brunt of dislocation. However, it is important to temper this now familiar chain of reasoning with caution, particularly when it comes to prediction. Rapid technological changes have been effectively continuous since the industrial revolution began a couple of centuries ago – rather like urbanization in this respect – so it is hard to claim it as a factor explaining recent shifts in inequality or to be confident that its future impacts will be markedly different from previous epoch-making changes. A more prudent approach is to consider the channels through which technological change can affect the distribution of income and wealth.

First, there are direct financial rewards to the innovators themselves. Vast profits and royalties have flowed to people like Bill Gates and Steve Jobs for their innovations in information and communications technology. The rewards flowing to innovators like these often exhibit strong winner-takes-all characteristics. As Jonathan Rothwell (2016) writes, 'Some entrepreneurs grow enormously rich as a result of founding a company with an innovative product. This applies to Mark Zuckerberg, as well as to Bill Gates and other mega-stars of the hi-tech sector.' However, looking at Brookings Institution data on which industry sectors feature most prominently among the top 1% income earners reveals that the highest proportions of the very highly paid people are to be found in offices of physicians, hospitals, legal services and securities and financial investments. Innovation may sometimes generate huge rewards, but the top 1% of income recipients are not usually significant technological innovators.

Historically, the waves of technological change that swept through different sectors of industry, from agriculture and mining into manufacturing industries and on to service industries, have changed both the nature and forms of work and have often shifted the balance between highly remunerated and more poorly paid labour. In the more developed countries, technological changes and the nature of modern industry have already led to a decline in the number of middle-income jobs. Employment growth has been concentrated at one pole in professional, scientific, executive, managerial and other high-paying positions and, at the other pole, in casual and part-time work in the secondary labour market. A 'precariat' has developed and 'gig work' has proliferated, compounded by casualization of jobs in the so-called 'sharing economy' with the rise of businesses like Uber and Airbnb (Standing 2011). Meanwhile the proportion of middle-income positions, such as skilled blue-collar jobs, has tended to shrink: jobs for barristers and baristas may be buoyant, but many middle-income blue-collar and white-collar jobs are evidently on the line.

Nothing new there, you might say: the implementation of technological change in industries always displaces jobs. The key question is whether new ones will provide a similar number of job opportunities and comparable incomes. Because that has usually been the case in the past: technological unemployment has been mainly a transient problem as people shift to re-employment in different fields – although the transition has sometimes taken a generation or two to complete. Young people in education today are usually well aware that the labour market conditions offer little certainty for future years. It is not just the number of jobs, however; it is also their nature and remuneration. Technological change that increases flexibility, for example, facilitates the further proliferation of casual jobs rather than full-time ones.

Who gets the benefits of productivity gains arising from technological and structural changes is crucial. If the fruits of productivity improvements are captured mostly by employers as profits, that reduces the share of wages. Indeed, a plausible explanation of labour's declining share in the functional distribution, shown in Figure 2.3, is that the technological and structural shifts have increased the bargaining power of employers relative to employees. In class terms, it has put labour more on the defensive relative to capital. Trying to bargain collectively for wage rises is difficult where substantial levels of unemployment have become a seemingly permanent feature of the economic landscape. It is yet more difficult where employers import immigrant labour, often short-term. For the displaced workers, the prospect is exclusion from the mainstream of economic (and therefore social) life, perhaps seeking work in informal labour markets or becoming dependent on social security in the absence of wage incomes. In this case, the distributional inequalities predictably widen.

The household distribution of incomes in the more affluent societies is also vulnerable to the polarization between 'two-income households' (where both partners are working) and 'no-income households' (where all are unemployed). The latter tend to be spatially concentrated too, compounding the inequality between winners and losers in labour markets where technological and structural shifts are ongoing. These factors accentuate – and give distinctive socio-spatial shape to – the underlying tendency towards a growing disparity in economic rewards. Technology itself is not the driver of greater inequality. More crucial is how technological change is managed – and in whose interests. As Harvey emphasizes (2010: ch. 7), technology is best understood in terms of its place in the web of capitalist relations, leading into an analysis of the material factors shaping technology itself. A capital-centric approach is quite different from a labour-centric approach to distributing its fruits more equitably. For the latter purpose, strong institutions for organized labour and committed social democratic states are necessary countervailing influences.

Countervailing forces

Figure 7.1 recaps this chapter's principal themes. It identifies circular and cumulative causation, compounded by the effects of globalization, financialization, neoliberalism, urbanization and technological change, as interacting elements shaping the forms and extent of modern economic inequality. This is a constellation of powerful and pervasive economic processes.

Perhaps what really needs explaining is why capitalist societies are not more unequal than they actually are. Some consideration

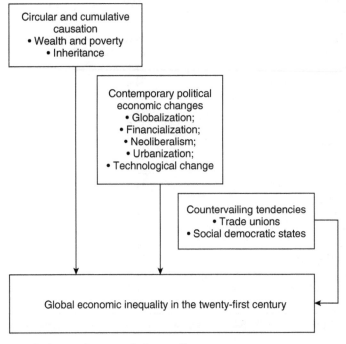

Figure 7.1 Drivers of economic inequality

of labour organizations and social democratic states, broadly interpreted, is necessary for this purpose. During much of the twentieth century, these institutions provided a significant countervailing power to the forces driving inequality. The 'great compression' that Piketty identifies as the dominant feature of the three decades after the Second World War was surely the high-water mark of their influence. Trade unions and reformist governments played roles in the political economic drama by: (1) establishing better wages and working conditions; (2) developing the institutions of the welfare state; (3) extending the provision of and access to education; (4) macroeconomic management, helping to ensure full employment; and (5) progressive taxation as a vehicle for redistribution.

Trade unions usually have more power when most of the workers are union members. As Table 7.1 shows, the OECD countries vary considerably in this respect; but most have experienced

Table 7.1 Trade union coverage of the workforce, selected OECD countries

Country	2000	2016
Denmark	73.6	67.2
Sweden	79.0	66.7
Belgium[a]	56.2	54.2
Norway[a]	54.1	52.5
Italy	34.4	34.4
Austria[a]	36.9	27.4
Canada	28.2	26.3
UK	29.7	23.7
New Zealand	22.4	17.7
Japan	21.5	17.3
Netherlands	22.6	17.3
Germany	24.6	17.0
Switzerland[a]	20.2	15.7
Australia	24.7	14.6
Spain[a]	16.5	13.9
Mexico	16.9	12.5
Czech Republic	27.2	10.5
USA	12.9	10.3
Republic of Korea	11.4	10.1
France[a]	8.0	7.9

Note: [a] Figures in the right-hand column for these countries are for the latest available years.
Source: https://stats.oecd.org/Index.aspx?DataSetCode=TUD.

declining rates of union membership during this century, as comparison of the two columns shows. Coverage of the workforce has declined in every case other than Italy (where it has flat-lined), even in Denmark and Sweden, although those two countries still top the league table with about two-thirds of their workers unionized. Notable plunges in union density have been evident in Australia and the Czech Republic. This weakens workers' capacity to maintain the overall wage share in the national income, giving freer rein to processes driving further inequality.

The countries in which unions have had high coverage of the workforce have generally had lower overall inequality of incomes (as measured by the 90:10 ratio), although the correlation is far from perfect (Wilkinson & Pickett 2018: 239). Figure 7.2 shows a compilation of data on this, with an indicative 'line of best fit' going through the scatter to indicate a generally inverse relationship between union coverage and inequality. Although not strong evidence, these cross-sectional data are consistent with time-series data on how, during the twentieth century, inequality waxed and waned with unions' expansion and contraction. Looking at the US experience over that last century, for example, the growth and then decline in unions' coverage of the workforce was an almost exact

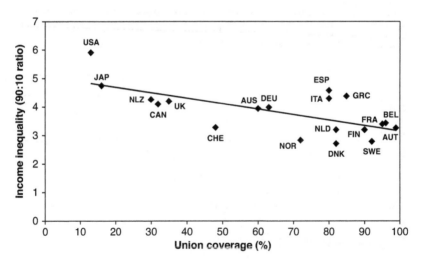

Figure 7.2 Trade union strength and inequality, cross-country comparison, 2009

Source: The State of Working in America, Economic Policy Institute (Washington DC, 2011). Under Creative Commons License CC BY-SA 3.0.

mirror image of the decline and then growth of income inequality (Wilkinson & Pickett 2018: 239). Because the direction of causation is ambiguous, however, it is best to interpret this historical experience as showing long swings in the economic and industrial relations 'culture' of the society. Trade unions' struggles for better wages and working conditions, although primarily focusing on the interests of their members, significantly influence (and are influenced by) these long swings in the general character of societies over time. Unions' continuing struggles for better wages and rights for workers operate now in a more difficult context in most of the developed nations. As Verity Burgmann (2016) notes, unions are trying to develop effective tactics to combat the effects of corporate globalization and neoliberalism. Concurrently, the international shifts of production to lower-wage countries, such as China and India, open up new possibilities for labour organization and political economic action.

The story of social democracy in recent decades has been somewhat similar. Historically, the development of the 'social state', as Piketty (2014a: ch. 13) calls it, was crucial in reducing income inequalities in the developed countries. During the twentieth century, most of them increased taxes to finance expenditure on provision of public goods and services and the payments to welfare recipients, including the elderly, people with disabilities, unemployed people and people needing financial assistance to bring up children. Figure 7.3 shows the dramatic changes that occurred in four

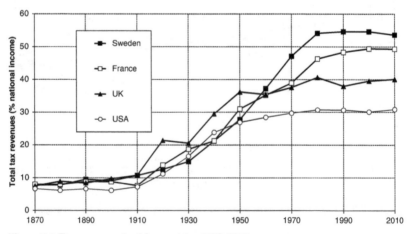

Figure 7.3 Tax revenues in rich countries, 1870–2010

Source: Piketty (2014a: 475). Reproduced with permission.

of those countries during the period 1910–80. Total tax revenues as a percentage of national income increased more than six-fold in Sweden and France and four-fold in the UK and the USA. Each country had its distinctive political economic drivers. In the Swedish case, a thoroughgoing social transformation was created by the concerted efforts of its trade unions and leading lights within the Social Democratic Party such as Ernst Wigfors (Higgins & Dow 2013). In the US case, facing the economic calamity of the Great Depression of the 1930s, President F.D. Roosevelt explained to businesspeople and the rich that it was necessary to reform the system in order to preserve it (Wilkinson & Pickett 2018: 239). In the UK and France, the development of a strong public sector was an integral part of the politics and economics of post-war reconstruction after the devastation of the Second World War. We tend nowadays to emphasize the cross-country differences, contrasting Sweden's well-developed welfare state and high taxes with the USA's poorly developed welfare state and lower taxes, but it is pertinent to recall some of these historically common elements in the national trajectories when starting from a very low base.

Since about 1980, the political economic situation has been quite different. Throughout the developed nations, the influence, even the existence, of reformist governments with social democratic inclinations has become weaker. Neoliberal policy practices have been more dominant. Both 'roll-back' neoliberalism and 'roll-out' neoliberalism have had explicitly anti-egalitarian characteristics (Peck & Tickell 2007). An international wave of right-wing populism is now making further inroads into previous social democratic gains. An OECD study of taxes and income transfers across OECD countries shows the extent to which redistribution has changed during the last two decades (Causa & Hermansen 2017: 9). Reduction of top income tax rates and more targeting of transfer payments has created a significant pause in the development of the progress of 'social state'. Yet, as Figure 7.3 shows, while the rapid growth of state taxing and spending that occurred in the previous half-century levelled off from the 1970s (and earlier in the USA), it has not generally declined.

One research study, setting out to refute the popular view of 'welfare state retrenchment' since the 1970s, indicates that most welfare states actually became more redistributive during the 1980s and 1990s (Wang, Caminada & Goudswaard 2014). Notably, though, that was mainly the effect of increased inequality in market incomes. Where market inequalities are rising, welfare states normally become more redistributive, unless there are major changes to benefit entitlements. Such changes as have occurred have often involved more emphasis on targeted policies and less on universal provision. A balanced view, generalizing across OECD nations, is that the forward march of the 'social state' has been interrupted but not sharply turned around. Whether a renewal of a more egalitarian policy push is desirable and possible is a central theme for the rest of this book.

Conclusion

Several interacting processes have been driving disparities in the distribution of income and wealth, both within nations and globally. The brief survey of them in this chapter shows the following:

- Pervasive processes of circular and cumulative causation, such as inheritance, reproduce and magnify economic inequalities.
- In the modern capitalist economy, the interacting effects of globalization, financialization, neoliberalism, urbanization and capital-centric technological change compound the tendency.
- Countervailing tendencies exist but labour organizations and social democratic states have had reduced traction in recent decades.

Does this matter? On what grounds might we be concerned about the consequences of growing inequality? It is to these questions that we next turn.

Problems

8

Hazards to Handle; Opportunities to Grasp

Why should we be concerned about the growing intra-national economic inequalities? Even if they cause some social tensions and resentments, aren't they conducive to economic dynamism and social progress? Isn't inequality, in the last resort, a 'necessary evil'? Views like these are widely held – and promulgated by conservative commentators – so they need to be carefully considered in relation to the evidence. This requires scrutiny of the connections between inequalities and economic performance, whether judged in terms of productivity, growth or stability. It also requires looking at other connections with social problems, mobility and cohesion, the intensity of environmental problems, the prospect of more peaceful societies and the effectiveness of our democratic institutions and human rights.

This chapter considers each of these connections by reviewing evidence drawn from diverse sources. As the chapter title foreshadows, such an investigation can take either a problem-saturated or solution-focused approach. We can look at whether, why and how inequality tends to create hazards. Alternatively, we can look at whether, why and how greater equality would create opportunities for a better society. These are two sides of the same coin, or – to use a different metaphor – two views of the same glass, as half empty or half full. Let's examine both.

Fostering higher productivity

Beginning with the economic issues takes us directly to the grounds on which conservatives commonly seek to justify inequality. Their key claim is that inequality is 'good for the economy' because it creates strong work incentives and encourages the productivity from which our overall standards of living derive. You might be surprised to know that this 'incentivization' view actually has little analytical support in neoclassical economic theory. As enunciated in the microeconomic textbooks, the standard theory recognizes that changes in people's remuneration have two effects, known formally as the *substitution* and *income* effects. The former involves people substituting work for leisure time as the rate of pay for their work increases: that is, the familiar 'incentivization' view that higher reward produces more effort. However, the latter effect – the income effect – operates in the reverse direction. This is because people may work fewer hours when their hourly rate of pay is higher, while still generating the same total income as before. They will tend to respond in this way if they place a high personal value on leisure time. Since both substitution and income effects operate simultaneously and pull in opposite directions, the actual outcome depends on their relative strength. This can vary from case to case, from person to person, from industry to industry, depending on people's personal preferences for extra income or leisure. In other words, the net effect of pay changes on work effort is indeterminate. We cannot say whether, in general, the net effect of a wage increase for a lowly paid worker – or the reduction in the hourly rate for a more highly paid worker – will increase or decrease their work efforts.

The conservative arguments for having big inequalities in rewards probably work better in terms of the incentive to innovate. Indeed, higher pay-offs may inspire more vigorous efforts. Yet there are many other personal and environmental factors influencing whether innovation occurs, including the degree of autonomy that innovators may enjoy, their sense of vocation and their personal proclivity for risk-taking or risk aversion. There is a significant school of economic thought, deriving from the pioneering contributions of the Austrian economist Joseph Schumpeter (1934, 1942), that points to innovation having more complex institutional dynamics than are implied by the simple 'incentivization' view. Indeed, for both work and innovation, monetary considerations are only part of an array of influences on how much effort is expended. Attitudes to work reflect the nature and location of the job, the social character of the workplace, the opportunity costs that impact on non-work time and much else besides. Not all workers have flexibility of working hours anyway: many, if not most, cannot adjust their work hours in response to changing rates of pay. Moreover, the motivations of innovators may have more to do with personal ingenuity or professional goals than the simple prospect of economic gain. For all these reasons, a simple linear relationship between effort and reward is implausible.

US political economist Sam Bowles (2012) has cast further light on these matters by pointing out that the incentive structures in highly unequal societies can actually tend to undermine productivity. If workers do not feel adequately compensated for their contributions, they may tend to 'go slow'. Cooperative relations generally produce more productive work environments. The growing gulf between managerial remuneration and average wages is particularly problematic from this perspective. As Bowles also notes, productivity depends on trust and loyalty in overcoming the coordination problems that recur in businesses. In his own words: 'In addition to the invisible hand of competition and the fist of command, a well-governed society must also rely on the handshake of trust' (Bowles 2012: 8). Moreover, markedly unequal societies have to allocate many resources simply to defend the status quo. Private expenditures on security equipment and guards, together with public expenditures on police, prisons and surveillance, constitute a major drain on modern economies. For these three reasons – the dilution of work incentives, the discouragement of trust and the diversion of resources to unproductive uses – the overall productivity of an economy tends to be impaired, rather than improved, by a high level of economic inequality.

The liberal economist Joseph Stiglitz takes a similar view, arguing that 'policies that aim for growth but ignore inequality may be self-defeating, whereas policies that decrease inequality by, for example, boosting employment and education have beneficial effects on the human capital that modern economies increasingly need' (2015: 288). An OECD report (2016) confirms that inequality tends to impede capacity for productivity improvements within individual nations and calls for greater international recognition of the 'policy nexus' between higher productivity and greater equality.

Attaining better macroeconomic performance

Macroeconomic performance depends on more than personal productivity anyway: it also depends on the efficiency with which nations use their resources of land, labour and capital. Mainstream economists, especially following Arthur Okun (1975), have commonly talked of an 'efficiency–equity trade-off', implying that efficiency will be impaired if too much emphasis is put on distributional equity. The argument would be plausible if the incentive to generate more income were weakened by part of the incomes being redistributed to the poor or if there were a strong tendency to featherbedding. However, broader social and environmental factors apply here too, affecting personal behaviour and economic outcomes. Over three decades ago, Robert Kuttner (1984) pointed out the fallacies in the efficiency–equity trade-off argument, giving examples of public policies that perform well in terms of both equity and efficiency (or perform poorly in both). No general trade-off need apply.

Empirical studies undertaken by researchers at the usually conservative IMF have confirmed that greater equality can actually improve national economic performance. One widely cited IMF study indicates that countries with high inequality are less likely to sustain economic growth over the long term (Berg & Ostry 2011). Another shows that policies to redistribute incomes more equitably tend to go hand in hand with beneficial economic outcomes, not the negative effects on productivity and growth that opponents of redistribution have claimed. It explicitly rejects 'the Okun assumption that there is a general trade-off between redistribution and growth' (Ostry, Berg & Tsangarides 2014: 21). Studies like these, especially because they come from such a generally conservative institutional source, significantly shift the balance of economic debate about the effects of inequality.

How damaging is this evidence for the economists' traditional assertion of an efficiency–equity trade-off? Very: the posited inverse connection looks increasingly untenable. However, governments have been generally slow on the uptake. The continuing belief that economic inequality 'works' for capitalism is reflected in current neoliberal and right-wing populist governments pushing to create 'jobs and growth' by cutting taxes on business profits while simultaneously restricting welfare and keeping unemployment benefits below the poverty line. As the institutional political economist J.K. Galbraith wryly remarked when similar policies were previously pursued many decades ago, the underlying presumption is that the rich will work harder if their incomes are increased while the poor will work harder if theirs are reduced (cited in Davidson 1987). It is, to say the least, a somewhat perplexing behavioural postulate.

Creating more economic stability

The relationship between inequality and economic stability is a third economic concern. Are highly unequal societies more or less vulnerable to cycles of boom and slump? This is a big issue because economic instability is a major source of social stress. When recessions occur, people lose jobs, savings and businesses. A good society avoids this situation if it can. Would greater equality help? All capitalist societies, from the most egalitarian to the most unequal, have been troubled at various times by the problem of cyclical instability. It is therefore difficult to point to inequality, rather than capitalism in general, as the source of the problem. However, there is some international evidence that high inequality is associated with shorter cycles of growth and recession (Berg, Ostry & Zettelmeyer 2012); and there are some significant political economic reasons for the more pronounced cyclical tendency in the more unequal societies.

Post-Keynesians, such as Engelbert Stockhammer (2012), explain economic downswings as the result of insufficient demand for the goods and services that the economy would be capable of producing if firms and industries were working at full capacity. Inequality increases the likelihood of that demand deficiency situation arising, because wealthier people tend to have a higher propensity to save. If most of the fruits of economic growth go to them, the overall level of consumption in the economy will be less than it would be if the incomes were more widely dispersed. The rich people's higher propensity to save causes 'leakage' from the circular flow of income that depresses the overall level of economic activity. Growth slows, workers are laid off, productive capital is under-utilized and the recession deepens. Post-Keynesians say that less inequality would help to avoid economic downturns and be conducive to more consistently buoyant macroeconomic outcomes. Overall consumption spending would be higher, tending to raise the level of output and employment throughout the economy. This is not to say that recessions could never occur: only that the problem of periodic demand deficiency would be lessened. As Keynes wrote, '[T]he redistribution of incomes in a way likely to raise the propensity to consume may prove positively favourable to the growth of capital' (2018 [1936]: 332). If so, it is a win-win situation.

Marxist political economists point to deeper, contradictory causes of economic fluctuations and crises. They observe that capitalist businesses, each seeking to minimize their costs of production, try to resist paying higher wage rates, even though they would collectively benefit from the extra demand for their products that those higher wages would generate. On this reasoning, wages tend to be simultaneously too high (from the viewpoint of capitalists seeing to produce surplus value) and too low (from the viewpoint of those same capitalists seeking to realize the surplus value by selling their products). A deep-seated contradiction like this inhibits the likelihood of any equilibrium or steady growth path. Yet there is no easy resolution of crisis tendencies through redistributive policies. Win-win outcomes are elusive.

General propositions like these – whether Keynesian or Marxian – offer useful explanations of instability and crisis tendencies in capitalist economies, but they need to be set in historical context. The experience of the global financial crisis a decade ago is a case in point. Among the numerous analyses of its causes, Stockhammer's is particularly helpful in showing the influence of inequality and its links with debt and speculation. As he points out, increased inequality causes lower-income households to incur more debt while it also fuels speculative activities undertaken by rich people with surplus wealth. This constellation created unstable conditions, culminating in the crash (Stockhammer 2012).

The tendencies to debt and speculation are ongoing. Stagnation in levels of real wages has been widespread in the affluent capitalist nations, causing heavier borrowing among low- and middle-income households trying to maintain their living standards. Much of the borrowing is to pay for housing, the high prices of which force aspiring home owners to go deeper into debt with mortgage-backed loans from financial institutions. While this debt-based consumption helps temporarily to offset capitalism's systemic tendency to insufficient demand, it creates an increasingly debt-laden economy. Meanwhile, the same economic conditions work very differently for richer households, businesses and financial institutions. Their accumulated wealth is available for diverse speculative purposes: 'investing' in hedge funds, derivatives and other new financial products as well as real estate. The result is a multi-layered arrangement of financial assets of uncertain value – rather like a house of cards. As Stockhammer (2012) notes, these conditions came to a head in the lead-up to the global financial crisis in 2008, which would have been even more catastrophic had it not been for some national governments implementing emergency Keynesian-style bailouts.

While some minor financial reforms have taken place since the crash, there are no ultimate safeguards against a recurrence. We are expected to accept a volatile and vulnerable economy as normal. Looked at now through this political economic lens, however, we can see that economic inequality is integral to the situation: it was at the core of the last major global crash and it continues to be an ongoing source of instability, making future economic crises more likely.

Reducing social problems

Turning to broader social considerations, some other important reasons for concern with economic inequality come into view. A growing volume of social science research shows the connections between inequality and the intensity of social problems. Broadly speaking, the social problems form three clusters: physical and mental health; anti-social behaviours such as criminal activities; and failure to achieve desirable social outcomes such as improved educational outcomes. Research by the British epidemiologist Richard Wilkinson paved the way for a deeper understanding of these issues. Medical researchers had known for decades, if not centuries, that particular health problems can be strongly associated with poverty, but Wilkinson (1996, 2005) showed that economic inequality, more generally, tends to be associated with unhealthy behaviours. Countries with high economic inequality have a higher incidence of various illnesses.

Wilkinson's most widely cited book, co-authored with Kate Pickett, is *The Spirit Level: Why More Equal Societies Almost Always Do Better* (2009). Like Piketty's book, it provides an engaging blend of statistics, commentary and policy implications. It parades evidence of significant correlations between nations according to their level of inequality and the incidence of social problems such as crime, prison incarceration and low educational attainment, as well as obesity and poor physical and mental health. The authors calculated a summary index of these problems, based on nine indicators of wellbeing that they surveyed. Their key findings were that (1) there is no significant correlation between country scores on this index of social problems and level of national income per capita, but (2) there is a stronger correlation with the extent of economic inequality in those same countries. In other words, differences in the incidence of social problems align much better with differences in inequality than with differences in overall per capita incomes. These are significant findings, even though the correlations are less than perfect, as is almost invariably the case with cross-country comparisons of this sort. Figure 8.1 shows the pattern, with the 'line of best fit' superimposed on the scatter. Among the developed nations, Japan and the Scandinavian nations are at the lower left end with relatively low inequality and a low score on the index of social problems. The UK and Portugal are towards the upper right with greater higher inequality and greater social problems. The USA, being the extreme case, is almost out of the picture.

A correlation between inequality and the intensity of social problems cannot be the full story, though. It is also necessary to

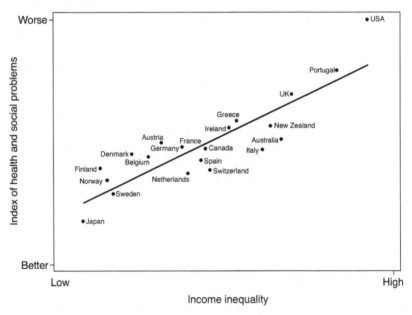

Figure 8.1 Health and social problems related to inequality, OECD countries
Source: Wilkinson & Pickett (2018: xix).

identify causal connections. These vary for each of the social problems being studied – and Wilkinson and Pickett present plausible hypotheses and evidence for each of those that they analyse, as have other studies of health standards that are negatively influenced by inequality (e.g. Bose 2013; Deighton 2015; Marmot 2016). Responding to critics of their earlier book (e.g. Leigh 2013: 99–101), Wilkinson and Pickett's more recent book, called *The Inner Level: How More Equal Societies Reduce Stress, Restore Sanity and Improve Everyone's Well-being* (2018), provides more empirical evidence and explores causal links more thoroughly. It puts particular emphasis on stress and status anxiety as factors shaping unhealthy and anti-social behaviours. This puts the behaviour and wellbeing of individuals back at the core of the analysis, but they are individuals shaped physically and emotionally by their positions in hierarchies. The analysis indicates that, in general, the greater the social distinctions, the more entrenched are the problems and the greater the difficulties in climbing the ladder of social success.

Increasing social mobility

For proponents of equality of opportunity, it is axiomatic that people should be able to move between different occupations or different locations in order to take advantage of the available economic and social opportunities. On this, liberals and social democrats are in accord, notwithstanding their different views about the political responses and programmes to achieve the goal. The problem is that, in practice, the impediments to economic and social mobility are diverse and pervasive. These impediments may be geographical or occupational. They may result from racism, sexism and other forms of discrimination that obstruct meritocratic outcomes. The interesting question is whether these impediments tend to be greater in the more economically unequal societies. Or does high social mobility in unequal societies enable people from all walks of life to become rich? Unhappily, the evidence suggests that the former is the usual case – that the more unequal societies also tend to have less social mobility.

Figure 8.2 shows the results of one such study of 22 countries for which data on both variables are available. Social mobility (on the vertical axis) is measured by comparing parents' incomes with their children's income in adulthood: a big gap denotes high mobility. Income inequality (on the horizontal axis) is measured

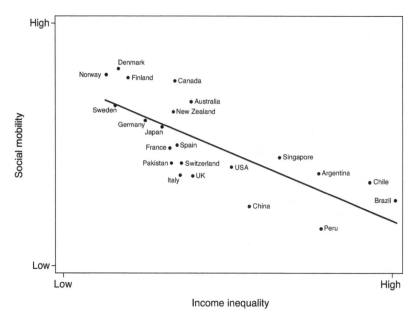

Figure 8.2 Social mobility and income inequality, international comparison
Source: Wilkinson & Pickett (2018: 177).

by the quintile ratio. The correlation between the two variables is inverse, although far from perfectly so: in general, the greater the economic inequality, the less the social mobility. The polar cases are the four Nordic countries, all of which have low inequality and above-average social mobility; and an array of South American nations with high inequality and low mobility, with China and Singapore in quite close company with them. Of the more affluent nations, the USA has the most troubling combinations of high inequality and low mobility, although mobility is also notably low in Italy and the UK.

One may infer that social mobility is generally lowest in the societies where, on liberal principles, it would be most needed. It is a particularly troublesome finding for those who would wish to claim about a country, such as the USA, that 'sure, it's an unequal society but anyone can make it to the top'. The rhetoric of mobility (sometimes described in the USA as the 'Horatio Alger' syndrome or, simply, the 'American dream') is clearly at odds with the reality. The combination of substantial economic inequality and low mobility thwarts the meritocratic ideal. The implications are considerable, especially for liberals who are willing to tolerate high inequality of rewards but want to increase equality of opportunity. On this evidence, that is not a tenable stance. Equality of opportunity tomorrow requires greater equality of outcome today.

One form of mobility *is* positively associated with economic inequality. This is not social mobility within nations, however: it is geographical movement between nations. Huge numbers of people recurrently try to relocate, whether as refugees from war and oppression or simply to seek better economic opportunities. Where the income gaps between countries are huge and growing (as is the case in the countries of Europe and Africa that are geographically very close), further growth in these flows is inevitable, as Branko Milanovic (2018) points out. Worldwide, this poses major challenges for border protection arrangements, settlement processes, social cohesion and the practical application of humanitarian values.

Encouraging social cohesion

A socially cohesive society is one in which there is mutual respect, goodwill and some sense of both solidarity and common purpose. A concern to achieve this goal differs from the liberal meritocratic ideal in that it pays more attention to the conditions for cooperation and harmony within social groups. However, as with social mobility, inequality can be a big impediment to its achievement. Institutions – whether households, workplaces, sporting teams or other community organizations – normally function better when their members work well together because of their willingness to cooperate. For this to occur, the people must expect reasonably equitable sharing of the fruits of cooperation. Where just an individual or a sub-group of participants is likely to capture most or all of the benefits, trust is fractured and willingness to cooperate is far less likely to be forthcoming. Instead, a greater incidence of social problems and pathologies is likely, as documented by Wilkinson and Pickett (2018). If there is an uneven incidence of winners and losers according to differences of gender and ethnicity, the ten sions tend to be even greater.

Social scientists have probed the extent of social discord in societies having varying degrees of inequality. One study, undertaken jointly by psychologists from universities in Denmark,

Norway, the USA and New Zealand, was published in the *Proceedings of the National Academy of Science* in 2017. Based on studying the behaviour of 45,000 people across 27 countries, it found a significant connection between inequality and beliefs that influence social behaviour, usually for the worse. As the authors wrote: '[S]ocietal inequality is reflected in people's minds as dominance motives that underpin ideologies and actions that ultimately sustain group-based hierarchy' (Kunst et al. 2017). In other words, inequality comes to be accepted as a social norm that justifies the behaviour of those at the top at the expense of those with inferior status. The result, to quote the authors again, is 'greater racism, sexism, welfare opposition, and even willingness to enforce group hegemony violently by participating in ethnic persecution of subordinate out-groups'. This is not a pretty prospect.

The incidence of crime is a further indicator of poor social cohesion. It is a form of anti-social behaviour that one might expect to be associated, both statistically and causally, with inequality. As social geographer Danny Dorling argues in his book *The Equality Effect*, 'There is less need to commit crime in a more equal society where fewer people are impoverished and everyone is less desperate about their financial situation' (2017: 152). This expectation of a positive correlation between economic inequality and the prevalence of criminal behaviours is borne out by the evidence. Dorling's own compilation of international comparative studies shows the generally positive correlation between income inequalities, general crime rates and homicide rates across the OECD countries (2017: 152, 218), although he also advises against drawing strong conclusions because of variations in the definition of offences and ways of recording and counting crimes in different countries. A high homicide rate, for example, may also be more attributable to permissive laws relating to gun ownership than to inequality per se. These cautionary comments add to the interest in a recently published statistical analysis of crime in the US states between 1978 and 2013 because a state-by-state study within one country has the advantage of having fewer cultural variations influencing behavioural patterns than is the case with international studies. The study's authors report their general findings that 'income inequality and unemployment have a positive impact on crime' and that 'inequality plays a crucial role in affecting all types of crime' (Constantini, Meco & Paradiso 2018: 565).

Reducing environmental stresses

The importance of inequality is also borne out in relationships to the bio-physical environment (e.g. Baland, Bardhan & Bowles 2007). Inequality correlates positively with indicators of environmental stress and negatively with the capacity to respond to environmental challenges. The former link is not surprising to the extent that the higher incidence of environmental damage results from the extravagant consumption of goods and services by rich people and their reluctance to reduce their consumption to 'a fair earth share' for the good of the planet (Dauvergne 2016: 11). We now have quite good empirical evidence of the links between levels of economic inequality and the incidence of environmentally damaging behaviours. Again, the book by Danny Dorling (2017) provides a useful compilation, showing that, for the OECD nations, the levels of carbon dioxide emissions, water consumption, waste production and the estimated 'ecological footprints' all have positive correlations with the degree of economic inequality (measured by the decile ratio of income). The relevant scatter diagrams for the first two of these variables are reproduced here as Figures 8.3 and 8.4, with the size of each circle being proportional to the country's population.

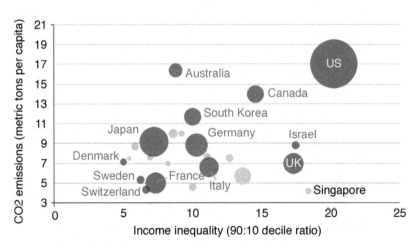

Figure 8.3 Economic inequality and carbon dioxide emissions
Source: Dorling (2017: 139).

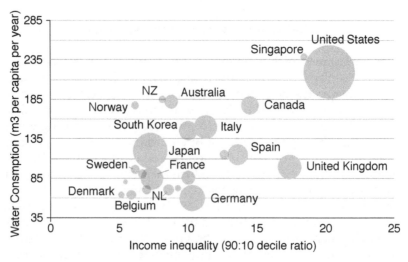

Figure 8.4 Economic inequality and water consumption (domestic), 2009–13
Source: Dorling (2017: 139).

A quick glance at these two figures reveals quite a wide 'scatter' of the country scores. Of course, there are many nation-specific factors bearing on the behaviours associated with environmental stress. In Figure 8.3, for example, Singapore's appearance as an 'outlier' in the scatter, with notably low CO_2 emissions, probably reflects its character as a small city-state with a public transport system that reasonably effectively serves the needs of its people. The big, car-oriented Australia, on the other hand, has higher levels of emissions than countries with a similar level of inequality such as France and Germany. However, there is evidently a broad association between economic inequality and environmental impact. The single most striking feature of the two figures is the dominance of the USA as a nation with high inequality and a high incidence of environmentally damaging behaviours, including high CO_2 emissions and high domestic water consumption. It also has a particularly high level of domestic waste production. Japan and the Nordic states are at the other end of each scale. Politically, the presence of these polar cases is important because, as we all face the prospect of environmental catastrophes that ultimately do not 'respect' national boundaries, it is to them that the rest of the world looks either as exemplars or with dismay.

Does inequality also affect the likelihood of finding solutions? If the environmental challenge, particularly climate change, is to be effectively addressed, the key requirement is cooperation in formulating and implementing remedial action. Cohesion matters in this context too. International deliberations on how to reduce or mitigate the problem of climate change have shown the problems that arise when extreme inequalities fracture cohesion and common purpose. The willingness of diverse nations to work together to produce an ecologically sustainable future needs an egalitarian perspective and a commitment to redistributive policies (Parr 2013). Poorer countries, understandably, are generally less willing to reduce their carbon emissions if doing so would effectively lock them into perpetual economic disadvantage.

There is also evidence that the willingness of business leaders to comply with international environmental agreements is higher in more economically equal countries (Wilkinson & Pickett 2018: 229). A broad public acceptance is necessary, too, for policies like emission trading or carbon taxes: unless poorer households are compensated for the impact of the increased energy costs, social and political resistance is inevitable. Bolder attempts to create transitions to sustainability, like moving to 100% renewable energy or reducing environmentally damaging consumerism, require yet stronger emphasis on having an egalitarian dimension in public policy. For these reasons, environmentalists commonly talk of the need for 'just transition' to sustainability (Stilwell 2012). It is not simply a matter of feeling that 'we're all in the same boat' when threatened by the prospect of climate change: it is a matter of actual winners and losers. If the wealthy can simply pay to pollute, the necessary collective agreement to change our patterns of production and consumption is much harder to achieve. Without equity there is unlikely to be sustainability.

Improving prospects for peace

Do egalitarian societies also tend to be more peaceful? Of course, all reasonable people want a peaceful society. Yet the world is bedevilled by tensions that frequently spill over into violent confrontations, including terrorism and war. While it would be facile to characterize all such conflicts as products of socio-economic inequality, it is evidently a pervasive influence. Powerful economic players often have a stake in, and profit from, war, whether directly by supplying the means of destruction or by creating post-conflict regimes that are conducive to their interests (Doran 2007; Klein 2007; Stilwell, Jordan & Pearce 2008). Inequalities deriving from the ongoing effects of colonialism and imperialist exploitation are cases in point. Anti-imperialist struggles, sometimes violent in nature, have challenged the political economic advantages gained by affluent nations at the expense of the people in the poorer regions and countries that they dominated. Conflicts within post-colonial societies are also often the legacy of such inequalities.

While being sceptical about a general correlation between civil violence and economic inequality, Joseph Stiglitz points to evidence of links between the incidence of violence and the presence of 'horizontal inequalities' associated with race, ethnicity, religion or region. He notes that, when the poor are from one group and the rich from another, 'a lethal, destabilizing dynamic often emerges' (Stiglitz 2015: 289). One study cited to support this claim found that the greater the inequality between ethnographic groups, the greater the likelihood of civil war being experienced in that nation (Cederman, Weidmann & Gleditsch 2011).

The effects of inequality are also increasingly evident on a global scale as groups who perceive themselves as exploited, oppressed or marginalized by wealthy nations and classes elsewhere have recourse to violence. The recurrent hostility towards 'the west', the USA in particular, commonly involves resentment against structures of political economic power (and their supporting ideologies) that are insensitive to the conditions, culture and aspirations of poor people in other countries. Looking back to the last century, Dorling (2017: 55) probably overstates the case in postulating a causal link between its two great world wars, the inequality peak that occurred in Europe just before the first war and the abrupt rise in inequality in Germany and Japan just before the second. In both catastrophic instances, so many other contingent factors were involved. Yet the broader question he poses has strong and ongoing resonance: 'What will be a safer world less likely to resort to war – one with more or less inequality?' (Dorling 2017: 55). Indeed, it is hard to conceive of a peaceful world without emphasis on dealing with the processes that have created unjustified and unacceptable inequalities. This was well put in 1943 by Dr H.V. Evatt, the Australian politician and later President of the UN General Assembly, when he said that 'unless it has an adequate basis in economic justice', no system of security 'can be permanent' (cited in Plant 1967: 405).

Enhancing democracy

A further aspect of the case for equality concerns the relationship between economic structures and *political* institutions. This touches the perennial question: are capitalism and democracy natural partners? Democracy is widely held to be the most desirable political arrangement – or, as a cynic might say, the 'least worst' arrangement. We tend to think of democracy as operating mainly through voting procedures in which a majority of votes determines the outcome. In its simplest electoral form, this means 'one person, one vote'. This is an essentially egalitarian principle. Capitalist economies, on the other hand, operate on the quite different basis of 'one dollar, one vote'. In the marketplace, those with the most money send the strongest market signals about what firms should produce. This principle, cherished in mainstream economics as 'consumer sovereignty', has an anti-egalitarian character when applied in societies with markedly uneven distributions of income and wealth. That is why democracy and capitalism are such uncomfortable bedfellows. The former political ideal is egalitarian; the latter economic arrangement is anti-egalitarian. Only if the distribution of income and wealth were to be substantially less unequal could there be less tension between capitalism (as an economic system) and democracy (as a political system).

The relationship is yet more problematic if we recognize that there is more to democracy than voting and more to capitalism than markets. The deeper democratic principle is that each person should be entitled to participate equally in collective decision-making. Markedly uneven distributions of political economic power obstruct the realization of this ideal. Moreover, capitalists express their interests not only through markets: class power has political expression that tends to corrupt the institutions of the state. Many of the tangible problems of modern politics illustrate these tendencies. Donations from corporations or wealthy individuals to political parties, for example, recurrently influence government policy agendas and priorities. Lobbyists for corporate interests continually ply their trade with similar intent. On those infrequent occasions when governments try to introduce policies that would go against powerful interests, they are almost invariably subject to immense pressures to reverse those policies. Thus, as Stiglitz (2013: ch. 5) argues, the concentration of wealth in modern capitalist societies has a corrosive effect on nominally democratic

political institutions. Systematic research in the USA has shown
that 'when Americans with different income levels differ in their
policy preferences, actual policy outcomes strongly reflect the
preferences of the most affluent' (Gilens 2005: 778).

Luke Petach (2017) usefully summarizes four channels through
which these processes work: (1) greater responsiveness by governments to the preferences expressed by the rich, rather than
the middle class or poor people; (2) increased political instability;
(3) the ability of the wealthy to subvert government policies; and
(4) altering the preferences of the electorate in ways that favour
authoritarianism. The current rise of right-wing populist leaders
may be interpreted in the latter context. Country-specific histories
matter, of course, but the inherent tensions between capitalism
and democracy generally loom larger where large economic inequalities exist. As Paul Krugman (2011) has written, '[E]xtreme
concentration of income is incompatible with real democracy. Can
anyone seriously deny that our political system is being warped
by the influence of big money and that warping is getting worse
as the wealth of the few grows ever larger?' Stiglitz calls it 'the
evisceration of our democracy' (2013: 171).

Achieving human rights

Human rights are the final consideration in this chapter. They
come last not because they matter least: on the contrary, they
are fundamentally important, although recurrently elusive. The
Universal Declaration of Human Rights, drawn up in 1948 by the
UN with Dr Evatt as President, illustrates the point. As a set of
global principles, the Declaration remains the paramount statement of the centrality of rights in international discourse and
provides a strong basis for judging how far we are failing in our
attempts to make the world secure and sustainable, peaceful and
prosperous for all people.

Article 1 of the Declaration states: 'All human beings are born
equal in dignity and rights.' This establishes a fundamentally egalitarian principle that transcends differences of gender, ethnicity,
class, location or family circumstances. Yet we know that the real
world has extreme inequalities of material conditions that clearly
violate the realization of this ideal in practice. People's individual
opportunities and 'life chances' (even their chances of life) are systematically shaped by conditions beyond their personal control,

resulting in vast differences in both opportunities and rewards. The point of Article 1 is not to gloss over these glaring material differences. Rather, the contrast between its clear statement of the ideals and the violations resulting from actually existing inequalities highlights the need for remedial social and political action. Tackling unwarranted inequalities is an essential ingredient in the achievement of universal human rights.

Human rights are not purely abstract expressions of values. When specified in terms of particular socio-economic standards, they become practical guides to social entitlements. They thereby become a basis for developing purposeful actions, including by national and international institutions of governance, and potentially a focus for judicial determinations by international courts. For example, Articles 21 and 23 of the Declaration spell out more specific rights to work, fair remuneration and a reasonable standard of living. These are economic avenues for progress towards the achievement of universal equality in dignity and rights. The effect of the UN Declaration is to give moral legitimacy to that quest.

Conclusion

Figure 8.5 on the following page presents a retrospective road map for the chapter. It summarizes the channels through which inequality impacts on wellbeing and the possibility for social progress. As we have seen, hazards are evident in each case. Concurrently, each is a reason why a good society needs to try to reduce inequality. From the arguments and evidence, we may conclude the following:

- Egalitarian societies generally produce superior economic outcomes.
- Greater economic equality would be conducive to societies that are democratic and peaceful, less troubled by social problems and more ecologically sustainable.
- Concern with the equality of human rights gives moral legitimacy to redressing inequalities that impede that ideal.

This is not to say that reducing inequality would solve all contemporary economic, social, environmental and political problems. In the real world, unlike in video games and action movies, there is no 'silver bullet' capable of annihilating all threats. No existing

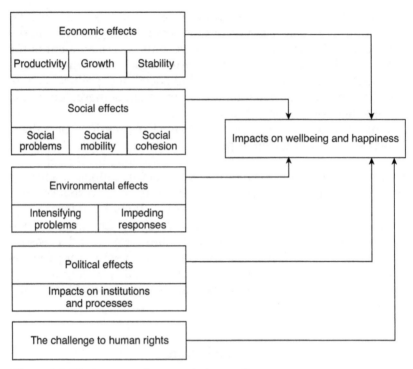

Figure 8.5 The impacts of economic inequality

society has resolved all the economic, social, environmental, political and human rights issues. However, reducing inequality could
ameliorate many of the stresses and help pave the way towards
happier societies.

9

Towards Happier Societies?

'I've been rich and I've been poor; believe me, rich is better' are words variously attributed to actress Mae West and vaudeville artist Sophie Tucker. They probably ring true to you, maybe eliciting a knowing smile. But if we all got richer, would we all be happier? If we had previously been living in absolute poverty, we almost certainly would. Otherwise, perhaps not, especially if our personal happiness depends on what we have relative to other people. The endless pursuit of riches may not be ultimately satisfying anyway because, while it is surely good to escape poverty, the process of getting more and more income and wealth may take time away from ultimately more pleasurable personal and social activities. Yet people commonly act as if there is a direct, strong and continuing connection between income and happiness. Indeed, the drive by rich people to be even richer is an integral part of the economic inequality story.

This chapter asks whether increasing incomes and wealth, beyond the escape from poverty, produces happiness – and whether reducing economic inequality would be better. It differs from the preceding chapter, which considered the impact of inequality on economic, social, environmental and political outcomes. Here we look at subjective considerations bearing on human happiness. This is a shift from what Tony Atkinson (2015: 12) calls the 'instrumental' case for greater equality to the 'intrinsic' case. Our primary focus is on the links between the extent of inequality and happiness, as reported in social surveys and discussed in the field of happiness research. We also look at some interesting ways in which the relationship between inequality and wellbeing has been treated in economic and social analysis.

What is happiness?

The right to the pursuit of happiness is famously enshrined as the highest social goal in the US Declaration of Independence. But what does happiness entail? In their day-to-day lives, people commonly talk of whether they are happy or not as the key indicator of their wellbeing. Yet it is rather difficult to pin down an unambiguous definition. The economic historian Eric Hobsbawm called happiness 'a term which causes its definers almost as much trouble as its pursuers' (1962: 236). As a condition that concerns the human state of mind, it is inherently subjective, having different meanings for different people. Is it a matter of feeling elated or contented, euphoric or fulfilled?

One way of conceptualizing happiness is in terms of how adequately we are meeting our personal needs. Being free from want and distress gets the process started. Over and above that, happiness may be a more socially relative or even existential matter, such as having a positive experience of one's place in society or, more broadly, the universe. Making a transition from satisfying basic needs in life to those higher elements of subjectivity is a qualitative shift. The well-established pyramid of needs identified by behavioural psychologist Abraham Maslow (1943) shows what may be involved. At the base of Maslow's pyramid are the fundamental physical needs, such as food, housing and material comfort. Next come safety and security, followed by love and belongingness, including the desire to feel accepted by one's family and community. Then comes the need for esteem and other people's respect and admiration. At the top of the pyramid comes what Maslow calls self-actualization, where people start enjoying what they have and finding happiness in their own attainment, without any strong tendency to compare or compete with the achievements of others. Each level of need has to be broadly satisfied before progressing to the next, moving from mere survival to self-fulfilment. This implies a positive correlation between economic circumstances and wellbeing, one that diminishes in strength after basic material needs have been satisfied. Achieving a more comprehensive sense of feeling good would require successful progression through all the other levels of the pyramid.

Somewhat differently, we may see the nature and causes of happiness as related to *time*. As the American economist Richard Layard (2005) argues, some aspects of happiness have transient characteristics while others are more enduring. A distinction between gratification and contentment is implied. Gratification is the short-term, pleasurable sensation brought on by a recent success or happy event – or even by alcohol or drugs. In the longer term, however, the state of personal contentment is what matters, and this typically depends on whether people feel fulfilled in their lives. There is a physical basis in the functioning of the brain for the distinction (Lustig 2017). The effect of dopamine on the brain is to stimulate a pleasurable feeling, perhaps a temporary euphoric state, but with waning effectiveness. Serotonin, on the other hand, has a quite different chemical effect, creating a more tranquil and longer-lasting form of contentment. The former is the feeling of pleasure; the latter is a more durable happiness. Too much emphasis on short-term gratification may actually work against long-term contentment.

So what elements can sustain our sense of feeling good? Sources of pleasure found at the hedonistic level and outside of ourselves may be inherently short-lived. Attaining the deeper and longer-lasting form of happiness is more fundamentally important if our concern is with societies in which people experience and enjoy sustainable wellbeing.

Personal income and happiness

The most direct way of finding out whether people feel happy and why (or why not) is to ask them. To see whether their answers reflect their economic circumstances, we can then seek evidence of statistical correlation with their incomes or wealth. Survey-based analyses of this sort can help us to see which types of society are happiest at a point in time and to see how reported happiness varies as economic conditions change. There are hazards and pitfalls in interpreting the survey responses, of course, especially where there are significant cross-cultural and linguistic differences in the meaning attached to the concept of happiness. Some broad patterns recur, however. Broadly speaking, the findings from such studies suggest the following:

- Within any society, the rich are usually happier than the poor, although many rich people are unhappy and many poor people are happy.
- While there are differences in happiness between rich and poor societies, they are generally rather small: some poor countries have average happiness levels similar to much richer countries.
- As countries get richer, the happiness of the people does not substantially increase: economic growth does not reliably create happier societies.

The first of these findings is not surprising: one would expect a positive but less than complete correlation because income is one of many factors likely to influence happiness. Health, for example, is more fundamentally important: it is hard to feel happy when unwell. The second finding is rather more troubling, inviting further investigation of why the cross-country correlations between income and happiness are sometimes weak. The third is yet more deeply problematic, especially for economists, politicians and other people who have uncritically assumed that economic growth would be the principal means of making societies happier. It is not a new finding, however, and should cause no surprise. The economist Richard Easterlin pointed out, more than four decades ago, that the conventional economic assumption of a continuously positive connection between income and wellbeing did not hold well in practice (Easterlin 1974, 1985). The 'Easterlin paradox' and its implications have been contentious ever since, provoking discussion about the nature of the evidence and its interpretation (Frey & Stutzer 2002; Stevenson & Wolfers 2008, 2013). Although contested by critics, the three general propositions seems to have been broadly borne out by subsequent experience.

The role of economic inequality in explaining the Easterlin paradox has come increasingly to the fore in social research. One study, seeking to identify the conditions under which economic growth may have net beneficial effects for wellbeing, showed that this is so when there is increasing social trust and less economic inequality (Mikucka, Sarracino & Dubrow 2017). Others point to economic growth having much less positive consequences when it impairs the quality of human relationships and social cohesion (Bartolini & Sarracino 2015; Piekalkiewicz 2017).

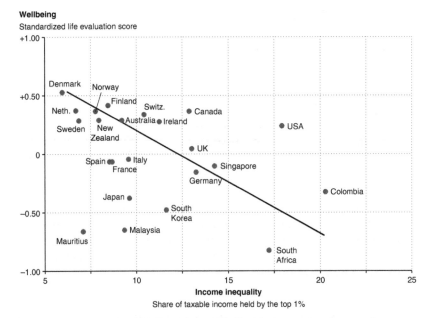

Figure 9.1 Income inequality and wellbeing for an array of countries

Source: de Neve & Powdthavee (2016).

Another study, focusing directly on the relationship of people's life satisfaction to economic inequality, has generated the evidence shown in Figure 9.1. Taking the share of taxable income held by the top 1% as the measure of inequality, it reveals evidence of some positive association with a standardized life evaluation score, albeit not strongly so. Drawing a 'line of best fit' through the scatter of observations may be drawing a long bow in this case: countries with similar inequality scores show very different scores on life satisfaction. However, most of the countries with high life satisfaction scores do seem to be relatively egalitarian. The Nordic countries come out looking best.

Further exploration requires engagement with both economic theory and practical implications. This chapter proceeds according to the organizational framework set out on the next page in Figure 9.2, identifying two principal economic influences affecting wellbeing and happiness: the level of personal income and the extent of economic inequality. In the former case, the effect of rising incomes is interpreted in three ways: through the study of impacts on consumers' utility; through habituation; and through the effects

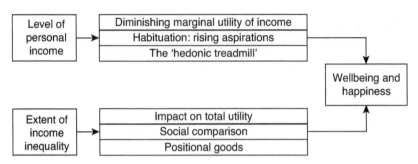

Figure 9.2 Income, inequality and happiness: possible connections

of a 'hedonic treadmill'. In the latter case, the effect of income inequality is interpreted as operating through three channels: its impact on consumers' total utility; its influence on the process of social comparisons; and in relation to the welfare implications of seeking 'positional goods'.

Needs, wants, utility and wellbeing

It is not hard to posit reasons why rising out of absolute poverty makes people happier, while further income increments produce less reliably beneficial effects. Escaping from poverty enables people to buy things that are essential for their wellbeing, while luxury goods that would be bought with further income are less fundamentally important. Thus, after meeting basic material needs, additional income yields diminishing personal benefits. Underlying this argument is the presumption that we can distinguish between needs and wants. In his pioneering work on consumerism, political economist J.K. Galbraith made this distinction in his analysis of what consumption adds to wellbeing in an affluent society (Galbraith 1962), but also emphasized that it is harder to maintain it when commercial advertising is rife (Galbraith 1976). Advertisers' main aims are to convert wants (things you might like to have) into needs (things you *must* have). Thus, in a world of consumer capitalism, to reach a level of consumption where no further increments of satisfaction are attainable is a receding prospect.

Mainstream economists have been reluctant to make judgements on these matters because dualisms like needs/wants or necessities/luxuries are hard to define or quantify precisely.

Instead, consumers' implicit self-assessment is preferred, building on the assumption that utility (or satisfaction) derived from consumption is purely subjective – only the individual consumer himself or herself can know and value it. Yet economists also posit that the subjective evaluation has a general characteristic: the principle of diminishing marginal utility. Every first-year university economic student studies this core proposition. It implies that happiness comes directly from consumption – but at a diminishing rate for each product purchased. Thus, a person's increased consumption of any one commodity will lead to a less than corresponding increase in that consumer's utility. In economics textbooks, the principle of diminishing marginal utility is held to apply to each individual commodity, not to the total consumption of all commodities. Yet that latter aspect is crucial if we want to know the impact of increased incomes on a consumer's total utility. Only if we can talk about 'marginal utility of income' can we use the theory to infer anything about how consumers' happiness relates to their overall consumption (Layard, Mayraz & Nickell 2008).

Putting a subjective concept – utility – at the centre of the mainstream economic theory of consumer behaviour, but then having no consistent means of aggregating the utility derived from consuming the different products, leaves us at an impasse. We cannot simply assume that more income and consumption adds to total utility, nor know in general the rate at which increments of utility diminish. We therefore need to consider alternative, heterodox traditions of economic thought that may yield more insight into consumers' wellbeing and happiness. Looking at the societal context within which individual preferences and aspirations develop is a way forward.

Habituation and rising expectations

Income, consumption and wealth are key markers of social position and success (or failure), especially in modern societies where advertising messages permeate nearly all of the media and most aspects of our lives. Demand is seldom, if ever, satiated. There is always something more expensive to purchase – with the expectation of gratification coming variously from the act of purchase, from owning the item and from using it (whether wearing, eating, watching, sailing, driving, flying, listening to, playing with, living in or just displaying it). Thus, if happiness reflects the relativity between aspiration and achievement, it is not surprising that it does not reliably rise over time in a consumerist society. Getting a bit richer can make people initially happier, because it enables them to consume more or better goods and services, but the benefit wears off over time, sometimes quite soon. They become *habituated* to the standard of living that they attain, seeing that as the new base-line. They then aspire to more – and happiness comes only if more materializes.

According to Clive Hamilton and Richard Denniss, this constitutes a process of serial disappointment that has given rise to the phenomenon of 'the suffering rich' (2005: 63). No matter how much people have, they usually believe they need more to be happy. As a cynic might say, too much is never enough. In a poll conducted in the USA, for example, respondents were asked what is the smallest amount of money a family of four needs to get along in their community. Over time, the average amounts that people nominated rose in line with the increase in actual incomes (Layard 2003: 4). As Hamilton says, most people continue to believe that 'to find happiness they must be richer, regardless of how wealthy they already are' (2003: xvi). This pervasive tendency for aspirations to rise along with their incomes helps to explain at least part of the Easterlin paradox.

A hedonic treadmill

If people need a rising income just to maintain their existing state of happiness, they can be said to be on a hedonic treadmill: running hard to attain more pleasure but making little, if any, sustainable progress. They fuel disappointment and discontent while directing their personal energies away from pursuits that might actually enhance their wellbeing and happiness. Robert Frank, the author of *Luxury Fever* (1999), posited that, increasingly, people are locked into a competitive race for the trappings of status and success, making their lives less comfortable and less satisfying.

Some political economic critics of consumerism go further, arguing that the process actually creates an unhealthy social syndrome that generates other disorders. 'Affluenza' is a concept used in this context to describe a pervasive 'sickness of affluence' (de Graaf, Wann & Naylor, 2005; Hamilton & Denniss 2005). Among the definitions of affluenza are 'the bloated, sluggish and unfulfilled feeling that results from efforts to "keep up with the Joneses"'; an 'epidemic of stress, overwork, waste and indebtedness' caused by dogged pursuit of consumerism; and an 'unsustainable addiction to economic growth' (Hamilton & Denniss 2005). As they say, consumerism encourages people to buy things they do not need with money they do not have to impress people they do not like.

Studies of what more reliably enhances wellbeing and happiness suggest that these items are often 'beyond the market'. Robert Lane's books on *The Market Experience* (1991) and *The Loss of Happiness in Market Democracies* (2000) are classics on this theme, pointing to the collision between the process of commodification and the activities that actually enhance people's contentment. Because consumer capitalism is a want-creating system, not geared to the latter goal, we should not be surprised at the weakness of the connections between incomes, consumption and wellbeing.

Inequality and happiness

Is inequality of incomes, rather than the overall level of income, more significant in shaping wellbeing? There are different ways of approaching this question, of course. One draws on the mainstream economic theory that we considered a little earlier in this chapter, which can have a surprisingly radical implication when considered in relation to inequality. It all hinges on the question: what if the principle of diminishing marginal utility applied to people's total incomes? One might infer that, as a person's income rises, she or he would receive less additional satisfaction from each increment. Thus, the first $10 received by a poor person would give enormous satisfaction: it might mean the difference between starving and eating. However, an extra $10 received by someone who already has $1 billion would hardly be noticeable. It is therefore likely, if not certain, that taking that $10 from the rich person and giving it to the poor person would enhance the total utility of these two people. The economist A.C. Pigou (1928), who held the Chair of Economics at the University of Cambridge prior to John Maynard Keynes, famously took this view. Indeed, one could hardly imagine a tidier utilitarian rationale for progressive redistribution of income and wealth.

It may seem ironic that neoclassical economic theory, usually seen by its critics as pro-market and politically conservative, indicates (even 'proves') the desirability of progressive income redistribution. Lo and behold, Robin Hood endorsed by main-stream economic theory! Indeed, *if* the principle of diminishing marginal utility applies to income, and *if* we can compare the utility of different individuals, progressive income redistribution looks like it has a strong neoclassical economic rationale. These are two big 'ifs', however. Both of them provide escape routes for mainstream economists troubled by the 'interventionist' implica-tions of their theory. In the first case, they can (and do) simply say that the theory of utility applies only to individual goods, not to all of a person's income and consumption. In the second case, they may (and do) say that *interpersonal utility comparisons* are impossible because we cannot compare the satisfaction that different people derive from their consumption. Because utility is subjective and specific to each person, it cannot be compared between people. Thus, we cannot know the welfare implications of the sort of redistribution that Pigou envisaged. Rather, the only safe conclusion is agnostic, providing no basis for redistribution of income, nor indeed any public policy.

Is it necessary to wind up in this conceptual cul de sac? Clearly, there *is* a basis for expecting people to satisfy their most intense needs first and then to allocate additional income to buying things that are less important for their personal wellbeing – call them necessities and luxuries, if you will. Equally clearly, the greater the economic inequality, the more difficult it is for a society to ensure that everyone gets the basic goods and services necessary for their material wellbeing. These propositions do not need to be formal theorems to be useful for helping us understand why more people are unhappy in extremely unequal societies. They give us a basis for developing further insights into the socially relative character of people's wellbeing.

Social comparisons

When people's happiness depends strongly on how their own situation compares to others, the adverse effects of economic inequality become yet more evident. The pioneering American institutional economist Thorstein Veblen (1970 [1899]) paved the way for an analysis of consumerism in an unequal society. He argued that the consumption of the fabulously rich 'leisure class' in the USA in the 'gilded age' of the late nineteenth century was primarily motivated by the quest to display wealth as a means of attaining social prestige. The profligate consumption patterns of the elite thereby set the aspirational standards for other social groups, notwithstanding their general incapacity to afford the luxury status items. The 'conspicuous consumption' of the leisure class fostered 'social emulation' and, in effect, made social dissatisfaction endemic. Seeing the consumption process as both want-satisfying and want-creating has been a significant current in political economic analysis ever since, most notably in the work of J.K. Galbraith. In the modern social context, the process of emulating the life-styles of the rich and famous is an obvious feature. Television and other media bring images of those affluent life-styles into the homes of people in diverse economic and social circumstances, while commercial advertising promotes the products necessary for their pursuit. For people on low incomes, this is a recurrent reminder of what they cannot have.

As social beings, our wellbeing tends to depend, subjectively, on whether we think we are doing well or poorly relative to others. People's aspirations and satisfactions are shaped by the reference group with which they compare themselves. Beyond a low level of material affluence, income differences relative to reference groups have stronger effects than absolute income. The key element in perceived wellbeing arising from this form of social comparison is relative incomes rather than absolute incomes. This is the basis of the *relative income* hypothesis. It undermines the conventional economic assumption that, because people's preferences are independently determined and stable, increases in income and consumption will increase utility (Headey & Wooden 2004). On the contrary, if people's preferences also depend on what others have, increases in income or wealth beyond a certain point will generate no necessary increase in satisfaction if an unequal distribution of income and wealth persists.

Various empirical studies have tested the hypothesis. A frequently cited one, by Andrew Clark and Andrew Oswald (1996), calculated 'comparison incomes' for UK workers, these being the average incomes of people with similar jobs, education, and so on. They found that absolute incomes had small effects on satisfaction but comparison incomes had a much greater impact. The bigger the difference between their own incomes and those of people performing comparable jobs, the less satisfied they were. Low levels of satisfaction were also associated with a high incidence of promotion among fellow workers and having spouses or other household members who earned more than they did. Another study, undertaken in the USA, asked graduate students whether they would prefer (a) $50,000 a year while others received half of that or (b) $100,000 a year while others received double that. A majority chose option (a). Evidently, they thought that they would be happy with less than the maximum attainable as long as they were better off than others (Layard 2003). The implication is clear: if some people get higher incomes, this can have adverse consequences for other members of the society, making them feel relatively worse off even if their incomes have not actually fallen.

Positional goods

A complementary explanation of why a markedly unequal society is unlikely to be a generally happy society derives from the concept of positional goods. Fred Hirsch introduced this in his analysis of *Social Limits of Growth* (1977) to describe goods whose possession conveys status but whose supply is necessarily restricted. General increases in incomes cannot enable everyone to consume such goods. Relative income, rather than absolute income, determines a person's access to the scarce items that confer social prestige.

Houses in affluent suburban areas are a classic example. As more people want to live in a socially prestigious locality, the higher the house prices there will tend to be. Unlimited demand and fixed supply is a reliably inflationary recipe. The result is that the affluent areas become even more exclusive and highly sought-after. So the aspiration of the least well off to live in the 'best' suburbs is continuously thwarted. They can only get the prestige residence there by becoming so very rich that they join the elite. Other people who might have nearly got there find themselves further away from achieving their goal.

By their very nature, positional goods are those things that we cannot all have even if we all get richer. To continue to pursue them in an unequal society is inevitably frustrating. Yet, once basic material needs are satisfied, consumers' spending patterns increasingly emphasize this kind of conspicuous consumption, in the attempt to signal economic success and social status. If most people could afford these items, other, more expensive goods would then become the sought-after status items. It is a never-ending spiral, creating recurrent disappointment rather than widespread fulfilment of aspirations.

It is not only a problem for individuals. It is also a societal problem because public investments that would more reliably give social benefits run a poor second to the pursuit of personal gains. Again, housing is an obvious illustration. The inflationary process in housing markets, driven by people aspiring to buy houses in affluent suburbs, makes people feel that they must increase their disposable incomes if they are to be able to afford good housing. They are then more unwilling to pay the taxes that would finance the provision of public goods, including good-quality public housing. In effect, they come to regard all tax as an unwelcome impediment to consuming the private status goods to which they aspire. Meanwhile, the lower-income groups, recognizing that they cannot compete for properties in the most desirable locations, seek somewhere they can afford, perhaps on the fringe of the cities in which they work, but they then face long and often expensive commuting trips. Transport systems become overcrowded and congested, reducing average travel speeds. Social stresses cumulate.

A viable solution to circular and cumulative causation processes like these could come through expanding the provision of public goods, so that all may then enjoy access to good facilities. J.K. Galbraith famously wrote of the social imbalance in US society between 'private wealth and public squalor' (1962) that has since become a ubiquitous phenomenon. Redressing it through better public sector provision remains the best response. Otherwise, inequality becomes an ever-bigger problem. One could hardly imagine a clearer recipe for unhappiness than the combination of economic inequality, social emulation, a limited supply of public goods and the futile quest for positional goods.

Towards happier societies?

Two themes stand out from this brief engagement with the evidence and arguments in happiness studies. First, striving to get rich, beyond a certain point, tends to produce disappointing outcomes. Continued efforts to attain the material affluence of the wealthiest members of society tends to be self-defeating. Various studies suggest that people who pursue materialistic life-styles have lower levels of happiness, life satisfaction and psychological wellbeing, sometimes associated with an increased incidence of depression, anxiety and neuroticism (Burroughs & Rindfleisch

2002; Hamilton & Denniss 2005). Second, the process of striving for greater income may take time away from other activities that would more reliably contribute to personal wellbeing. As Clive Hamilton argues, economic growth 'not only fails to make people contented [but it also] destroys many of the things that do' (2003: x) by fostering hollow consumerism, degrading the natural environment and undermining social cohesion.

These tendencies, it should be emphasized, relate primarily to generally affluent societies and particularly to people in middle- and upper-income brackets. Poor people have understandably direct concerns with increased income. Yet, even in countries with modest per capita incomes, it is pertinent to reflect on the likelihood of the ultimately disappointing pay-off from emulating the excesses and contradictions of consumer capitalism.

So what does make us happy? When asked, people commonly cite intimate, loving relationships with family and friends as primary influences, as well as being of service to others, finding work that engages their skills and supports their values, and taking the time to renew the spirit and pursue the activities they enjoy (Gittins 2010: 13; Nelson, Pike & Ledvinka 2015). These may be common-sense notions, but even materially comfortable people often do not make them a priority in practice. This is a societal, as well as a personal, challenge that requires reduction of the glaring inequalities that condemn many people to poverty while fuelling a sense of insecurity even among those with most of the available material comforts.

Considerations like these help to explain aspects of the Easterlin paradox. They do not deny the crucial importance of escaping from conditions of absolute poverty. Those at the bottom of the income and wealth distribution surely have a pressing need to secure what material comforts they can. Indeed, they have a reasonable expectation that higher income will contribute to their happiness. However, beyond that, seeking personal fulfilment through trying to get higher incomes or accumulate more wealth is more predictably self-defeating. It usually leaves people with insufficient time for building better social relationships and pursuing the activities they enjoy. It is often the perception of relative disadvantage that drives people, even quite affluent people, to pursue more income and wealth well beyond the point at which physical needs are satisfied and at which social relations tend to suffer.

Conclusion

The issues reviewed in this chapter raise challenging questions about individual and societal wellbeing. They add to the case made in the preceding chapter for trying, as a society, to reduce the inequalities of income and wealth. For individuals, there are a range of social-psychological reasons why getting richer, beyond the escape from poverty, does not reliably increase personal happiness. For whole societies, getting richer but becoming more unequal may intensify many of the pressures that undermine collective wellbeing. Key findings of this chapter are as follows:

- Relative incomes have a major bearing on people's perception of their success and wellbeing.
- Inequality and consumerism are a potent mix in modern capitalist societies, creating a 'hedonic treadmill' and tending to fuel 'affluenza'.
- More individual and social benefit would come from reducing inequalities, improving the provision of public goods and refocusing on what more reliably produces personal and social contentment. Redistribution, rather than continually striving for more economic growth, seems to offer (if you'll pardon the expression) a bigger bang for society's buck.

Ethically, the identification of social problems conveys the requirement to act, or at least to consider acting, for their remediation. The political implication is clear: that we should be concerned with developing strategies and policies for reducing inequalities through collective endeavour, including progressive public policies.

Policies

10

Redistribution

Turning from the analysis of patterns, processes and problems to consideration of public policies raises big questions about what could or should be done. Could we have more egalitarian societies? If so, by what means? And who would effect the change? Looking to governments for that purpose is the normal first response. All governments tax and spend; and they commonly claim to be adjusting those taxes and expenditures to ameliorate inequalities. Critics of extreme inequality commonly call for more vigorous redistribution. Some go further, arguing that governments should not just be redistributing the existing 'market' incomes and wealth: they should also be trying to reduce the pre-tax inequalities.

To provide a framework for considering these various aspects of the state in the economy, Figure 10.1 on the next page sets out the types of policy that currently operate in most countries, giving examples in each category. The focus of this chapter is on policies for *redistribution* that appear in the top row of the figure. These are primarily *fiscal policies*: comprising government taxes, transfer payments and other forms of government expenditure. Among the array of tax options are income tax ('pay as you earn'), business tax ('pay as you profit'), inheritance tax ('pay as you go'), wealth tax and land tax. Among the different types of expenditure are the provision of social infrastructure and services.

This chapter considers the policy instruments that governments could use for redistribution if they had the political will to act.

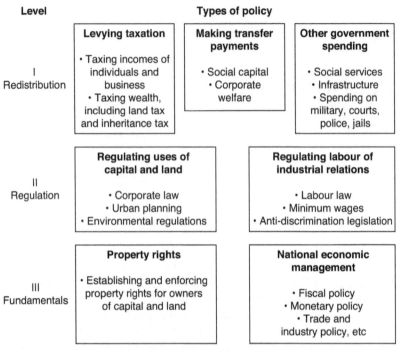

Level	Types of policy		

Figure 10.1 The state and economic inequality

Principles for taxation

The tax system is an obvious place to start when seeking to create more equality in the distribution of income and wealth. 'Too little, too late', some might say, because, by the time people have received their incomes and (in some cases) accumulated their wealth, the inequality already exists. 'Well, better late than never' is a reasonable response, because the tax system can make the post-tax distribution significantly less unequal than the pre-tax distribution. Because national governments always have tax policies of some sort, the key questions in practice are 'How much redistribution?' and 'By what means?'

The following four criteria are always relevant to judgements about how the tax system should function and the purposes tax reform should serve:

- *Potency*: taxation needs to be effective in generating revenue to pay for spending on public infrastructure and public services.
- *Simplicity*: the legitimacy and effectiveness of any tax system depends upon it being widely understood; simplicity also reduces opportunities for tax avoidance.
- *Efficiency*: the tax system should neither discourage productive economic activity nor encourage unproductive pursuits.
- *Equity*: tax rates should be consistent with social justice, relating to people's capacity to pay and broader concerns about reasonable equality of sacrifice.

While the distributional aspect of taxation is most explicit in the last of these four criteria, governments need to think carefully about what combination of taxes balances all four concerns. There are many options, including taxes on incomes, profits, land, wealth and inheritance.

Income tax

Taxing incomes is the most obvious way of aligning revenue collection with people's ability to pay. A broad definition of taxable income, including income from all sources and with few allowable deductions, is generally best in this regard. The first part of income received, up to a threshold where the tax scale begins, needs to be tax-free – otherwise, people would be taxed into poverty. Above that threshold, the rates of tax may vary from a flat rate to a steeply progressive rate.

How progressive can income taxes be? The highest marginal rates of income tax in many of the advanced capitalist countries used to be very much higher than they are today. That was particularly so during the three decades after the Second World War when the 'great compression' in post-tax income inequalities occurred (Piketty 2014a: ch. 14). Progressive taxation generated revenues that financed substantial welfare state initiatives, helping to create a more equitable distribution of income after both tax and transfers.

Figure 10.2 on the following page, reproduced from Piketty's *Capital in the Twenty-First Century*, shows the top marginal income tax rates that prevailed during that period in four of the biggest capitalist nations. It is worth inspecting carefully because it shows

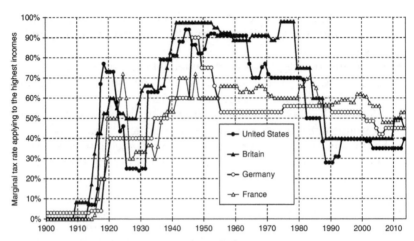

Figure 10.2 Top income tax rates, 1900–2013

Source: Piketty (2014a: 499). Reproduced with permission.

that there used very much higher tax rates than most people can now imagine. Neoliberals commonly warn that a top marginal income tax rate of, say, 50% would create a major disincentive to effort, putting a brake on economic growth, yet top rates were over 70%, and sometimes 80% or even 90%, during the 'golden age' of economic growth from the 1940s to the 1970s. It was from the 1980s onwards that the tax rates were cut to the levels with which we have grown familiar in recent years – and which have prevailed during a period of lowered economic growth rates in the developed nations. Between 1963 and 2017, the top marginal rate of the income tax scale in the USA fell from 91% to a mere 40%. As shown in Figure 10.2, the reductions in the highest marginal tax rates in other countries, particularly the UK, have also been dramatic.

Could or should income tax rates be raised? Tony Atkinson (2015), writing his last book towards the end of a life immersed in the study of inequality, posited a 65% rate as appropriate for the UK. Although modest by historical standards, that would be well above what currently prevails and, if ever adopted as policy, would surely provoke dismay, derision and draconian responses from conservative opponents. However, not only the top marginal rate in the tax scale matters. Other ways to make the income tax system more progressive, even at existing tax rates, include:

- broadening the base to which income taxes apply, so that income from all sources is included;
- reducing the number of allowable deductions, thereby removing advantages that usually accrue primarily to recipients of income from the ownership of capital;
- taxing income from capital gains at a rate no lower than incomes from labour;
- aligning income tax rates and company tax rates, thereby reducing tax avoidance that currently occurs by representing personal income as business income, or vice versa, whichever has the lower tax rate;
- restricting the use of trusts, currently widely used as vehicles for tax avoidance; and
- taxing inheritance and substantial gifts as income to the recipient.

Policies like these could make the distribution of post-tax incomes much less unequal than the distribution of pre-tax incomes. They also have the capacity to reduce tax avoidance. Such policies could also help to restore faith in the taxation system. At present, complex forms of tax minimization are rife in many jurisdictions, reducing revenue and making many people disillusioned with tax arrangements that they regard as unfair in practice.

From an equity perspective, direct taxation (on incomes) is always preferable to indirect taxes (on goods and services rather than people). This is because sales taxes are inherently regressive, taking a higher proportion of poor people's incomes than rich people's incomes. They can be made less regressive if they are applied selectively to goods and services mainly consumed by rich people, although potential anomalies can arise from how products are classified as necessities or luxuries. Currently, most nations rely quite heavily on uniform sales taxes (variously called sales tax, goods and services tax or value added tax) that earn their place as part of the tax mix because they are reliable and effective revenue-raisers even though their distributional effect is regressive. Societies that want well-funded public sectors therefore usually need to have both incomes taxes and sales taxes. Yet income tax is the much more effective vehicle for progressive redistribution on the revenue side of government budgets.

Business tax

Taxing business profits also has a strong rationale as a means of redistributing incomes. However, there are important differences in principle. Because profits form part of an economic surplus, there is a distinct political economic logic in slicing off a share for public purposes. Profits arise from the power of those who own capital to appropriate part of the revenue arising from business activities, the value of which results from the use of labour, land and the products of nature. More indirectly, they also arise, in part, from the use of public goods. The provision of public infrastructure (public utilities, roads, railways and communication systems, for example) is a foundation without which most businesses would find it harder to generate their profits. Even more fundamentally, as the bottom row of Figure 10.1 signals, the state safeguards the property rights on which the very existence of businesses depends in a capitalist economy and it conducts the macroeconomic policies that help to ensure growth in the overall demand for their products. Some payment to the state for these contributory services is appropriate. Moreover, as we have seen in chapters 2 and 5, the growing share of incomes to capital, relative to non-labour incomes, has been one of the key drivers of the growth in intra-national inequalities during the last few decades. Some rebalancing through business taxation needs consideration.

The 'agents of capital' who have a direct stake in the ownership and management of the businesses do not usually accept this logic because it runs counter to their interests as a class. Neoliberalism and 'trickle-down' economics may be regarded as their supporting ideologies. Their strong influence has encouraged governments to substantially reduce the rates of business tax. In the USA under Donald Trump's presidency, slashing corporate tax rates has further accelerated, while governments in many other countries are trying to follow suit, causing a race to the bottom. It is not surprising that governments elected with big business support reward their backers by pursuing this agenda. Yet its effectiveness as a means of stimulating investment and faster economic growth is dubious.

Cutting rates of business tax increases the post-tax income of capitalist enterprises, of course, but it does not necessarily result in corresponding increases in productive investment of the funds. It will do so only if the expected rate of return on that investment is positive – which depends on expected demand for the product – and if it exceeds the expected rate of return from alternative uses of the post-tax profits. Other options for businesses are using extra post-tax incomes for share buy-backs or takeovers of other businesses, purchase of real estate and speculation in financial markets. If the increased income flows through to these activities, there is no productive societal benefit. Rather, the effects are increased economic volatility and a reduced fiscal capacity of governments to use stabilization policies to deal with the consequences of that volatility.

It is also pertinent to note that the actual rate of tax that businesses pay on their profits is seldom the so-called 'headline' or official rate. This may happen in small to medium-sized businesses by disguising business income as personal income (or vice versa, depending on which has the lower tax rate). Aligning business tax rates with personal income tax rates can help to deter this. Large corporations may engage in complex tax minimization schemes and sometimes conceal their assets and profits in international tax havens. Policing these practices more vigorously is necessary if business taxes are to be a significant part of the overall tax mix.

Land and resource taxes

The capacity to conceal business profits, and high wealth more generally, has fuelled interest in applying more extensive land taxation. Land is a reasonably reliable tax base because it cannot be physically shifted, nor hidden from tax collectors. This enhances its attraction in an era where the owners of internationally mobile capital are often able to avoid paying tax. Yet that is not its principal rationale. It is a means of collecting the site rent that otherwise flows to the private owner rather than the community as a whole whose activities create the rising land values. Residential and commercial land values often rise dramatically when public infrastructure improvements occur nearby. Landowners can also receive tremendous windfall gains when their land is re-zoned to allow more intense urban development. Yet more generally, population and urban growth drive rising land values. Growing demand for sites for residential or commercial activities, while the supply of land remains fixed, predictably results in a long-run tendency for inflation in land values. Unless land tax recoups this social dividend, the effect is to increase the wealth of existing landowners, while those unable to afford land are further excluded from the market.

These processes are a major contributor to economic inequality. People and companies who are fortunate enough to have owned land in desirable areas capture the economic surplus at the expense of future generations who are saddled with higher prices for access to urban land. Land tax, levied on the site value of the land, would create a disincentive for hoarding unused land and stabilize land prices by reducing the attraction of real estate for speculative investment. It can also be a significant driver of regional policy because a uniform land tax generates more revenue from regions where land price inflation has been strongest. Thus, land in metropolitan areas tends to be more highly taxed than that in non-metropolitan areas, particularly rural areas. In these circumstances, land tax tends to encourage regional decentralization of population and industry.

Taxes based on land values exist in many countries, typically at very low rates, and they are commonly used by local governments to raise revenue to fund locally provided services. Should they feature more substantially in the tax mix? Writing more than a century ago, the American author and activist Henry George made a strong case, arguing that land tax should be the principal source of government revenue. This was the central plank in his professed policy programme to create a fair and prosperous society – creating 'progress without poverty' (George 1879). George advocated levying land tax rather than taxes on labour and capital, which he held to be economically distorting. Modern proponents of Georgist principles continue to put this case, while other advocates of economic and social reform argue for land tax being a bigger component in the total tax mix (Obeng-Odoom 2015b; Ryan-Collins, Lloyd & McFarlane 2017) and extending a similar land tax principle to all natural resources.

Extending land tax to the collection of rents from *natural resources* more generally has particularly strong resonance in economies oriented to resource extraction (Obeng-Odoom 2018). Public ownership of natural resources is the most direct means of capturing the economic surplus arising from their use. Where the resources are in private hands, however, effective resource rental taxes may achieve similar effects. If revenues are put into a sovereign wealth fund, that can be enormously beneficial as a reliable long-term source of public finance, as has been the case in Norway (Cleary 2016). There is also an environmental logic in linking taxation to the use of land and other natural resources since tax of this type constitutes a charge on private monopoly over a gift of nature.

Wealth taxes

What about broader wealth taxation that covers all asset classes? As already noted, aligning the rate of tax on incomes from capital with incomes from labour would reliably produce more egalitarian distributional outcomes in nations where capital gains are currently more lightly taxed than wage incomes. Redistribution of accumulated *wealth* is more fundamental but harder. Class interests are directly at stake and political resistance to progressive policy initiatives is inevitable. A focus on wealth is socially desirable, however, because accumulated wealth is at the root of cumulative economic inequalities. While progressive income taxes can stop the rich–poor gap from widening, ownership of assets underlies long-term earnings capacity. Taxes on wealth need careful design, of course: as a report from the OECD (2018) notes, their potential for progressive redistribution is negated if poor and middle-income people hold their (modest) wealth in more highly taxed forms.

Piketty (2014a: ch. 15) advocates an international capital levy (or, to be more precise, 'a progressive annual tax on individual wealth levied by national governments and supervised by an international tax authority'). A tax of this sort has a clear logic from an egalitarian perspective, especially where the concentration of wealth is the most important factor fuelling economic inequality. It could take the form of an annual charge based on the current value of assets held. Such taxes have existed in various places in the past, but is Piketty right in thinking that the time has now come for their more general application? Almost in the same breath as advocating it, he concedes that it is unlikely to happen (Piketty 2014a: 515). Indeed, there are many impediments, quite apart from the general difficulty of getting international agreement to apply the tax. The assets would need to be regularly valued for tax purposes, which can be a source of considerable friction and legal contestation. A capital levy can also be difficult for any 'asset-rich but income-poor' household to pay, although any such household might be permitted to defer the tax liability until the assets are sold or passed on as a gift or legacy. In general, taxing wealth is easier when assets are being transferred.

Over time, taxing wealth transfers may produce similar effects to annual wealth taxes, in terms of both revenue generation and distributional equity. If so, the challenge that Piketty identifies – to shift the focus of the tax system towards wealth taxation – may be more readily achievable by capital transfer taxes than by capital levies. This is not to deny annual wealth taxes a role in progressive tax reform, merely to note alternative means to similar economic and social ends. On this reasoning, taxes on capital gains, inheritance and large gifts should be components in any progressive tax system. Capital gains should be taxed no more lightly than other incomes: allowing preferential treatment for capital over labour is neither economically nor socially logical. According to a similar logic, assets transferred through inheritance could be liable to progressive income tax.

Inheritance and gift taxation

Most, but not all, developed countries impose tax on the transfers of wealth through inheritance (Alvaredo et al. 2018: 293). There are strong economic grounds for doing so. Even orthodox economists commonly express the view that inheritance taxes are more efficient than most other forms of taxation. Taxing inherited wealth does not have the 'distorting' economic effects that other taxes are sometimes said to produce. Income received from inheritance is a windfall gain. It has no relationship to the economic efforts of the recipients, so inheritance tax is unlikely to have significantly adverse effects on economic productivity and economic performance.

Inheritance taxation also has a strong ethical justification. Inherited wealth is unearned income. It differs in this respect from wealth personally generated through thrift, enterprise or hard work. Looked at from the donors' perspective, inheritance tax may be seen as infringing their freedom to pass on wealth that may have originally resulted from productive economic efforts. However, that 'infringement' already applies in respect of other taxes, such as income tax. As always, concerns about individual economic freedom need to be set against broader issues of social justice. The latter elements are strong in this case. Inheritance perpetuates economic inequalities inter-generationally and therefore obstructs egalitarian ambitions for a fair society. Inheritance and gift taxation can prevent, or at least reduce, the inter-generational transmission and intensification of socially damaging inequalities.

How should the taxes be structured? The usual concern is whether to tax the estate left by the deceased person (generally known as estate tax or death duty) or the income received by the beneficiaries of the will (generally known as inheritance tax). Taxing the estate is the more administratively straightforward option. In principle, however, it is better to levy the tax on the beneficiaries. Indeed, there is a strong case for simply taxing whatever they receive at the prevailing income tax rates. Then there would be no need for separate inheritance tax arrangements. All such receipts would be subject to the same income tax as any other income from labour, land or capital. As a necessary corollary, ensuring that transfers made before death do not avoid the tax, a gift tax is necessary. Otherwise the 'boat becomes too leaky' and the tax revenue too small.

When considering tax reforms, the devil is often in the detail. That applies here: to ameliorate predictable concerns about high inheritance taxation, some practicalities would need to be resolved. First, the transferred assets, where not in the form of cash, would need to be valued for tax assessment purposes. This can be contentious, of course, but no new principle is involved: government agencies already make official asset valuations for estate and land taxes. Second, there would probably need to be some 'smoothing' of tax liabilities because gifts and inheritance tend to come in large lumps. Spreading the value of the receipts over, say, three to five years could be permitted for determining the annual income tax payable. Third, there are grounds for making inheritance of family businesses, especially farms, tax-exempt because it would be undesirable for a tax liability to drive their new owners out of business. The socially sensitive question of inherited family homes needs similar attention because housing is often the largest single item in inherited wealth. A general exemption from taxation for family homes, up to a specified threshold value, is probably necessary, recognizing that houses vary enormously in value and that there is no general reason for a tax system to favour people who keep their wealth in one particular asset form.

Taxing transfers of inherited wealth and large gifts meets all four criteria for tax reform listed earlier in this chapter: it is a potent revenue-raiser; it has readily understood simplicity; it is efficient because it creates no distortions between forms of income and wealth subject to different taxes; and, most importantly, it is equitable in directly relating tax to ability to pay. At a time of receiving windfall income, passing on some part to the government is straightforward. Taxing inheritance and large gifts as income could also encourage people making the payments to distribute their wealth more broadly, thereby minimizing the total tax paid by the recipients. Leaving legacies to tax-exempt philanthropic institutions might also be encouraged.

A role for philanthropy?

Do we really need governments to redistribute incomes and wealth? What about entrusting all, or some part, of the process to rich individuals of good intent? Can philanthropy do the trick? Using personal or corporate wealth to support good causes, either through foundations established for the purpose or through charitable institutions, is quite widespread. The philanthropic tradition, moreover, has a long track record. In medieval Europe, wealthy people were expected to provide social protection and a modicum of aid to the poor. One popular saying in England was that 'a rich man that doth not give alms is but a thief' (Hunt 1990: 11). A tradition of Tory paternalism continued after the appearance of capitalism, but only on the margins of private wealth accumulation. In the USA, a more modern philanthropic tradition emerged from the era of the 'robber barons' in the nineteenth century, led by business leaders and families such as the Rockefellers and Carnegies. The means by which their wealth was accumulated often involved brutal exercise of corporate power – doing 'whatever it takes'. A cynic would say that recycling some of that wealth for socially benevolent purposes was in order to clear their consciences and improve their chances of being admitted through 'the pearly gates'. Yet a strong US philanthropic tradition was established, exemplified today by multi-billionaires Bill Gates and Warren Buffett. Individuals such as these can, and do, use some of their wealth – however it has been derived – for substantial social benefit. Few other countries are comparable to the USA; indeed, as noted in chapter 3, none have so many wealthy billionaires, nor as much wealth that could be used for philanthropic purposes.

Philanthropy is worthy and to be encouraged, but relying on it to turn the tide of growing inequality is unrealistic. It has major limitations when regarded as a policy for progressive redistribution. One concern is simply a matter of scale: it is inconceivable that voluntary transfers would ever be sufficient to make more than a minor difference to inequality, whether nationally or internationally. A second limitation concerns goals: some donors seek to reduce poverty, but not all philanthropy is of this kind. Much donated money goes to the support of the arts and culture, animal protection and pet care, support of elite educational institutions and scientific research. One estimate puts the proportion of philanthropic contributions in the USA going to poverty alleviation at a mere 2% (Lord 2015).

At best, private philanthropy is an ameliorative influence. It does not address the systemic origins of economic inequality; indeed, to do so would be to challenge the political economic power and accumulation processes from which much of the donated wealth derives. Moreover, the bulk of rich people's giving is not philanthropic. Most takes the form of gifts to family members, particularly to children, and the transmission of wealth through inheritance. The dominant effect of these wealth transfers is to perpetuate inequalities inter-generationally. Private philanthropy is clearly not a substitute for redistribution through public policies.

Redistribution through government expenditure

Equity needs to be a paramount concern on both sides of government budgets. On the expenditure side, two aspects are particularly pertinent: funding the provision of public goods necessary for the wellbeing of all the people; and making transfer payments according to social need. Both are recurrent features of welfare states – what Piketty (2014a) calls 'the social state'.

Historically, the development of welfare states, especially following the Second World War, was a clear expression of the social commitment to progressive redistribution through public spending. The architects of welfare states sought to create greater social security and more widespread prosperity than would otherwise exist in capitalist societies (Spies-Butcher, Paton & Cahill 2012; ch. 5). Both components mentioned above – redistributive transfer payments and provision of public goods – are always present in welfare states. The case made by Roger McCain (2017: 51) for establishing a national social endowment fund financed by a capital levy makes the link particularly explicit. In practice, welfare states are unevenly developed. Significantly, the best performers in terms of equity have been the more coordinated social market economies in Europe, doing appreciably better than the 'Anglo' countries. The best of all are the Nordic states. Even P.J. O'Rourke, the self-declared US 'Republican Party reptile', has described Sweden as 'good socialism' (1998: ch. 4). Combining high-quality public infrastructure with broadly based welfare expenditures produces the most egalitarian results.

Countries vary considerably according to whether their welfare provision policies embody principles of universality or use greater selectivity in targeting transfer payments only to the poor and needy. The former give benefits 'as of right', whereas the latter provide them only if claimants can satisfy 'means tests'. The latter policy approach has obvious resonance as a means of reducing inequality, and the general trend in most countries has been to put increasing emphasis on transfer payments of that type. However, universal provision is more conducive to building social solidarity and avoiding the costs of policing conditional, means-tested payments. Notably, Tony Atkinson (2015) makes a strong case for more universal provision, as part of his wide-ranging analysis of social policies for progressive redistribution.

A lot of welfare redistribution is inter-generational, rather than cross-class. Child payments and retirement pensions, which are typically major components in income transfers, shift resources between stages in people's lives rather than between rich and poor people per se. Similarly, public health systems steer resources to people with above-average public health needs (Hill 2014). These are important means of preventing hardship for vulnerable people and at stages in the life-cycle that would otherwise be more stressful. However, they are rather different from policies aimed at reducing the overall inequalities of income and wealth. Complex 'social states' with multiple policies need good procedures to track the redistributions.

Equity auditing and the politics of recognition

Whenever government expenditure has distributional goals, it is important to monitor its effectiveness and its impact on different sub-groups in the population. Who benefits from particular public spending programmes? Rich people or poor people? Men or women? Indigenous people or immigrants, who? Equity auditing can be useful for this purpose. Its three elements are:

- specifying the inequalities to be redressed (e.g. a particular target group);
- identifying potentially appropriate redistributive policies;
- analysing how effectively each policy contributes to the overall goals.

A strong case can be made for *all* public policies having to undergo this type of equity assessment before implementation. An equity audit process identifies which policies have desirable distributional effects. Some countries have made tentative steps of this sort, drawing up gender budgets that examine the differential effects of fiscal policies on women and men (Sharp & Broomhill 2002). This could be made an ongoing feature of all public policy formulation and implementation, thereby making more explicit the criteria for public choice. Thus, where the primary goal is to reduce distributional inequality in general, the focus needs to be on whether the policy creates more benefits for poor households than rich ones or vice versa. Where the goal is to reduce inequalities according to gender, race, disability or any other social attribute, the focus needs to be on how target groups fare relative to the population at large. In the latter case, equity auditing can work as part of a broader 'politics of recognition'.

The distinction between public policies that focus on redistribution and recognition owes much to the contributions by Charles Taylor (1994) and Nancy Fraser (1995). Redistribution, as discussed so far in this book, involves narrowing the gap between rich and poor. It is neutral as to the circumstances of people in the latter category, avoiding selectivity in policy, perhaps because giving special attention to minority groups might enhance the prejudices that contributed to their disadvantage in the first place. On the other hand, emphasizing recognition acknowledges the different circumstances and needs of different sub-groups. It may involve recognition of the distinctive history and current circumstances of Indigenous people, for example. Or the special needs of other groups identified by ethnicity, gender or sexual orientation. Such recognition acknowledges the calls for special attention that these groups express and can result in policies that redress their disadvantage.

In practice, recognition and redistribution can be mutually supportive (Fraser & Honneth 2003). In both cases the onus is on governments to create a more equitable society by formulating policies that redress unwarranted and socially unacceptable inequalities.

Thus, policies can recognize the distinctive situation of minority groups while also seeking to create overall social cohesion through greater equality of opportunity and economic outcomes. A suite of policies is implied, including education, symbolic elements (official apologies for past complicity or neglect), legislation on rights, provision of targeted services and fiscal transfers. Introducing regular equity auditing is one means by which 'recognition' can be embedded in some of the latter processes, helping to assess the redistributive impact of existing government programmes and to identify other programmes that might be more effective. As an aid to more comprehensive redistribution, it would get a yet more systematic role if government were to introduce 'distributional accounts' linked to the conventional national income accounts (Piketty, Saez & Zucman 2018).

Redistribution: its effects and limits

Balancing optimism of the will with pessimism of the intellect is necessary in all considerations of social states. Yes, progressive tax and transfer payments can be highly effective in reducing economic inequalities. Figure 10.3 shows how much they affect the extent of economic inequality across the OECD. For each country, the crossed bar shows the Gini value for 'market' income inequality, while the downward-pointing arrowhead shows the Gini values after taxes and transfers. Thus, the length of the vertical

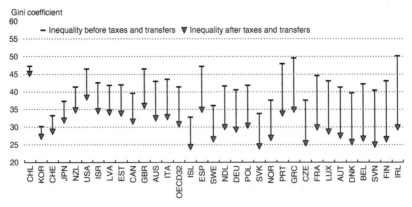

Figure 10.3 Fiscal redistribution in OECD countries

Source: Causa & Hermansen (2017: 30).

lines shows the reduction in inequality as the result of redistribution in each case. The authors of the report from which this information is drawn conclude that 'cash transfers, personal income taxes and social security contributions mitigate slightly more than one quarter of market income inequality among the working-age population, on average across the OECD' (Causa & Hermansen 2017: 8). There is much variability – ranging from a mere 5% reduction in inequality in Chile to a 40% reduction in Ireland – but some progressive redistributive effect occurs everywhere.

The diversity of international experience shows that there are no inexorable mechanisms or 'economic laws' that prevent progressive redistribution – which fuels optimism of the will. As Richard Wilkinson and Kate Pickett say, '[P]olitics and policy have played a central role in determining the distribution of income' (2018: 241). However, pessimism of the intellect requires that we also recognize and deal with significant limits.

First, there is the problem of widespread tax minimization. This reduces the revenue base that a state requires if it is to implement redistributive policies (while simultaneously increasing the incomes of tax consultants). For corporations and high net worth individuals, there are many sophisticated options for tax avoidance (which is legal) and tax evasion (which is not). Transfer pricing can 'reposition' profits in the accounts of affiliated and subsidiary organizations located in countries with low tax rates. Transnational corporations and high-wealth individuals are also notorious for their use of tax havens to evade tax altogether. Gabriel Zucman (2015: 43) estimates that at least 8% of total wealth is concealed in tax havens, totalling $7.6 trillion in 2014. He also estimates that about two-thirds of the decline in the effective corporate tax rate between 1998 and 2013 was due to businesses shifting income to low-tax nations (Zucman 2014: 133). These practices have created widespread social concern, especially since their exposure in 2016 by the publication of the 'Panama papers' and the 'Paradise papers' (Piketty 2016; Zucman 2016). Governments concerned to close loopholes have been developing international agreements on data-sharing to identify untaxed incomes and sources of wealth. At present, however, the tax system remains a leaky bucket.

Second, also working against the effectiveness of redistributive social states are neoliberal ideologies and policies that favour slimmed-down states and trickle-down economics. This makes mounting the case for progressive redistribution an uphill struggle. It also makes the reform process more vulnerable to the influence of vested interests. Thus, somewhat paradoxically, large economic inequalities reduce the political economic capacity of states to engage in redistributive policies. Rich and powerful people, commonly organized in institutions that engage in vigorous lobbying, put strong pressures on governments to back off from reforms that would make the tax system more progressive. Confirming the effectiveness of this process, one research study, spanning nearly 150 years, found that 'rising income inequality is associated with a declining income tax ratio in OECD economies' and that it curbs government spending as a share of GDP (Islam, Madsen & Doucouliagos 2018). Here again we see the significance of processes of circular and cumulative causation, indicating the need for some sort of circuit-breaker.

Conclusion

Redistribution results from the ways in which government taxes and expenditures are constructed. Well-designed fiscal policy can simultaneously reduce inequality and improve the provision of public goods. Potentially potent policies include:

- increasing the progressivity of the tax system by broadening the tax base; treating transfers of inherited wealth as income; aligning the taxation of incomes from capital, land and labour; taxing accumulated wealth through wider application of capital and land taxes; and reducing tax evasion;
- increasing government expenditure on public goods such as public health, education, child care, transport and housing, thereby making inequalities of personal income less crucial determinants of people's standard of living;
- using distributional accounts and equity auditing to monitor the redistributive effect of government tax and expenditure programmes.

A progressive approach to redistributive fiscal policy is necessary – but is it sufficient? A glance back to Figure 10.1 reminds us of the broader array of state functions that influence how income and wealth disparities develop over time. Digging deeper into policies of *pre*-distribution deserves comparable attention.

11

Progressive Pre-distribution

Is more than redistribution needed if we are to create more equitable societies? Do we also need to change the processes that create inequalities of market incomes? Posing these questions shifts the focus from redistribution to pre-distribution – to the institutional processes that shape the initial distribution of wealth and incomes before government taxes and transfers occur. It also directs attention to how value and wealth result from processes of production and to the inequitable character of exploitation, discrimination and imbalances of class power. It shifts the politics from redistributive reform to more radical transformations.

Policies for progressive pre-distribution require attention to both 'floors' and 'ceilings'. Floors eliminate poverty, while ceilings limit top incomes and extreme wealth accumulation. This chapter considers three examples of each. For higher floors: guaranteeing jobs for all, legislating for minimum wages and providing basic income. For lower ceilings: policies to cap executive salaries, change corporate organization and expand the commons. Discussing the pros and cons of these types of policies leads into consideration of how greater equality of opportunity might be created in the intervening space between floors and ceilings. Considering these issues directs attention to the all-important questions of ends and means: 'What sort of society do we want?' and 'How should the economy be restructured so that the desired social outcomes can be achieved?'

Creating jobs for all

The primary source of most people's income is wages. However, capitalist economies do not guarantee that paid work is available for all who seek it. The vagaries of the marketplace shape the number, location and type of employment opportunities. It is therefore appropriate to begin our consideration of structural reforms by asking what could be done to ensure that sufficient jobs are available for all job-seekers.

One reformist option arises from the economics of Keynes, developed between the twentieth century's two world wars. Confronted with the Great Depression of the 1930s, which imposed huge and persistent unemployment throughout the capitalist nations, Keynes showed what governments could do to attack the underlying problem: insufficient demand for goods and services relative to industry's capacity to produce them. Ever since, Keynesian and post-Keynesian economists have consistently argued that governments should step in where the market fails to create the necessary conditions for full employment. After the Second World War, governments in most capitalist nations formally committed to this goal and used Keynesian macroeconomic policy in the attempt to achieve it.

Fiscal policy is the most obvious policy instrument for job creation. As considered in the previous chapter, this relates to the composition of taxes and expenditures. In the context of Keynesian economics, however, the more crucial aspect is the total amount of those taxes and expenditures. By adjusting these volumes, governments can affect the overall demand for goods and services. Assuming a reasonably stable relationship between output and employment (which is not always so in practice), a stimulatory fiscal policy can generate more jobs. Concurrently, a monetary policy that keeps interest rates low helps to encourage private sector investment, so long as business decision-makers expect ongoing demand for their products. All being well, the resulting growth of output, employment and incomes creates a sustainable economic upswing. Implementing fiscal and monetary policies like these is better than letting recessions run their course. It avoids the social hardships that unemployed people suffer and the economic wastage that results from leaving human and capital resources idle.

Governments can also target interventionist policies to where they are most necessary. Regional development policies, for example, can steer expenditures to where unemployment is particularly pronounced. Industry policies can stimulate sectors of the economy that are job-creating. Selective government interventions in workforce retraining and relocation can also help to restructure the economy on a more ecologically sustainable basis. In these ways, the applications of Keynesian economics go beyond macroeconomic management to a broader array of policies concerned with regions, industries and structural transitions. A more long-term perspective is implied, with governments using expanded public investment as the driver for prosperity.

Economists and politicians of a neoliberal inclination regard this as all much too 'interventionist'. Their dominant influence in policy formulation in recent decades has marginalized the Keynesian approach to employment creation. Seeking faster economic growth by cutting business tax rates in the hope of encouraging more private sector investment in job-generating expansion has become the main policy. Persistent unemployment has been the result. Theories about the existence of a 'natural rate of unemployment' have sought to legitimize this source of ongoing hardship and waste.

Could a *job guarantee* scheme be an effective revival of Keynesian 'interventionism'? Some modern heterodox economists think so (e.g. Mitchell & Watts 2002; Komlos 2018). Under this scheme, governments would guarantee to provide jobs directly for all otherwise unemployed people, acting as 'employer of last resort'. This direct job creation would help to maintain the level of effective demand, thereby preventing the recurrent tendencies to unemployment. It would also prevent the atrophy of workers' skills. Significant questions need addressing, though. What type of jobs would people get under a job guarantee scheme, and would they have the requisite skills to do them? Would the scheme be voluntary and, if so, what would be the fate of non-compliant people? What would be the wage rate for the guaranteed jobs – presumably below those generally prevailing in the market, but how much lower? Being essentially counter-cyclical, would the temporary nature of the jobs be a problem? Would there actually be suitable private sector jobs for people with temporary public sector jobs to transition to during an upswing? All these practicalities need careful consideration alongside the broader political economic logic of Keynesian macroeconomics as a means of eliminating the effect of unemployment on economic inequality.

The overall cost of the job guarantee scheme is also an important consideration. Some of its proponents draw on what has come to be called 'modern monetary theory' to argue that there is actually no budget constraint on a government's ability to pay for the scheme (e.g. Wray 2015, 2016). They contend that government expenditure is self-financing. Even if that theoretical proposition is not accepted, however, standard Keynesian economic reasoning indicates that the net cost is likely to be quite modest because government revenue rises when people are working and earning incomes. A self-financing element tends to occur in all policies that employ otherwise idle economic resources, especially when macroeconomic multiplier effects are considered. As Keynesians have always emphasized, it makes sense to mobilize a society's resources for useful work rather than leaving people unemployed while important social needs – for better public infrastructure, social services, community care and improved environmental quality – go unfulfilled. Reducing unemployment combines egalitarian and broader macroeconomic goals.

Developing incomes policy

On post-Keynesian reasoning, getting people into jobs and earning incomes is only part of the story. Reducing economic inequality requires comparable attention to narrowing disparities in wage payments. This is hard to achieve in a capitalist economy, where market determination of wage rates is the norm. It is the coverage and strength of trade unions that is crucial in practice, as discussed in chapter 7. So too are the 'rules of the game' that governments set. Incomes policies that seek to narrow wage differentials can form part of these arrangements.

The most basic form of incomes policy is a comprehensive minimum wage. This is common, at least in the more affluent nations. Table 11.1 shows the ranking of OECD countries according to the minimum wage they currently require employers to pay, expressed as a percentage of median wages in each of those countries. The USA is right at the bottom: it is little wonder that it is so notorious for its prevalence of 'the working poor', although its situation is complicated in practice by differences between states in the minimum wage settings.

A minimum wage policy is a direct means of setting a floor for wage incomes. Yet, to be effective, two specific concerns about

Table 11.1 Ratio of minimum to median full-time worker wage, OECD countries, 2016

Country	Ratio of minimum wage to average median full-time worker wage
Colombia	0.86
Turkey	0.76
Chile	0.69
Costa Rica	0.69
France	0.61
New Zealand	0.61
Slovenia	0.59
Israel	0.58
Portugal	0.58
Romania	0.57
Luxembourg	0.55
Australia	0.54
Lithuania	0.54
Poland	0.54
Hungary	0.51
Latvia	0.51
Belgium	0.50
Republic of Korea	0.50
UK	0.49
Greece	0.48
Slovak Republic	0.48
Germany	0.47
Canada	0.46
Ireland	0.45
Netherlands	0.45
Estonia	0.41
Czech Republic	0.40
Japan	0.40
Mexico	0.37
Spain	0.37
USA	0.35

Source: https://stats.oecd.org/Index.aspx?DataSetCode=MIN2AVE.

its implementation need attention. First, employers have to be checked to ensure that they do not pay less than the required minimum. Second, it needs to be decided whether to focus on a minimum *hourly* rate or a minimum *weekly* wage. Setting a weekly minimum is more desirable from an anti-poverty perspective, but it does not easily translate into an effective requirement on employers employing workers on casual or part-time bases. Increasing flexibility ('casualization') of the workforce in many industries has made working hours highly variable.

Setting minimum wages is not the be-all-and-end-all of incomes policy anyway. A more comprehensive approach has to deal with the broader disparities among wage incomes. This means narrowing the gaps between high-paid and low-paid jobs. Piketty's research shows that the widening of these gaps during recent decades has been a big factor in the overall growth of inequality (see Figure 6.3). Trying to influence the overall shares of labour and capital in the functional distribution of income is a yet bigger challenge. To control that, incomes policy would have to regulate non-wage incomes too (from rents, interest, profits and professional fees).

Even with incomes policy limited just to wages, cooperation between governments, unions and employers is necessary. Employers have to be willing to work within agreed guidelines and to create the expansion in output, incomes and employment. Employees have to agree to limit wage demands in exchange for getting steady progress in wages, working conditions and what-ever improvements in social policies (the 'social wage') that the government offers in order to secure their compliance. This, in turn, may require trade unions to exert control over groups of workers who might otherwise try, from time to time, to 'break away' from the wage guidelines to pursue more direct wage bargaining with their employers. These are difficult requirements to maintain in capitalist labour markets. It is not so much that guidelines violate market processes that have an intrinsic distributive logic; rather, they cut across the power relationships that currently prevail in industrial relations. Incomes policy is possible, but it is a political economic challenge.

Introducing basic income

The introduction of a universal basic income (BI) is another way of setting a floor, not only for wages but for incomes in general. The common feature of BI proposals is payment of state income to all people without means tests and irrespective of whether they undertake waged work. If set at the poverty line (or preferably a little above) for each society, BI would provide a comprehensive floor to income inequality, ensuring that all people have enough to live on in modest economic conditions while leaving them free to seek higher incomes according to their abilities and inclinations. It is a radical reform proposal that has recently been generating strong surges of interest in many countries. It challenges conventional assumptions about poverty, rights and responsibilities.

The policy is simultaneously more modest and more ambitious than Keynesian and post-Keynesian employment and incomes policies. It is more modest in that it is only concerned with an income 'floor', but it is more ambitious in that it partially severs the nexus between income and paid employment. It also has elements of both redistribution and pre-distribution, as we have been using those terms in this book. It is a redistributive policy in that it uses government expenditure to reduce economic inequalities. It is a pre-distributive strategy in that it changes the rights and social norms relating to income entitlements. Discussion of it is located in this chapter because of the latter features: BI is radically different from the other redistributive measures discussed in the previous chapter. It is about much more than redistribution because it is essentially a different form of social contract. Introducing BI would affect how individuals relate to work and welfare and it would have broader implications for economic and social security.

Advocates of BI recognize various forms that it might take. The most general form is where the government pays every person over a specified age (say, 18 years) a regular income, set at a level sufficient to avoid poverty, according to the prevailing conditions and social norms in that country. People below that age would get a reduced amount paid to their parents (replacing any existing child allowance payments). For older people currently receiving state pensions, the BI could be a direct replacement, unless the pensioners are deemed ineligible for BI because their needs are already catered for. At first sight, it might seem odd to propose a payment that goes equally to both wealthy and poor people, but BI is about more than poverty alleviation. It is about income adequacy, but it is also about achieving a better work–life balance and shifting social priorities from unsustainable economic growth to more secure and equitable arrangements. Fundamentally, it is about widening freedoms. This can help to explain the support for BI coming from people on both the political left and right.

For the libertarian right, the attraction of a BI is that it could replace other welfare policies, thereby simplifying the form of the social safety net. Milton Friedman (1962) was an early supporter of a 'negative income tax' variant of BI for this reason. People concerned about how welfare states, seeking to meet a variety of social needs and intentions, have produced complex provisions for determining entitlements and payment levels have looked to BI as a less intrusively paternalistic – and possibly cheaper – policy. Meanwhile, on the libertarian left, leading proponents of BI such as Philippe van Parijs and Yannick Vanderborght (2017) also base their arguments on freedom, but with a broader emphasis on freedom from the constraints of need and from other oppressive characteristics of life in a capitalist society. The radical social scientist Erik Olin Wright (2010, 2016), moreover, regards BI as a key instrument for 'eroding capitalism' because it would give people more freedom and allow them to choose alternatives to conventional waged work.

Other advocates of BI, such as Guy Standing (2017), make the case for it in relation to conventional employment's uncertain future. Emphasis is put on how rapid technological change, more capital-intensive production and AI are causing traditional jobs to diminish in many industry sectors. This creates anxiety about the future of work and the prospects of technological unemployment. It also raises questions about how higher productivity may have public social benefit and what will be the source of demand for the goods and services produced in an economy with less waged work. The BI proposal has resonance in this political economic context as a means of adjusting to the technologies that open up possibilities for 'postcapitalism' (Mason 2016).

At a time of persistent government fiscal deficits in most capitalist nations, could BI be affordable? The direct monetary cost would depend on the level at which it is set and the extent to which it would replace existing welfare entitlements. The net cost of a BI would also depend on how much of the government expenditure is 'clawed back' through the rest of the tax system. There would be extra sales tax revenue when BI recipients spend their income. More income tax would also be paid if BI were included in taxable income (as it sensibly should be). These substantial offsets would reduce the net cost of the policy. Whatever its precise form, however, BI would surely comprise a large share of government spending in any nation, probably at least a quarter of the total. It would therefore require strong government revenue to fund it. That means serious tax reform, as discussed in the preceding chapter. For developing nations, it would usually require external funding through the international development assistance process, as discussed in the next chapter.

How a BI relates to the cyclical character of capitalist economies has important fiscal and macroeconomic implications too. Because the government has to make the BI payments whatever the economic conditions, volatility in revenue would create difficulty in funding it during periods of recession. At such times, BI would be an excellent short-term 'Keynesian' cushion, helping to maintain aggregate demand and ensure macroeconomic buoyancy. Less positively, the funding problem in a cyclically unstable economy could create uncertainty about the longer-term sustainability of a BI expenditure commitment.

The question of whether a BI would adversely affect national economic output is complex. Orthodox economists predictably warn of its adverse effect on work incentives. As previously noted, however, the availability and nature of jobs is changing anyway: many more people are in precarious jobs and there are big questions around the future of work. We could all face the future more positively with a BI in place. In an economic system based upon advanced modern technology, tying income to a conventional concept of work makes less sense. Welfare states already produce substantial redistribution: a BI would de-stigmatize that process. It could also eliminate many of the current complexities of targeted welfare arrangements and provide a general safety net that does not depend on each individual to demonstrate eligibility for selective assistance. Looked at from the perspective of social progress and work–life balance, therefore, we should not be alarmed if a BI were to drive some behavioural changes. It is part of adjusting to the opportunities created by economic and technological progress.

What behavioural changes might be expected? Three types of response are predictable, the principal uncertainty being the number of people in each category. First, many, probably most, people would want to supplement their modest BI with wages, depending on what is available and accessible to them. Second, some people would choose not to seek paid work, preferring to spend their time in personal pursuits of various kinds: they need not be subject to social opprobrium for doing so. Third, some people would take the opportunity to do socially useful but unpaid work, such as caring for children, the elderly and infirm, voluntary work in community organizing or further education and skills development. Starting small businesses and working family farms would become a more attractive option because the BI sets a base-line income, reducing the risk and uncertainty that otherwise deters such activities. Creative and artistic people would have the freedom to pursue their crafts and thereby benefit the nation, as the philosopher Bertrand Russell (1917) emphasized when making his case for a BI a century ago. Society could thereby facilitate a flowering of artistic and cultural development by liberating those with creative talents from the need for regular wage labour.

The more general public benefit would be BI's contribution to creating a more egalitarian society, with a lower incidence of the socio-economic problems linked to inequality, as discussed in chapter 8. Any increase in the socially beneficial work undertaken could be a secondary benefit. To the extent that these effects would contribute to a healthier and more flourishing society, they are what orthodox economists would call 'positive externalities'. They need consideration in any cost–benefit analysis of a BI, set against any negative economic impacts of the policy on the budgetary balance and paid work.

All forms of public (and private) expenditure have costs in terms of the opportunities forgone. If the introduction of a BI were at the expense of public spending on infrastructure, public housing, public education or other public services, the net social benefit could well be negative. Yet this need not necessarily be the case. There is a political choice to be made about economic and social priorities. A right-wing version would use BI as the basis for withdrawal of most, if not all, welfare state spending by governments. A social democratic version would have BI as a supplement to a strong public sector in which the social provision of public health, education, housing, transport and utilities is a top priority. A contest between these right-wing and left-wing versions of BI may therefore be anticipated.

Could a BI operate concurrently with a job guarantee scheme? If so, that would mitigate some of the conservative concerns about the future of work and work incentives. Indeed, combining the two policies could be possible if the job guarantee were to take the form of a guaranteed offer of public sector employment, perhaps centrally funded but administered by local governments (as proposed by FitzRoy & Jin 2018). Unemployed people would then have the choice of taking the job offer or declining it, in the latter case opting to subsist on the lower BI. That would comprise a three-tier arrangement, with universal basic income providing the floor, a guaranteed job offer providing a higher income for people choosing to take it, and then the more general labour market opportunities, whether in public or private sector employment, for those seeking the highest attainable incomes. This combination could prove to be an attractive and workable means of setting an income floor while maintaining paid work incentives.

Capping executive salaries

Lowering the ceiling is another aspect of pre-distributive policy, complementing a BI or other measures to create an income floor. It is a huge challenge, however, because there are so many forces pushing in the opposite direction. The obvious place to try to turn the tide is with the reward structures of corporate CEOs, whose extraordinary income growth has been such a prominent feature in recent times (Piketty 2014a: 333–5). Reducing the gap between their remuneration and the wages of lower-paid workers would lessen the need for subsequent redistribution though taxes and transfers. It is also pertinent to recall that economies operated no less effectively when the gap was much narrower, just as they did when top income tax rates were higher, as noted in the previous chapter. Evidently, the income relativities are not the product of a purely economic imperative. Governments, if so inclined, could change the 'rules of the game'.

Some governments, responding to calls for action, have required full public disclosure of CEO remuneration, relying on shareholders to constrain the size of payments made to company directors and CEOs. Shareholders' meetings do occasionally refuse to approve executive payments that have no obvious justification in terms of corporate performance. At best, however, that empowers one section of capital (owners) against another (managers). There is no direct benefit to other stakeholders, such as the firms' workers (Schofield-Georgeson 2018). A more assertive policy would be for governments to allow companies to claim executive remuneration as business expenditures only if they are within a specified multiple (say, 20:1) of average workers' wages. Continuing to make managerial payments above that limit would then add to the tax liabilities of the corporations. This would be a tougher stance, and national governments are understandably reluctant to make such a move, fearing economic destabilization by multinational capital and its agents. One may infer that limiting top managerial remuneration may need to be part of a broader process of corporate transformation. As Susan Holmberg and Mark Schmitt (2016) say, '[U]ntil we rethink our deepest assumptions about the corporation, we won't be able to master the challenge of excessive CEO pay, or the inequality it generates.'

Civilizing the corporation

What happens within companies is crucial to shaping the extent of inequality and wealth in modern economies and societies. Changing business behaviour requires digging deeper into legal foundations. Corporations enjoy remarkably favourable treatment in capitalist economies. Historically, allowing them legal status comparable to individuals – and endowing them with the remarkable right of limited liability – created the potential for systemic bias against the public interest. The question now is what could be done to constrain that power and change corporate behaviour to produce less inequitable outcomes.

This concern was central to twentieth-century writing about corporate behaviour in an era of managerial capitalism, including by J.K. Galbraith. It has recently been revisited by Roger McCain (2017) in a book specifically focused on wealth inequality. McCain makes the case for more emphasis on workers' ownership of businesses or, failing that, on hybrid forms of capital–labour arrangements, including employee stock ownership plans, workers' participation in management and co-determination. The latter element has for a long time been a distinctive feature of business in Germany, where industrial organization puts more emphasis on worker participation than elsewhere in the Anglo-American sphere, with evident benefits in terms of productivity (Rogers & Streek 2009). Other alternatives to private ownership of businesses include non-profit organizations, benefit corporations and solidarity cooperatives.

Worker cooperatives are particularly attractive in that they have less inherent distributional inequality. Differences in remuneration can be set through democratic processes rather than by managerial fiat. Thus, concern with distributional equity is integral to the functioning of the institution. Advocates of this organizational form commonly point to the positive experience of the long-running Mondragon cooperative in the Basque region of Spain (Herrera 2004). Also in Spain, the Catalonia region has a strong and proud tradition of cooperative enterprises. In the UK, the Lucas-Aerospace plan developed by workers at an advanced technology manufacturing business, though not long-lived, continues to inspire people seeking socially responsible business models (Holtwell 2018). It has to be conceded, however, that trying to operate a cooperative as a 'socialist island' in a predominantly capitalist economy is seldom easy. The extension of democratic practices into the enterprise creates benefits in terms of working relationships, but there can be problems of vulnerability to macro-economic and market conditions that impinge directly on workers' security (Errasti, Bretos & Nunez 2017). Stresses of this sort would be substantially eased if a BI system were also in place, because then the worker-owners would be better able to survive any such difficult periods without threatening the continued existence of the enterprise.

There have been many other proposals for strategies to make corporate behaviour more compatible with broad social and environmental goals. Time-limiting asset ownership, for example, as proposed by Shann Turnbull (1973) and in a more limited form by David Colander (2014), is one proposal that would have the effect of eventually returning asset ownership to the community. Administrative issues need careful consideration in any such schemes but the bigger obstacle is political economic: the power of the corporate giants that make states reluctant to pursue policies that provoke their predictable opposition. Politicians are usually reluctant even to consider mild options for reform. However, an alignment with community concerns about social justice and sustainability can occur when manifestly anti-social corporate behaviours create social opprobrium and reduce share values. In addition, the combined stresses of inequality and the environment could add to more pressure for action and provide a focus for challenging the authority and legitimacy of corporate power. The tensions between corporate interests and broader social interests also put questions about the commons on the political agenda.

Extending the commons

The notion of the commons looms large in modern social science discourse, primarily because of its association with land. Central to such discourse is Garett Hardin's (1968) well-known proposition about the tendency for common property to be degraded. Neoliberals have extended Hardin's analysis to argue that individual property rights are necessary to ensure efficient management of land. It is a simplistic view that has been widely criticized. As Elinor Ostrom (1990) and other writers have emphasized, there are multiple ways in which communities can manage common property efficiently and effectively, and indeed many examples of them having done so. Private property rights are neither necessary nor sufficient for achieving equitable and sustainable management of land and other socio-economic resources.

People concerned about creating more equitable distribution of income and wealth commonly argue, contrary to neoliberal interpretations of Hardin, that common property is an important part of progress. David Harvey, for example, writes of the need for 'the absorption of private property rights into a comprehensive project for the collective management of the commons' (2014: 50) as a key element in challenging contemporary capitalist contradictions. This approach runs directly counter to the process of privatization that has marked the period of neoliberal dominance in public policy throughout capitalist nations. Opposing the further privatization of public land and pushing for democratic control of an expanded commons is the most obvious implication.

Public policies also have to ensure that the owners of already privatized land make due contribution to public revenue. The ideas of the political economist Henry George, introduced in the previous chapter when discussing land tax, are relevant here. Indeed, wherever there is private property in land, land tax is an important means of reducing inequality. It is not merely an instrument for redistributing the income originating as rent; in the longer term, it also takes away the incentive and opportunity to seek wealth through private land ownership. Perhaps some landowners might even prefer to relinquish their land to the state rather than continuing to pay tax on it. Even if the land is privately retained, state revenues can capture the lion's share of the gains that private landowners currently receive when societal developments drive up land values. That revenue may then be spent on expanding public infrastructure, public housing provision or acquisition of land for public purposes elsewhere.

Public ownership of natural resources has a similar rationale. As political economists have argued, it is bizarre that the mining industry in many countries is allowed to extract resources with so little of the revenues from their extraction flowing into public funds (Collins 2018). Norway shows the possibility of an alternative approach, having set up a sovereign wealth fund into which much of the wealth generated by the mining industry has gone (Cleary 2016). Egalitarian goals and extending the commons are mutually reinforcing elements in seeking progressive pre-distribution and changing the economic system to one that has a more cooperative and collectivist character.

Increasing equality of opportunity

The liberal goal of creating greater social mobility also has an important role in this context. Whatever the heights of floors and ceilings, it is important to increase equality of opportunity in the intervening space. Such concerns have been a consistent feature of liberal arguments for greater equality of opportunity (UNRISD 2010).

Anti-discrimination policies are the most obvious example of policies serving this goal. A good society is one where social mobility is not constrained by class, race, gender and other anti-meritocratic impediments discussed in chapter 5. Preventing discrimination against people on the grounds of gender, race or any other personal attributes not directly relevant to their ability and potential is not just a matter of fairness. Any society that allows ongoing discrimination is also acting against its own collective economic interest: talent is wasted when people of lesser ability get preferment. Effective legislative measures are necessary to prohibit discrimination in labour and financial markets, as are constant vigilance, education and cultural change.

There are also particular policy fields where public provision and/or funding can increase equality of opportunity. *Early childhood (pre-school) education* is an obvious example because that is where strong foundations can be laid. Affordable and good-quality child care is not just necessary to make life easier for working parents; it is fundamental for developing the personal and social skills of all young people, irrespective of their socio-economic background.

Educational policy that provides funding to schools according to their students' needs – rather than perpetuating class privilege – is another important avenue for achieving greater equality of opportunity. Educational provision needs to ensure that young people in each generation have the best available learning opportunities. It should not foster the inter-generational transmission of economic inequalities, as it currently does in many countries.

Urban and regional policies can also play a role by targeting public expenditure on social services, job creation or the provision of infrastructure to localities with high unemployment or other concentrations of social problems. Within cities, policies to increase the supply of affordable housing for lower-income groups and to moderate inflation in housing costs can also be effective, enhancing geographical mobility and making poorer segments of society less vulnerable to social exclusion. Regional decentralization policies may simultaneously 'take the heat off' the biggest cities and help non-metropolitan areas provide a comparable range of economic opportunities and social services.

That socio-economic policies like these can contribute to greater equality of opportunity is widely recognized. However, creating equality of opportunity tends to be hardest where needed most, as we noted in chapter 8. This is a potent reminder that strong social pressure for greater equality of outcomes is the precondition for a fair society.

Conclusion

Beyond conventional policies for income redistribution are some boldly pre-distributive initiatives that need consideration in any strategy for reducing inequality. This chapter has considered three clusters:

- policies that 'raise the floor' by guaranteeing jobs, setting minimum wages and providing basic income for all citizens;
- policies that 'lower the ceiling' by capping corporate managerial remuneration, developing cooperative enterprises and extending the commons;
- policies that foster more equality of opportunity and enhance social mobility.

These policies of progressive pre-distribution can contribute significantly to the creation of a more equitable society. While sharing a similar liberal rationale with the redistributive policies discussed in the preceding chapter, pre-distribution has stronger potential for reducing the fundamental sources of market inequality. The challenge of dealing with global inequalities is no less substantial, as we shall see in the next chapter.

12

A Global Challenge

The global shifts in the distribution of income and wealth described in earlier chapters have significantly changed the challenges of economic development. Some previously very poor nations, most obviously the two most populous nations in the world, have experienced rapid economic growth. Although that has led to reductions in poverty, it has dramatically increased inequality, with fabulously wealthy elites now dominating the distribution of income and wealth in China and India as they do in so many other countries. Meanwhile, particularly in much of sub-Saharan Africa, the problems of underdevelopment and poverty continue unabated or in even more intense forms (Obeng-Odoom 2015a, 2017). The challenges of dealing with inequality and underdevelopment are inseparable.

This chapter explores how we may understand the challenges, what is to be done and by whom. There is a global moral imperative to act, as Pope Francis, among others, has emphasized. But what actions – and undertaken by whom? Indeed, is there any institution capable of working directly on global inequality? International political economist Robert Wade has argued that 'it cannot be a direct objective of public policy, which has to focus on inequalities within nation states or (via trade rules, aid, etc.) inequalities among states' (2002: 59). That puts supra-national institutions such as the IMF and World Bank in the spotlight. Are they capable of helping poor countries lacking the wealth, resources and institutions necessary to enact policies like those described in the preceding two chapters? Or must poor people across the globe try to 'lift themselves by their own bootstraps'? Are there policies for development assistance that are genuinely pro-poor? This chapter looks at competing views about development through a lens that focuses attention on global economic inequalities.

Poor show

Conventionally, the high incidence of poverty and the pressing need for poverty alleviation dominate discussion of the problems of poorer nations. Poverty reduction, along with the elimination of hunger, has been a notable focus of the UN's commitment to the Millennium Development Goals (MDGs), succeeded since 2015 by the Sustainable Development Goals (SDGs). This focus is both analytically and politically significant because it emphasizes the floor rather than the gap between floor and ceiling. While the sheer scale of global inequality makes the narrower focus effectively inescapable, it is important to view poverty in the context of inequality. This requires both careful attention to its measurement and incidence and an understanding of how it relates to development.

First, the numbers: how many people live in poverty, and where in the world are they? The current standard global poverty measure is the number of people living on less than $1.90 per day, or its local equivalent. This is an austere measure of absolute poverty, identifying very poor people struggling for subsistence. They are the current equivalent of people whom Frantz Fanon (1961) famously called 'the wretched of the earth'. This term, although sounding uncomfortably stereotypical, has continuing resonance because, while being very poor does not deny personal dignity, it certainly makes it much more elusive. A $1.90 poverty line is surely very basic, setting aside the more subtle considerations of 'relative poverty' and 'capabilities' that we considered in chapter 2. Yet it is on this basis (and its predecessors, such as the $1 and $1.25 per day poverty lines) that claims about great strides in the elimination of world poverty have been made in recent years.

Table 12.1 presents data on what proportion of people fall below this standard (i.e. the 'head-count ratio') in eight broad regions of the world. Its bottom row shows that just under 11% of the whole world's population lives in poverty, according to this austere measure. Strikingly, the corresponding figure for sub-Saharan Africa is over 42%. The nations of the Pacific (Oceania, excluding

Table 12.1 The incidence of poverty by region: proportion of population below international poverty line of $1.90 per day, 2013

Region	Percentage of population below poverty threshold
Australia and New Zealand	0.7
Central Asia and South Asia	14.4
East Asia and South East Asia	3.2
Latin America and the Caribbean	5.4
Northern America and Europe	0.6
Oceania, exc. Australia and New Zealand	27.2
Sub-Saharan Africa	42.3
West Asia and North Africa	2.6
World	**10.7**

Source: http://data.un.org/Data.aspx?q=poverty&d=SDGs&f=series%3aSI_POV_DAY1.

Australia and New Zealand) have the next highest rate (although the absolute number of people in these island nations is much smaller). Central and South Asia has an above-average incidence of poverty too, but East Asia and South East Asia are well below the global average. Latin America and the Caribbean have poverty rates above West Asia and North Africa. In North America, Europe and Australasia, poverty also looks almost non-existent, affecting less than one in a hundred people. It is evidence like this that leads to the perception that concentrated poverty is primarily a problem of the 'Global South' and now centred in sub-Saharan Africa.

Broad brushstrokes often help to show a big picture, but we need to look more closely to discern the detail. In this case, we need further geographical disaggregation to see the incidence of poverty in individual countries. We also need to compare the definition of poverty with a less austere measure. Table 12.2 overleaf takes these two steps. It shows data on poverty rates for the same range of countries previously used for Tables 3.1–3, excluding a couple for which no official data are available and adding six other particularly poor countries. For each nation, it shows what proportion of the population is living on less than the standard $1.90 poverty line and on less than $5.50 per day (in terms of dollars adjusted for PPP). This latter figure for the poverty line can be regarded as a more 'generous' but perhaps more 'realistic' indicator of what constitutes a basic living standard.

Table 12.2 Poverty according to two measures of the poverty line (2011 PPP), selected countries

Country	% of population living on under $1.90 per day	% of population living on under $5.50 per day
Anglos		
Australia[a]	0.3	0.7
Canada[b]	0.3	1.0
UK[c]	0.2	0.5
USA[b]	1.0	2.0
Euros		
France[c]	0.0	0.3
Germany[b]	0.0	0.0
Italy[c]	1.2	2.8
Spain[c]	0.8	2.9
Sweden[c]	0.3	0.7
BRICS		
Brazil[d]	4.3	22.1
Russian Federation[d]	0.0	2.7
India[e]	21.2	86.8
China[b]	1.9	36.3
South Africa[e]	16.6	56.3
JINKs		
Japan[f]	0.3	1.0
Indonesia[g]	6.8	62.8
Nigeria[h]	53.5	92.1
Republic of Korea[i]	0.3	1.3
Poor nations		
Bangladesh[a]	18.5	87.3
Burundi[b]	73.7	97.1
Côte d'Ivoire[d]	21.3	81.8
Pakistan[b]	6.1	79.5
Sierra Leone[e]	52.3	94.7
World[b]	**10.7**	**48.4**

Notes: [a] Data for Australia and Bangladesh for 2010; [b] data for Canada, USA, Germany, China, Burundi, Pakistan and World for 2013; [c] data for UK, France, Italy, Spain and Sweden for 2014; [d] data for Brazil, Russian Federation and Côte d'Ivoire for 2015; [e] data for India, South Africa and Sierra Leone for 2011; [f] data for Japan for 2008; [g] data for Indonesia for 2016; [h] data for Nigeria for 2009; [i] data for Republic of Korea for 2013.
Sources: All data from *https://data.worldbank.org/indicator/SI.POV.GAPS*; *https://data.worldbank.org/indicator/SI.POV.LMIC.GP*; and from *https://data.worldbank.org/indicator/SI.POV.UMIC.GP*.

As the bottom row of Table 12.2 shows, approximately one in ten of the world's people live below a poverty line of $1.90 per day. Nearly half of the world's people do so when the line is set at $5.50 a day. These observations signal the enormous scale of the global poverty problem and bring into sharp focus the dramatic differences in the poverty head-count according to where the poverty line is set.

The dimensions of poverty in each of the country groups are contentious. Consider the Anglo and Euro nations in the top sections of the table. The incidence of poverty there looks negligible, even if the higher $5.50 figure defines the poverty threshold. Yet is this really the case? Consider an affluent nation like Australia, for example: surveys undertaken there in recent years usually report around 14% of people living in poverty according to a national standard that sets the poverty line at half the median income (Serr 2017: 22). Particular population groups, such as Indigenous peoples, single-parent families and homeless people, commonly experience a higher incidence of poverty. Some localities are renowned for their concentrations of social problems associated with poor economic opportunities, unemployment and low income (Dean & Broomhill 2018). This is typical of developed nations. Poverty amidst affluence is normal, as marginalized groups are vulnerable to poverty according to prevailing social norms. One International Labour Organization analysis of 37 developed countries indicated that 22% of people had an income below 60% of the median for each country (ILO 2016). So, if we interpret poverty as relative to prevailing living standards in particular nations, the low single-digit figures appearing in the first nine rows of Table 12.2 are evidently out of kilter with nation-based perceptions of what it means to be poor. This is not to say that the numbers are wrong; only that a universal poverty threshold does not pick up the incidence of poverty, as it is normally understood, within affluent nations.

What about nations at the other extreme? Does the global measure exaggerate the incidence of poverty there? Certainly, a relative poverty measure would produce lower numbers of people formally classified as poor (i.e. a lower head-count ratio), given that the average incomes in many of those countries are so very low. Yet, falling below an absolute poverty line is a sufficient condition for being classified as poor, is it not? Looking at the last five rows of Table 12.2, showing the situation in some of the world's severely impoverished nations, this is clearly borne out. In Burundi, for example, between 73% and 97% of people live in poverty, depending on whether the lower or higher poverty benchmark is set. It is reasonable to infer that living in poverty is the general condition for between three-quarters of the people and almost everyone. Pakistan is quite different: setting the poverty line at $1.90 shows only about 6% of the people living in in poverty, whereas setting it at $5.50 shows almost 80% of the people in poverty. This is because nearly three-quarters of the people live on between $1.90 and $5.50 per day: very low incomes are the norm. Other nations where more than half of the people live on between $1.90 and $5.50 a day include India, Bangladesh, Pakistan, Indonesia and Côte d'Ivoire. South Africa looks quite different because, while there are very many poor people (more than half of the population, according to the $5.50 standard), there is also a substantial stratum of middle-income and rich people. Of all the poorer nations, China stands out as the most remarkably successful because, although over a third of its people live on less than $5.50 a day, less than 2% have less than $1.90 a day, according to the official national data. The situation in Russia, meanwhile, looks to have more in common with the Euro nations than with the other BRICS.

How useful is this sort of analysis? Relying on data provided by national governments does not always inspire complete confidence and may raise doubts about the details of particular cross-country comparisons. More fundamentally, some critics are deeply sceptical of the use of global poverty lines. Jason Hickel (2016) posits that this approach, particularly the selection of a very austere universal poverty line, played a key role in inflating claims made by the World Bank about the success of poverty reduction to meet the MDGs. The use of the higher $5.50 poverty line may mitigate this concern, but the focus on absolute rather than relative poverty remains deeply problematic. No universal benchmark can adequately take account of national differences in what it means to be living in poverty. To illustrate the point, Hickel quotes a survey in Sri Lanka that found 40% of the people were living in poverty, according to the national poverty standard. Yet the World Bank, using the then standard international poverty line, recorded a poverty rate of only 4% (Hickel 2016: 753). Nation-by-nation aggregation of the number of people in poverty according to local standards tends to generate a higher total than using a single global benchmark. This is partly because the former approach identifies so many more people in developed nations where 'poverty amidst affluence' persists.

Table 12.3 World poverty according to two measures, 1981–2013

	% of population living on under $1.90 per day[a]	% of population living on under $5.50 per day[b]
1981	42.2	66.9
1990	35.3	68.2
1999	28.6	66.9
2005	20.8	60.5
2010	15.7	54.0
2013	10.7	48.4

Sources: [a]Data from *https://data.worldbank.org/indicator/SI.POV.GAPS*; [b] data from *https://data.worldbank.org/indicator/SI.POV.UMIC.GP*.

Of course, it is important to acknowledge the good news aspect of this story too. Table 12.3 shows what there is to celebrate. For the lower of the two absolute poverty lines, the progress in poverty reduction appears to have been steady over more than 30 years. For the higher poverty line, the situation is rather different: on this basis, there was no progress during the first half of the period but there has been significant improvement more recently. A situation where almost half of the world's population still lives on less than an income equivalent to than $5.50 per day does not constitute the end of chronic economic hardship – far from it – yet progress **is** progress.

Linking these findings to earlier chapters in this book, we can infer the following:

- Poverty is still a substantial problem worldwide but, when measured by various universal measures of personal incomes, it has become less pronounced during the last two decades.
- This reduction is substantially the product of China's strong economic growth, but also reflects significant economic improvements in other highly populated countries like India and Indonesia.
- Other developing countries have had an uneven experience of economic growth, development and poverty reduction. Particularly in sub-Saharan Africa, poverty remains acute and chronic.
- Concurrently, economic inequalities have increased within almost all nations. This tendency is particularly strong in the nations where absolute poverty has fallen most, such as China and India. Wealthy elites have prospered and distributions of

income have become more 'stretched'. Global inequality, seen in terms of the changing distributions of income and wealth between rich, middle-income and poor people, has not fallen despite the reductions in absolute poverty.

- The current challenge is to find paths to development that are more equitable between and within nations so that global inequality can be reduced.

These observations indicate the need for fundamental rethinking about progressive strategies for development.

Conservative, liberal and radical perspectives

The various competing views of poverty and development, like other issues in political economic analysis, can be considered in relation to the now-familiar trilogy of conservative, liberal and radical approaches. Conservative viewpoints tend to identify the problem of poverty in terms of the attributes and plight of poor people. This usually involves study of the living conditions of the poor, their health, education, homelessness, and so forth. However, as radical political economist Howard Wachtel (1971) pointed out, 'It is important to differentiate between the manifestations of poverty – normally called "the poverty problem" – and their underlying causes' (1971: 1). Liberals look at causal factors but typically interpret them in terms of market failures. Hence, they focus on the impediments to market forces that prevent the spread of prosperity, and the prescription of remedial policies that could help to produce better economic outcomes for poor people, all presuming that the state is well intentioned and has the institutional capacity to make the reforms effective. Radicals, not surprisingly, challenge the latter assumptions, seeing poverty more deeply rooted in class, gender and race relations and the class-biased character of the capitalist state. Thus, poverty is seen as an innate consequence of the 'basic institutions of capitalism – class, labour markets and the state' (Wachtel 1971: 16), leading to advocacy of struggle for non-capitalist alternatives.

The different viewpoints clearly show up in the debates about policies for development. Most discussion has had a common theme: the need to raise living standards for poor people in poor nations. As such, there is at least the semblance of a shared egalitarianism. Yet the egalitarianism has two obvious limits. Its focus is usually on the reduction of poverty, not inequality, and it typically stops at the national borders, not engaging with the nature of global capitalism. Implicitly accepting the necessity, even desirability, of intra-national inequality and not challenging the broader systemic character of inequality are the hallmarks of conservative approaches to development. This shows in the conventional view that all countries have to pass through a phase of widening inequalities en route to a higher stage of development when the fruits of affluence are shared more equitably – growth first, redistribution later. The inference is that time and self-correcting market processes should do the trick, perhaps nudged on by policies to encourage any structural adjustments necessary to conform to capitalist economic growth. It is a view that has claimed some academic respectability ever since Simon Kuznets (1955) and Jeffrey Williamson (1965) posited that economic inequality tends to widen during the early stages of a nation's economic growth, then narrows once a more developed state is reached. Although subject to sustained critique, the assumption of an 'inverted U-shaped' relationship between inequality and growth remains implicit in much policy practice.

In the late twentieth century, the 'Washington consensus' adopted mainstream economic reasoning about how efficiency and growth should be sought through reducing barriers to trade, privatizing public enterprises and increasing market competition while scaling back the regulatory role of the state. The IMF and World Bank's relentless pursuit of that agenda was criticized from both liberal and radical perspectives (Chossudovsky 1997; Stiglitz 2002; McMichael 2008; Ruccio 2011). Some critics now contend that the more recent 'post-Washington consensus', although more sophisticated, shares some similar assumptions, creating significant continuity in practice. In Paul Cammock's words, there has been a 'constant commitment to the systematic transformation of social relations and institutions in the developing world, in order to generalise and facilitate capitalist accumulation on a global scale, and build specifically capitalist hegemony through the promotion of participation and ownership' (cited in Engel 2010: 75).

Critics of the current Anti-Poverty Consensus (APC) contend that it is underpinned by a similar neoliberal inclination. Political economists expressing this concern include Ha-Joon Chang, Branko Milanovic, Thomas Piketty, Armartya Sen, Joseph Stiglitz and Robert Wade. Ben Selwyn (2017) describes them as helping to form an Anti-Poverty Counter-Consensus (APCC). Criticism of the World Bank and IMF's failure to drive more progressive and egalitarian development strategies is a recurrent theme. The smooth rhetoric of the agencies is contrasted with the continuing harsh realities in the poorest countries where major inequalities persist and flourish. Yet critics of the APCC, such as Selwyn (2017: 7), assert that the APCC's narrative 'shares much common ground with the APC'.

Selwyn's critique of both the APC and the APCC, while acknowledging good intent by the liberal contributors to the latter, leads into a more radical political economic analysis. More unites the APC and APCC than divides them, Selwyn claims, because they share common assumptions of 'capital-centred development': that economic growth is necessary for human development; that capitalist property rights should be the basis of the growth process; and that policies should seek to improve rather than replace exploitative capital–labour relations. Playing by these rules is not conducive to development, he says. Indeed, the globalization of corporate capital makes it increasingly difficult for developing countries to achieve higher economic prosperity without intensifying their inequalities. Hence Selwyn's advocacy of 'labour-led development' and 'democratic development'. Thus, rather than hoping for development to occur as a result of successful capitalist economic endeavours, the emphasis is put on strategies that seek to curtail the power of global capital, challenging capitalist social relations, their associated inequalities and the commodification of nature.

Selwyn's critique leads into the advocacy of strategies for economic democracy; new systems of banking that serve community needs; sharing and reducing work; protecting and learning from indigenous peoples; 'industrial policy for a green transformation'; and agrarian reform (2017: chs 5–6). Policies of land reform are also important in breaking the stranglehold on development that results from concentrated land ownership, especially in postcolonial regimes. Less concentrated ownership opens up possibilities for more widely dispersed distributions of income. As Tim Anderson (2015) notes, communal ownership and stewardship are conducive to more equitable sharing of the fruits of land use. In a similar vein, the Indian scholar and activist Vandana Shiva has also emphasized themes of empowerment and sustainability – replete with examples of practical achievements, particularly where women take the lead – in community-based development initiatives (e.g. Shiva 2005). Such views contrast strongly with mainstream economic thinking.

Recognizing that these differences of view – conservative, liberal and radical – pervade discussions of development helps when considering policies for promoting development. So too does recognizing what has 'worked' in practice and what has not. Identifying principles, strategies and policies that contribute to promoting development in conjunction with reducing inequality is a big challenge.

Going for growth

As we have seen in earlier chapters of this book, the previously poor countries that have achieved surges of economic growth have experienced greatly increased internal economic inequalities during the process. China's distinctive blend of an authoritarian state and increasingly capitalistic trade principles has achieved the biggest macroeconomic success story that the world has seen for half a century, perhaps ever. The surging economic growth in India has also been remarkable. What these two countries with markedly different political economic institutions have in common are huge supplies of cheap labour. Combined with increasingly advanced technology and high volumes of investment, both local and international, this has led to success in international market competition across a wide array of products, rapid macroeconomic growth and reduction in absolute poverty. However, such success has come at a significant cost in terms of economic inequality, as noted in previous chapters, as well as social dislocation, environmental damage and sometimes highly problematic employment conditions (Barnes 2015). The model is not generalizable, particularly once global economic limits are recognized. Moreover, new stresses arise: nations that have missed out in the competition for trade success and capital inflow now sometimes find themselves subordinated to the interests of the newly emerged economic giants. The downsides, as well as the upsides, of Chinese investment in poor African nations, for example, are increasingly of concern (Mohan 2013; Mohan et al. 2014).

Ha-Joon Chang (2002) famously identified 'kicking away the ladder' as a process whereby rich nations denied poor nations the opportunity to develop the processes by which they had themselves become affluent. Some have sought growth by other means. In the late twentieth century, 'developmental states' in South East Asia had considerable success in promoting industrialization and economic growth based on their own institutions, combining engagement in capitalist markets with a state-centric approach to planning structural economic change (Thurbon & Weiss 2016). Others have sought economic development through mining of natural resources, which looks initially like a very attractive option for countries blessed with valuable natural resource endowments. Taking advantage of oil reserves, mineral deposits and other natural resources to earn much-needed revenues seems to offer a straightforward means to boost economic growth and fund development. Countries in the Middle East and some in Africa and South America have sought to exploit this option. However, as even affluent capitalist nations have found, there are hazards in this type of economic specialization, leading to what has been called 'the resources curse' (Collins 2016). The pitfalls are particularly great in developing nations because of the imbalance of bargaining power with multinational corporations involved in developing the extractive processes (Obeng-Odoom 2018).

What about *'fair trade'*? Some see this as a way of getting the best of both worlds by engaging in trade but constraining it so that it does not violate environmental, labour or other community standards important for balanced development. The policy has been applied to the production and distribution of coffee and other agricultural products in some developing nations. However, there can be a downside when it locks poor nations into trading patterns where the exploitation of labour and nature can be just as intense as in so-called 'free trade'. Finding a compromise between market forces, social justice and ecological sustainability is difficult. Again, how concentrated is ownership and control is a question that looms large (McDonald & Marshall 2010; Valiente-Riedl 2013).

What about development that comes 'from within' by providing small-scale funding for local economic initiatives? Can local financial institutions help these 'bottom-up' processes of economic development? That was clearly the ambition of the pioneers of *microfinance* from the 1990s onwards, particularly Muhammad Yunus from Bangladesh, who has been widely fêted for his efforts, including the award of the 2006 Nobel Peace Prize. There were originally very high hopes for microfinance as a distinctively pro-poor form of development. Providing small loans directly to low-income families, particularly to women, had a significant 'grass-roots' appeal as a means of establishing and growing small businesses in poor communities (Yunus 2003). Early initiatives in Bangladesh seemed highly promising. The Grameen Bank, which Yunus had initiated, became synonymous with his ambition to 'create a world without poverty' (Yunis 2007). It increased its geographical range internationally and broadened its scope from the provision of microcredit to social business, comprising 'companies that focus on providing a social benefit rather than maximising profits for its owners' (Yunis 2007: 28).

Yet the experiences with microfinance over the last two decades have disappointed many of the original enthusiasts and its critics have become numerous and sometimes vociferous. Milford Bateman (2010), for example, argues that 'microfinance is largely antagonistic to sustainable development and also to sustainable poverty reduction' (2010: 1). While accepting that microfinance can provide benefits in individual cases, Bateman argues that its emphasis on individualistic solutions to poverty is inimical to building more solidaristic and sustainable local economic development trajectories. As he says, '[T]he poor are instead increasingly thrown back on their old, and largely unsuccessful, historical mission: to attempt vainly to rescue themselves from their own poverty and suffering though their own individual actions and meagre resources' (Bateman 2010: 2). Worse, from an institutional perspective, is the increasing commercialization of microfinance that took place from the 1990s onwards, whereby the original Grameen Bank was converted to a for-profit business model.

Development assistance, reparations and debt forgiveness

A different set of strategies hinges on *aid, not trade*. The assistance can come in various forms, including loans advanced by the World Bank, grants given through development agencies and funds channelled through NGOs specializing in poverty relief or development assistance. Its form and conditions are crucially important for its effects. Critics of dependence on foreign aid have long argued that its effect can be to reinforce a post-colonial straitjacket that constrains domestic development policies (Hayter 1981). The main beneficiaries of 'tied aid' can be the donor nations, whose economies benefit from the increased business (Anderson 2013). In recent years, there has also been a tendency towards the 'neoliberalization of development assistance', with a larger role for international private sector management consultants in the processes of tendering for, designing, managing and evaluating development assistance programmes.

The recent push for *international reparations* may be seen in this context as a means of both increasing the volume of financial flows and changing the nature of entitlements. Arguments for the payment of compensation to poor countries for the oppression, exploitation and suffering experienced by their people during the colonial era are becoming increasingly clearly voiced (Beckles 2013, 2016). For example, the 22 island nations that comprise the Caribbean Community are currently calling for official reparations from former imperial European nations as compensation for slavery and the genocide of their indigenous peoples. The general argument is strong: even Nozick's right-wing libertarian philosophy concedes it in principle, as noted in chapter 2 of this book. Legal cases have established precedents: for example, in 2013, the UK government agreed to compensate thousands of Kenyans for physical and psychological damage inflicted on them during the colonial regime in the 1960s (Lewis 2014). The valuation of country-to-country reparations and the form in which payments should be made are huge issues too. Even if not immediately successful in achieving claims for actual monetary compensation, the movement for reparations puts more pressure on former colonial powers, particularly those involved in the slave trade, to accept responsibility for providing more substantial aid to developing nations.

The arguments for *debt forgiveness* have been a parallel thrust. Under the 'Washington consensus' policies of the IMF and the World Bank, some developing countries got into a 'debt trap' situation, needing to borrow more in order to meet the servicing costs of their past borrowing and thereby rendering economic development effectively impossible. The Jubilee 2000 movement was formed to focus on this 'catch 22' situation and had partial success when the international financial institutions agreed to cancel debts held by some of the most deeply indebted nations. Yet the problem of the debt and interest burden remains. Indeed, it is not only in nations of the 'Global South' that the problem arises, as became evident during the negotiations between the Greek government and the 'troika' of European institutions in 2015. Based on economic logic (of the sort mounted by Greece's then Finance Minister, Yanis Varoufakis), a strong case can be made for sharing responsibility for creating situations with 'vicious circle' characteristics. Of course, financial institutions are always concerned to get the interest on their loans, and conservative economists warn of the 'moral hazard' tendencies that result from not penalizing defaults. Without some circuit-breaker, however, impoverished countries become locked into impossibly difficult situations when any economic surplus that they generate goes to servicing debt rather than financing development.

There is a case for raising the floor of pro-poor international development aid from the more affluent nations. The currently agreed UN target is for them to contribute at least 0.7% of their GDP as official aid. Tony Atkinson's last book advocated raising this to 1% of GDP (2015: 236). At first sight, this may seem a minor, even trivial, gesture. Only a few countries, such as the UK, currently meet the existing target. Some fall woefully short: the USA and Australia give only about a quarter of their proper share. Formally raising the target might therefore seem spurious, but it would be a significant international signal of good global citizenship. It would add moral suasion and, if accompanied by the withdrawal of particular benefits from non-compliant nations, could help to reverse the drift to aid exhaustion. What could inject a particular dynamic into the process is a corresponding commitment by the recipient nations to use the aid, in part if not wholly, for particular policy priorities, such as investment in improved public infrastructure and the provision of basic income.

The latter requirement may be particularly contentious because of its expense. A predictable response is to say that, if affluent nations cannot afford BI provision, developing nations certainly cannot. However, affluent countries could afford it, depending on the level at which the BI is set and on the tax-to-GDP ratio that governments are prepared to manage. Poorer nations generally cannot do so without significant external assistance, however. A commitment to global human rights implies the responsibility to try to bridge a gap of this sort. Moreover, it is important to take into account that the level of a BI would not be everywhere the same, since it would need to reflect prevailing social norms and living costs in different countries. In the poorer nations, somewhere in the range of $1.90 to $5.50 per day might be feasible (as per the poverty lines discussed earlier in this chapter). The volume and distribution of international aid to help each developing country to achieve that standard might be linked to its government's willingness to implement and efficiently administer it. As an incidental benefit, the universal application of a BI, even at variable payment levels, would help with eligibility for payment to people moving, temporarily or permanently, between countries.

These are tentative suggestions, illustrating how the processes of circular and cumulative causation that currently impede development might be reversed if there were sufficient political will to do so. They signal the importance of designing development assistance so that it contributes concurrently to reduction of intra-national inequalities and international inequalities. There is no magic wand. Development assistance programmes, however they are constructed, cannot avoid potential problems arising from public and private institutions that are vulnerable to corruption, for example. They need conditionality, constant monitoring and sanctions for non-compliance to ensure some degree of consistency between intention and outcomes. As an additional measure, countries continuing to operate as tax havens could be made ineligible to receive development assistance.

Reforming the institutions

Whether the existing international political economic institutions, such as the IMF and the World Bank, are up to the task of implementing and managing the processes of international development assistance also demands consideration. It is hard to imagine a worldwide assault on poverty and inequality that did not involve them in some way. Yet institutional critiques, sometimes arguing that the agencies are part of the problem and cannot be part of the solution, are familiar fare in political economic discourse (e.g. Chossudovsky 1997; Engel 2010; Selwyn 2017). Even the restrained assessment by Ngaire Woods noted that 'they evolved – particularly in the 1980s – into institutions increasingly financed by the poor and directed by the rich' (2006: 213). Can leopards change their spots? Eminent international figures have spoken out about the need for more attention to economic inequalities when designing, implementing and assessing development assistance policies. The IMF has been making statements about reducing inequality since 2010. Its senior executive, Christine Lagarde, has ramped up the rhetoric. However, one careful political economic study has shown that what the IMF actually does in practice, particularly in its country assessments and conditional lending practices, has not fundamentally changed to emphasize the redress of inequalities (Nunn & White

2016: 212). This echoes earlier accusations of 'organized hypocrisy' (Weaver 2008; Kentikelenis et al. 2016). Keeping in mind the longer history of the IMF structural adjustment programmes and its other austerity and neoliberal policy measures, it takes a big leap to see the institution in a new light.

While we may not look towards the international agencies to lead the way to a new era of redressing global inequality, perhaps preferring to embrace the 'bottom-up' approaches discussed earlier in this chapter, it would be better to have some institutional reform rather than none. It is also pertinent to reflect on the nature of policy change in large organizations like the IMF and the World Bank. Anyone with personal experience of large bureaucracies understands that public pronouncements by a senior executive do not necessarily change the behaviour of officials concerned with day-to-day policy implementation. Put in a positive light, it is like a big ship changing direction. Within the IMF research department, Jonathan Ostry and his colleagues have been generating important research papers, as previously cited in this book, that make the case for seeking greater within-nation economic equality. One may infer that, as in most organizations, there are progressive and conservative factions: institutional behaviour reflects their interaction. The ultimate test would be whether the IMF and the World Bank make specific changes that take their concern with inequality beyond speeches, research papers and pilot projects into the mainstream of their activities. The reasons for becoming more concerned about global inequalities are also pertinent: recognizing that growing inequality poses increasing risks to political stability and the expansion of the capitalist world market may be one quite conservative motivation.

Ultimately, the nature and extent of the international agencies' commitment to redress of global inequality can be judged by their institutional practices. Will their analyses and policies recognize the importance of inequalities in wealth and not just income? Will they add statistical measures of economic inequality to the economic metrics they use in assisting country performances? Will they implement distributional accounts as a regular component in national accounting and assess how structural economic changes affect inequality? These are modest tests of how serious the institutional responses are. The bigger test is the capacity of the international institutions to challenge the power structures of global capitalism of which they are themselves creations. To be part of the solution, not part of the problem, requires that private economic interests do not violate the societal and ecological requirements for global equity and sustainability.

Conclusion

Worldwide, economic inequality is greater than within any nation. Its redress requires a combination of international and intra-national redistributions. This raises profound questions about development strategies, finance, trade, aid and political economic institutions. The arguments and evidence reviewed in this chapter indicate the following:

- Recent reductions in international economic inequalities have been uneven and have been accompanied by sharp increases in intra-national inequalities.
- Development assistance programmes implemented by official international agencies have been constrained by their capital-centred assumptions; alternative strategies need emphasis on empowerment, sustainability and labour-centred development.
- A more comprehensive approach requires moving beyond poverty alleviation to reducing inequality worldwide. Payment of reparations and provision of development assistance by rich countries could focus on financing public sector infrastructure and universal basic income in poor ones.

Radical reform, whether focused on international and global inequalities or on inequalities within individual nations, is seldom straightforward. Its likelihood of success is enhanced by being aware of the impediments, as discussed in the next chapter.

Prospects

13

Impediments to Equity

There is a popular saying: 'Where there's a will there's a way.'
Indeed, there is no shortage of potentially effective policy instruments, as described in the preceding three chapters. However, the
persistence and growth of inequalities within nations and worldwide also suggests the presence of substantial obstacles. Indeed,
there are many barriers on the road to progress. Understanding
and addressing them is a key element in producing effective and
enduring change.

This chapter explores the most important impediments in terms
of four broad themes: ignorance, ideologies, interests and institutions. It looks at the nature of these obstacles, considers necessary
responses and ends by asking where the economics profession sits
in relation to the challenges.

Ignorance

Social surveys have shown a wide gulf between people's beliefs
about the extent of inequality and its actual extent (e.g. Hauser
& Norton, 2017; Kraus, Rucker & Richeson 2017). Most people
think inequality is much less than it actually is. Ignorance is, at
face value, a lack of information. Digging deeper, a connection
with psychological factors is evident, because beliefs intermingle
with hopes and fears. People feeling comfortable with their beliefs
about living in a classless, meritocratic society may tend to shun

evidence to the contrary (perhaps labelling it 'fake news'). Even when they acknowledge the existence of major inequality, they may deny that it is a problem, preferring to see it as justified. Thus, they may regard inequalities of gender and race as reflecting people's innate characteristics rather than systemic factors arising from racism and sexism. A lack of experience of 'how the other half lives', perhaps combined with wishful thinking, may also lead to vast overestimation of the extent of social mobility.

Interestingly, people in very unequal societies seem to be least able or willing to recognize the structural roots of inequality. Researching perceptions of inequality in a range of countries, Jonathan Mijs (2017) found evidence of a positive correlation between income inequality and the proportion of citizens who believe their country is meritocratic. This evidence is reproduced here as Figure 13.1, showing 13 countries for which the comparison could be made. The dot in the top right corner of the figure is the USA. The 'line of best fit' through these observations is suggestive of a perverse relationship. Thus, the greater the need for redress of inequality, the less likely are people to think it necessary.

Drilling down to analyse the formation of beliefs like these, research by the same author found that college students in the USA who had grown up in rich and white neighbourhoods were likely to interpret economic success as reward for merit. By contrast, students growing up in more sociologically diverse environ-

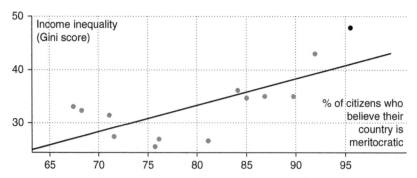

Figure 13.1 Actual inequality and beliefs about inequality; international comparison, 2009

Note: The countries are Australia, the Czech Republic, Germany, New Zealand, Norway, Philippines, Poland, Russia, Slovenia, Sweden, Switzerland, the UK and the USA. Data are for 2009.

Source: Mijs (2018).

ments were more likely to perceive a structural basis to inequality. Having a roommate at college from a different ethnic group also affected attitudes: students who shared a room with someone of a different race showed a better understanding of the structural sources of inequality (Mijs 2017). This evidence is suggestive of the environmental factors shaping awareness.

An inference is that, while ignorance is not an absolute obstacle to progressive reform, it can be self-reinforcing in the absence of conscious strategies for change. Education, in the broadest sense of this term, is therefore a precondition for collective action to reduce economic inequality. It is not just a matter of what is in the school curriculum, in university courses, or even in the media. It is everything that shapes understanding and discussion of inequality in the public domain. As Susan George says, 'Another world is possible ... if we know what we're talking about' (2004: ch. 1). There are some positive signs of a significant shift under way. Since the global financial crisis began in 2008, public awareness has been changing. Political leaders and religious leaders recurrently speak about the importance of reducing inequality. Researchers have also markedly improved the quality and availability of data. We are now at a stage when we know the dimensions of the issue and the case for action. Piketty's book was extraordinarily timely, tapping into the growing public concern and providing data, analysis and reflections on where we, as a society, are heading. Atkinson's final book (2015) and Wilkinson and Pickett's latest book (2018) have also added useful supplementary policy discussions, as have a number of other contributions during recent years. Maybe this modest volume will help maintain the momentum.

Ideologies

All political economic arrangements depend for their legitimacy on systems of belief. Ideologies work either to defend the status quo or to challenge it. Ideology, interpreted in this context, has two functions. One involves useful ideas that help us to structure our understanding of the world in which we live. The other, more problematic, aspect involves diversion or distortion of reality, usually to serve particular interests.

Nationalism, racism and sexism are particular ideologies that have the latter characteristic. Nationalism is an ideology that encourages social solidarity based on a common attribute: living in the 'best country in the world' (and aren't there so many of them!). As such, it can be a source of social cohesion and a focus of pleasurable rivalries in international sporting contests. However, there is a seamier side where more extreme nationalisms result in denigration of foreigners, including immigrant workers. When combined with racist ideology, the consequences can be highly problematic. Minority groups who have lived in a country for decades may be victims of terrible treatment, even genocide, if regarded as 'outsiders'. Thus, reactionary nationalism and racism are interacting ideologies that legitimize what might otherwise be regarded as abhorrent discrimination and abuse of human rights. Sexism is similarly pervasive as an ideology used to justify discrimination against women. Even people who are disadvantaged by such ideologies may accept them, perhaps grudgingly or even unconsciously, producing the fatalist attitudes by which underprivileged groups reconcile themselves to disadvantaged socio-economic positions.

Other ideologies are more explicitly political economic. Ideologies associated with meritocracy and reward according to productivity have commanded attention in previous chapters of this book. As Yanis Varoufakis (2016) writes:

> The economists (especially members of the so-called Chicago school, e.g. Gary Becker) aid and abet the self-serving beliefs of the powerful by arguing that arbitrary discrimination in the distribution of wealth and social roles cannot survive for long the pressures of competition (i.e. that, sooner or later, people will be rewarded in proportion to their contribution to society). Most of the rest of us suspect that this is plainly false.

Similarly, consider the priority accorded to economic growth. Solving the 'economic problem' is usually couched in terms of more efficient resource use to achieve greater abundance. This has been described as 'the dominant ideology of our times, with its supreme goal of unending growth in production and consumption' (Gittins 2010: 6). The belief that economic growth benefits everyone is a particularly effective ideology, diverting attention away from the inequalities of people's actual economic opportunities and experiences. 'We're all in the same boat' and 'a rising tide lifts all boats' are its folksy expressions. But do we all really have a common interest in prioritizing economic growth?

Critics of growth's assumed primacy have been many and varied. Political economist J.K. Galbraith (1962) led the way with his critique of the 'affluent society' and his advocacy of redressing poverty, reducing over-consumption and redressing social imbalance, rather than maximizing production. The pioneering report by the Club of Rome then demonstrated the unsustainable character of prevailing rates of economic growth (Meadows et al. 1972). Prominent mainstream economists Ezra Mishan (1967), Steffan Linder (1970) and Tibor Scitovsky (1976) added their voices to the growing chorus of concern about the downsides of economic growth, emphasizing its adverse 'externalities', the 'harried' society it creates and its 'joyless' character. Psychologists (e.g. Wachtel 1983), political commentators (e.g. Seabrook 1988) and thoughtful writers from business backgrounds (e.g. Bronk 1998) chimed in. Similar expressions of concern have continued to reverberate among leading social and environmental scientists, given extra strength and urgency by the concerns about climate change. There is ongoing momentum in social movements for a 'steady state economy' (Czech 2013; Daly 2014; Washington 2016) and 'degrowth' (Demaria et al. 2013), but the ideology of 'growthmania' remains deeply entrenched. Economic growth (or just 'growth') is regarded as self-evidently desirable: to argue against it is like trying to claim that less is more. To get traction for the view that distribution is at least equally important is still an uphill struggle.

A hallmark of pervasive ideologies is that they produce minds closed to views that challenge prevailing beliefs. Their deep-seated character may have stopped some potential readers of this book from getting this far. Anthropologists Peter Benson and Stuart Kirsch have coined the term 'politics of resignation' to refer to the ongoing acceptance of corporate capitalism, notwithstanding the social harms and inequalities that corporations may cause. They ask: 'How do we unlock the folded arms of cynicism?' and suggest paths to developing counter-ideologies based on 'a critique of capital that focuses on industry's avoidance of ethical responsibilities for the harms caused to humans and environments' (Benson & Kirsch 2010: 475). More generally, the antidote to ideologies is critique that relates directly to experience and current concerns. We know that reactionary nationalism, racism and sexism are socially divisive and inimical to achieving collective solutions to societal problems. We know that infinite economic growth is not a sustainable process, especially when associated with continuing global population growth, deletion of non-renewable resources and the (mis)use of the physical environment as a receptacle for the waste products of a consumerist society. Ideologies like these that are out of kilter with observable reality are vulnerable to challenge. Confronting conservative ideologies is integral to progressive social change.

Interests

What makes the contestation of ideologies more complex is its relationship to interests. The ideological contest does not occur on a level playing field. Those defending the status quo typically have greater wealth and power than do critics imbued with egalitarian goals. The connection of ideology to interests is therefore particularly pertinent to economic inequality. A wealthy stratum that has prospered under the current political economic arrangements has both the commitment and resources to frustrate distributional shifts that would threaten its economically privileged position. Some enlightened capitalists and high-wealth individuals, recognizing challenges to their legitimacy, redistribute part of their overall income through philanthropic donations, as noted in chapter 10. More commonly, however, those with control of vast wealth put their energies and funding into processes that defend existing political economic arrangements. Corporate propaganda has become a massive operation (Beder 2006), seeking to put a congenial face on the institutions and processes that have been increasing economic inequalities.

As inequalities of income and wealth gaps widen within nations, *concentrations of political economic power* further increase the difficulties of effecting a change of direction. Thus, circular and cumulative causation processes operate to strengthen the interests opposed to progressive reforms and to increase the resources at their disposal in resisting change. It is not all one-way traffic, though. Corporate capitalism, since the global financial crisis, does not enjoy the public support it previously had. The self-rewarding behaviour of CEOs is widely condemned. The growing divisions between the 1% and a broad middle-income group in the rich nations are a source of growing tension. The term 'trickle-down' economics has come to have almost universally pejorative connotations, seen as a hollow promise by vested interests and their apologists. In a rapidly changing world, the alignment of currently powerful interests and ideologies is contestable. Much depends on how these tensions play out in the shifting relationships within and between political economic institutions.

Institutions

As shown in Figure 13.2, most prominent among the institutions in which the interests contend are the state, corporate capital, trade unions, NGOs, think tanks, the media, educational institutions and the economics profession. How much attention is given to either redressing or reinforcing inequality depends on their internal structures and strategies.

The state is the institution with the greatest formal power, having the legislative capacity, resources and authority to either

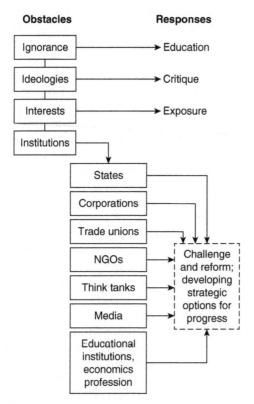

Figure 13.2 Analysing obstacles to progress

foster or limit inequality. There is a widespread reformist assumption that the state's power could be used for restructuring the economic system on a more equitable basis. The three preceding policy-oriented chapters of this book may be read as implying that this is so. Indeed, because more people would gain from progressive redistribution than would lose from it, you might think that democratic states would normally adopt some such reformist agenda. That they frequently do not do so in practice suggests that they may be captive of disproportionately influential interest groups. As the sociologist C. Wright Mills wrote, 'Across the bargaining tables of power, the bureaucracies of business and government face one another, and under the tables their myriad feet are interlocked in wonderfully complex ways' (2002 [1951]: 79).

It is useful to regard the modern state as shaped by three factors: the influence of democracy, the nature of bureaucracy and the interests of capital (Stilwell 2011). The influence of democracy varies. Some states pay it little heed in practice and dictatorships normally suspend any semblance of it. However, most nation states periodically seek renewal of governmental legitimacy through elections. Therein lies a significant impetus for egalitarian reform. Green, labour and social democratic parties recurrently promise, if elected, to deliver policies for progressive redistribution or even pre-distribution, as discussed in chapters 10 and 11. However, policies also depend on the nature of the public sector bureaucracy, whose managers shape much of what happens – or doesn't happen in practice. Elements of inertia are ever-present, creating obstacles to major policy shifts. The institutions of capital also directly shape political possibilities. Indeed, it is from the intertwining of the institutions of government and corporate capital that the most intractable obstacles to reform emanate. The prevailing economic conditions also constrain what is politically feasible. If capital accumulation slows and economic crises occur, an incumbent government is likely to be held responsible and may be ousted at the next general election. Because of the complex interactions between these democratic, bureaucratic and capitalist elements – and the corresponding shifting power relationships – the state is always and everywhere an arena of struggle.

For those who favour a more egalitarian society, these features of the state pose both opportunities and challenges. We know that, historically, important redistributive reforms have been achieved, albeit unevenly and never with any guaranteed permanence. We also know that it is difficult to get governments to sustain their commitments to progressive reforms when faced with a backlash from more conservative interests. It is not enough to posit liberal, progressive reforms based on rational argument about public policies (Berry 2017: 299). As J.K. Galbraith (1974) emphasized, the 'emancipation of the state' from the influence of powerful corporations is a necessary accompaniment, if not a precondition. Echoing Marx, Ben Selwyn's call for the 'reabsorption of the state by society' (2017: 130) has a similar ring. On this reasoning, the task for progressives is to try to 'subordinate and transform capitalist social relations' by social ownership of production and extension of democratic control, driving an agenda based on identified community needs and cooperative bottom-up decision processes.

The institutions of *corporate capital* have a different programme. Their enormous economic resources and collective class interest align in maintaining the capitalist status quo and the systemic inequalities embedded in its class relations. This is not to deny the recurrence of some elements of disunity. Inter-corporate competition may impede the development of a collective strategy for corporate capital. Senior corporate executives may be so preoccupied with seeking a 'healthy bottom line' for their businesses – or maximizing their own personal remuneration packages – that they have little time for the pursuit of broader class concerns. Some avenues for coordination do exist, however. On a global scale, organizations like the World Economic Forum provide institutional focal points for the reinforcing capitalist class interests. More locally, business and employers' associations exist primarily for this purpose. Overall, celebrating the 'creation of wealth', supporting the interests of capital and addressing common class problems are the priorities, strengthening the nexus between conservative economic ideas, economic interests and their political expression. The pursuit of a more egalitarian society is not on this agenda.

The institutions of labour, most obviously *trade unions*, exercise some countervailing power and have significant capacity to contribute to creating a more egalitarian society. Like the institutions of capital, they are not necessarily 'all on the same page'. Short-term sectional interests may dominate over the broader class interests of labour and concerns about international inequalities. Peak councils of unions provide focal points for attempts at coordination within individual nations, while the International Labour Organization gives some international reach. The potential for coordination is yet greater when trade unions operate in tandem with parliamentary labour parties – acting, respectively, as the 'industrial' and 'political' wings of the labour movement. Historically, the institutions of organized labour developed to defend and extend workers' rights, to improve wages and working conditions. The last few decades have been more problematic for unions, however, as noted in chapter 7. They have been on the defensive in the advanced capitalist countries, trying to deal with their declining coverage of the workforce and facing particular difficulties when faced with legislation and regulations intended to reduce their power and influence. There is, nevertheless, still plenty of action by organized labour, as Verity Burgmann (2016) emphasizes. The rise of developing nations as major manufacturing centres also creates possibilities for the growth of organized labour, with potentially game-changing implications.

NGOs are also important institutional players. Although lacking the industrial muscle of organized labour, they have been effective in mobilizing activists in numerous campaigns involving issues of inequality and social injustice. Among the many NGOs trying to mount pressure for progressive reforms are movements for development assistance in poorer countries, human rights, environmental protection, improved housing affordability, indigenous land rights and gender equality. Many have become notably proficient in using social media for their purposes. When working in tandem with political parties at the radical edge of social democracy, they are an important feature of modern political life. Social movement politics is different from class-based politics but can be effective in fostering and popularizing progressive ideas. As the slogan says: 'Be realistic, demand the impossible.'

Think tanks have also become important features of the modern institutional landscape. They sometimes link with progressive social movements. More typically, however, they serve the interests of high-wealth individuals and the institutions of corporate capital, producing information and perpetuating values conducive to the capitalist class interests that provide their funds. For this purpose, they disseminate pro-business information and 'free market' ideology through schools and the media, and lobby decision-makers in government and other public institutions. They make common cause in this endeavour with right-wing economists, including some of senior professional standing, whom they invite to speak at their public events. Their concern with economic inequality is usually to warn against policies that might reduce it.

Other institutions, such as the *media*, have a more ambivalent character. Some journalists, acting in the best traditions of the 'fourth estate', have a proclivity to dig the dirt on people and institutions who act in ways that violate a broader public interest. Yet the major media proprietors, most notoriously Rupert Murdoch, have prodigious personal wealth and power. Not surprisingly, they usually see their interests aligned with those of the dominant class in capitalism. Meanwhile, the proliferation of social media opens up great opportunities for information dissemination serving progressive social purposes, although the relentless influence of commercialization in social media – including the harvesting and sale of 'big data' – signals other, less attractive tendencies.

Educational institutions also have contradictory characteristics. Formally, they exist for the development of people's personal skills and for the expansion and dissemination of knowledge. Yet their administrators commonly emphasize 'safe' aspects that conform to the status quo. In schools and colleges, this takes the form of an instrumental approach to education that emphasizes 'teaching to the test' and prioritizes career preparation rather than the development of critical and creative personal attributes. In universities, the traditional commitment to teaching and research 'in the pursuit of knowledge wherever it may lead' now sits awkwardly in an academic environment when corporate funding is an increasingly important influence. It is in this context that we need to pay particular attention to the teaching of economics.

Where does the economics profession stand?

The members of the economics profession play a part in each of the 'four I's' discussed in this chapter. When teaching in schools and universities, *ignorance* is the ostensible target. The curriculum reflects the influence of particular *ideologies* that shape particular ways of seeing the economy. Like any profession, economists' *interests* are influenced by the broader structures of society in which they operate. The ideas they promulgate permeate *institutions* ranging from governments to corporations, think tanks and the media. The key question, in relation to economic inequality, is whether the economics profession is part of the problem or part of the solution.

Generalizing about a whole profession can be hazardous. There are normally diverse members with different priorities, methods and views, even if they mostly agree on general principles and procedures. Some would say this is what professions are for: to identify and enforce some degree of cohesion, if not conformity. In the case of the economics profession, the dominant theoretical orthodoxy produces its own distinctive element of cohesion. Notwithstanding some claims to 'internal heterodoxy', the mainstream of the profession operates with a fundamentally neoclassical 'worldview'. This emphasizes efficiency rather than equity, markets rather than social regulation, allocation rather than distribution, and equilibrium rather than cumulative imbalance. Like most orthodoxies, economics can accommodate some deviance (and deviants). Making minor variations to the standard theories can be a means by which individual economists establish their personal reputations. Yet a strong central tendency persists, especially in the teaching of successive generations of students. The core course components – macroeconomics and microeconomics – embody a particular set of assumptions and judgements. They reproduce an orthodoxy which mainstream economists themselves are proud to call 'thinking like an economist' (Mankiw 2015).

Some illustrations of this mainstream economic orientation have appeared in preceding chapters: marginal productivity theory, human capital theory and a posited efficiency–equity trade-off, for example. There are yet more general tendencies that have the effect of marginalizing the analysis of inequality. These are: (1) the economic discipline's primary concern with economic output; (2) its dominant focus on individual buyers and sellers in markets; and (3) the assessment of economic welfare in terms of individual utility. Together, these characteristics of economic orthodoxy create an implicit bias in the profession against the analysis and redress of inequality.

Defining the principal economic problem in terms of the amount of goods and services produced and consumed embodies a particular view of how economic progress is to be assessed. When Adam Smith wrote *The Wealth of Nations* in 1776, it was a reasonable presumption because most people had very modest material living conditions, by current standards. More production and consumption were key elements in increasing Britain's prosperity, if not the wealth of nations in general. Nearly two and a half centuries after Smith, however, to retain the primary emphasis on economic growth as the principal focus for economic analysis is more questionable. In the developing nations, the economic growth priority has continuing traction, of course, because producing more goods may improve the material wellbeing of people previously living in poverty – if only the distribution problem could be solved. In the more affluent nations, however, the situation has changed because two other aspects now loom larger: creating a more equitable distribution and a sustainable economy that does not ruin the planet. As previously poor countries proceed further along the path of economic growth, these latter concerns become yet more global in character. Undaunted, most mainstream economists, both in their teaching and in their public policy pronouncements, continue to focus their analyses on economic growth rather than on more equitably sharing its fruits or balancing economic goals with ecological concerns. The dominant impact of the last global financial crisis, unfortunately, has been to reinforce this bias.

A second, related feature of economic orthodoxy is its emphasis on markets. Mainstream economists sometimes claim that markets have an egalitarian character, saying that, because the personal characteristics of buyers and sellers (race or gender, for example) are irrelevant to market transactions, only money matters. In an ideal world, that might be so. In the real world, however, systemic connections between market power, class, race and gender create inequitable outcomes (Darity, Hamilton & Stewart 2015). People from disadvantaged socio-economic positions typically have few resources with which they can enter into market transactions, whereas the more economically advantaged groups have greater purchasing power and more impact on market supply and prices. They also have a greater ability to set the rules of the game. Markets seldom operate according to the textbook principles of 'perfect competition' anyway: elements of monopoly, collusion and corruption commonly intrude, as noted in chapter 6. Thus, while mutually advantageous exchanges may occur in markets, no reliably egalitarian forces shape market outcomes in practice. The cherished economic principle of 'consumer sovereignty' – seeing consumers' choices as the principal driver of what is produced – ignores the obvious fact that some consumers enter the market with much more spending power than others. Implicitly, it gives more weight to the preferences of rich consumers rather than poor ones. To the extent that consumer sovereignty rules, it is the sovereignty of the rich over the poor.

Third, the mainstream economists' conception of wellbeing, based on individual utility, deflects attention away from concerns about distributional equity. The concept of surplus appears in mainstream economic theory mainly in relation to the utility of individuals. When consumers derive more utility from a product than they have to pay for it, the economists say that a 'consumer surplus' exists. Extending this sort of reasoning, the economists say that expanding markets create more opportunities for increasing people's welfare through 'gains from trade'. Who gets those gains, however, does not get comparable attention because the economists' models usually take the existing distribution of income and wealth as given. Moreover, because the mainstream economists are resistant to making interpersonal utility comparisons, there is no adequate conceptual framework for making welfare judgements, other than in trivial ('Pareto-efficient') cases when all people are better off following a policy change. Such instances are very rare in the real world: even the reduction of barriers to trade normally creates losers as well as winners. Nor is there any professionally accepted basis for aggregating individuals' utilities into a social welfare function. Thus, mainstream economics has great difficulty in judging whether any economic outcome is desirable or not. In effect, there is no sound basis for conceiving of societal interests and societal wellbeing. Economic analysis of distributional considerations is a casualty of this sort of disciplinary construction, deemed 'better left to the political realm' (Cook 2018: 32).

Challenges to this dominant economic orthodoxy have been many and varied (e.g. Keen 2001; Schroeder & Chester 2014; Weeks 2014; Fullbrook 2016; Legge 2016; Thornton 2017; Reardon, Madi & Cato 2018). Some critics say that the economics profession acts like a priesthood defending orthodox dogma; others concede good intent but attribute the biases to professional socialization. There is innovation within mainstream economics, but the core of the discipline exhibits remarkable continuity and there is little interest in the views of political economists who challenge its underlying assumptions. When senior figures in the economics discipline speak publicly of the purpose of their analyses, they sometimes reflect on their wish to contribute to social progress, even to the reduction of economic inequality. However, notwithstanding possibly laudable social intentions, nothing fundamental changes. Economic growth retains its place as the assumed engine for the creation of jobs, redress of poverty and raising living standards. Markets, perhaps with a little fine-tuning, remain the preferred means to that end. Welfare judgements, including judgements about how public policies affect inequality (and they all do, of course), remain hobbled by the long-standing methodological individualism. This is business as usual.

Can the economics profession recognize its fundamental limitations and change in ways that put emphasis on real-world economics? Can the profession as a whole follow the lead of scholars like Atkinson, Piketty and Stiglitz who have embraced the need to focus on inequality and its redress? While there are some glimmers of hope, the particular construction of mainstream economics, including its separation from other social sciences, is deeply problematic and inhibits change. The practitioners of political economy and interdisciplinary social science need to step into the breach by offering alternative ways of understanding the world and changing it for the better (as argued more fully in Stilwell 2019).

Conclusion

This chapter has considered obstacles to the redress of inequality: ignorance, ideology, interests and institutions. Inertia is the product of these impediments. Indeed, inertia is always the normal state of affairs unless strategic interventions are effective in driving change. Happily, for each of the four obstacles, strategic responses are possible. Thus:

- The impediments to equity that arise from ignorance and ideologies can be countered through education, critique and exposure of the vested interests defending the status quo.
- Proposals for progressive reform can be driven by social movements, trade unions, intellectuals and activists, working in, through and sometimes against existing institutions.
- The biases of mainstream economics that currently impede serious engagement with equity can be challenged by critical political economic analysis.

The famous call for 'pessimism of the intellect, optimism of the will' indicates the need to face up squarely to obstacles while seeking pathways for progress. This chapter has focused on the former aspect; the final chapter of this book takes up the latter theme, seeking a way forward.

14

Making the Future

We live at a time of change and challenge. Indeed, ain't that always so? What matters is is not the existence of changes and challenges, but their nature. This book has considered the current national, international and global changes and challenges from a 'political economy of inequality' perspective. Engaging with these big issues can be daunting, but it can also be empowering. Many people, disheartened by the short-sighted and class-biased policies of their governments, are looking for alternatives. Some, alarmed and even angered by the growing concentration of incomes and wealth within the top 1%, see the need for a radical break with the past. Indeed, the current groundswell of public concern about economic inequality is probably on a scale unseen for over half a century.

This concluding chapter explores the prospects, seeking to develop a forward-looking perspective. Its structure is according to three Cs – challenges, contradictions and changes – before drawing conclusions. The big questions are 'What happens if nothing is done?' and 'What could realistically be done?' to make a difference. Answering them requires careful assessment of the conditions conducive to change and the agents that can drive it. Facing the future is always important, but this is not primarily a process of forecasting. More fundamentally, it is a pro-active process of making the future.

Challenges

The emphasis throughout this book has been on the inequalities in the distribution of incomes and wealth that compound the social, economic and environmental problems of modern capitalism. As we have seen, inequality is a major feature of the world economy and its constituent nations and regions. There are striking contrasts between the conditions in which rich and poor people live, both within individual countries and between countries.

Is it an achievable goal to have greater equality? In countries where neoliberal policies have been in vogue in recent decades, the political will to tackle economic inequality has been conspicuously lacking. Governments have implicitly formulated their policy priorities on the assumption that economic inequalities produce higher productivity and faster economic growth. The arguments and evidence in this book indicate reasons to question this assumption. As we have seen, extreme inequalities in income and wealth tend to undermine economic productivity, efficiency and stability. They also undermine social cohesion, public health, political legitimacy and environmental responsibility. This impedes the development of a more generally contented society. Because people's happiness also depends on what they have relative to other people, substantial economic inequality is a recipe for widespread social discontent even when average incomes are rising. Combined with the challenge of climate change and the need for more economic stability, these issues constitute powerful reasons for changing track to a more equitable, secure and sustainable social order.

There are signs of hope. Recognizing that national and international differences in the extent of economic inequality are the product of human intention and collective efforts, rather than an inexorable or 'God-given' process, can indeed be empowering. Because countries of similar economic prosperity vary considerably in their extent of inequality – compare the USA and Sweden, for example – we know that there is no absolute economic impediment to greater equality, even within the constraints of capitalism. Similarly, we can draw positive lessons from looking at history. Because significant strides towards the redress of inequalities occurred in many developed nations during the three decades following the Second World War, we know that a degree of egalitarianism is achievable through public policy processes, given the political will. This can generate 'politics against pessimism'

(Higgins & Dow 2013). It can provide ammunition and reasons for hope when faced with conservative ideologies, inequitable uses of power and regressive policy practices. Political economic conditions continuously change: the purpose of progressive politics is to steer the change along preferred paths. Tackling the drivers of inequality is part of this process.

Contradictions

Because extreme economic inequalities cause problems, they also create a need for solutions and generate agents of change. This is a dialectical process, driven by contradictory elements. Four are particularly significant in the current era, each opening up potential for challenge and change.

First, there is a deep-seated tension embedded in the relationship between wages and profits in capitalist economies. Wages tend to be simultaneously too low and too high because they play a dual role: as a cost of production and as a source of demand. This creates what Marxist political economists call the contradiction between the production and realization of surplus value. It has been manifest in the advanced capitalist countries in the last decade as prolonged wage stagnation, inhibiting the growth in demand for goods and services. Thus, inequality – at least that aspect of it arising from low wages – is proving problematic for capital. This is not to say that we can expect a flurry of businesses offering higher wages to their workers, only that there is a tense and uncertain, rather than stable, macroeconomic situation. As Jim Stanford writes, 'If the wealthy are capturing a larger surplus than ever, but consuming or wasting it rather than reinvesting it, the political stability of the system, in addition to its economic vitality, will be threatened' (2017: 75–6). It is a source of ongoing political economic instability.

Second, the capital accumulation process causes greater social and environmental stresses. The interests of capital, driving the process of commodification and the spread of markets, are dominant, while the quest for profit takes priority over other concerns with social stability, equality and sustainability. The exploitation of nature is a particularly pervasive tendency. Yet, as the economic system bumps up against ecological constraints, it is evident that these arrangements are not sustainable in the longer term. The rapid growth in countries like China and India, while narrowing international economic inequalities, compounds this economy–nature contradiction. Laudable efforts to reduce the damaging effects are evident, particularly in China (Matthews 2017), but the challenge is enormous, especially because of growing internal economic inequalities. Ultimately, it is inconceivable that the whole world's population could live at the material standards of the affluent Anglo and Euro nations – or of newly affluent Chinese and Indians – without massive environmental impacts.

A third tension is geopolitical, centred on the changing balance of political economic power between the largest nation states. The dominant feature here is the decline of US hegemony and the spectacular political economic ascendancy of China as a world power, with Russia retaining an awkward presence in ongoing conflicts. Other nations with less clout are sometimes battlegrounds for the superpower contests, variously seeking alignments – or disengagement – so that their people may live in relative peace and prosperity in an increasingly dangerous world. The politics of this situation are volatile, reminding us that the future is never a simple projection of the past.

Finally, and most directly arising from the trends in economic inequality, there is the political tension between the 1% and the rest of the society, both within nations and worldwide. Throughout the capitalist nations, and most especially in the USA, the increasing concentration of economic gains has few positive trickle-down effects for the middle-income group. Figure 14.1 over the page shows how the authors of *The World Inequality Report 2018* (Alvaredo et al. 2018) depict the inequalities underlying this tension. The upper line extrapolates the growth in the wealth share of the the top 1%. The lower part of the figure shows the yet faster expected growth of the wealth share held by the top 0.1% and the 0.01%. If this extrapolation from recent trends is borne out in practice, the result will be even more extreme concentration of wealth in an elite and a tiny elite-within-an-elite. The losers are likely to be a broad 'middle' stratum of people between the top 1% and the bottom 50%. The second line in the figure shows the projected decline in their share. It presages a divergence of interests between the elite and a broad upper-middle-income group: one may surmise that the latter may not be so supportive of the status quo in future, perhaps even seeing its interests more closely aligned with the bottom 50%, whose small share in total wealth is roughly constant. If so, the disproportionate concentration of wealth at the very top creates potential for a different politics.

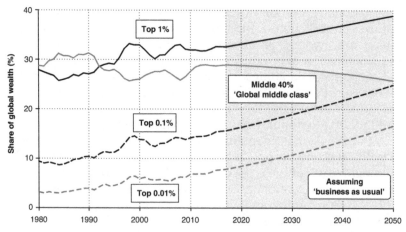

Figure 14.1 Changing shares of wealth: actual and projected, 1980–2050
Source: Alvaredo et al. (2018).

Piketty has turned his attention increasingly to these political implications, looking at the 'interplay between long-run inequality and the changing structure of political cleavages' (2018: 2). He has tried to assess the changing basis of support for political parties identifying as on the left or right. Traditionally, different types of party have had distinctive alignments, the left drawing support from low- to middle-income groups seeking social change, while the right's support comes from the middle- to upper-income groups wanting to maintain the status quo. Piketty's analysis of voting patterns reveals a shift, particularly on the left, where votes now come more from people who have had higher education. He labels these the 'Brahmin left' and notes the difficulty of unifying them with the more traditionally working-class base of left parties. Meanwhile, parties on the right draw their support from people running businesses or imbued with those business values – what Piketty calls the 'merchant right'. Although the two categories are not mutually exclusive, Piketty's thesis is that this 'structural evolution can contribute to explaining rising inequality and the lack of a democratic response to it, as well as the rise of populism (as low education, low income voters feel abandoned)' (2018: 3). It is an interesting way of explaining why increased polarization of incomes and wealth in most countries has not led to stronger electoral performance by parties of the left. On Piketty's reasoning, it would tend to do so if the growing numbers of tertiary-educated voters added to the more traditional working-class vote, but this is evidently not the usual case. Instead, the voters without tertiary education have become more 'free floating' in their electoral behaviour, increasingly swinging towards populist and demagogic candidates.

Looked at from a political economic perspective, these four contradictions have a common element: growing inequality, fuelling economic volatility, environmental stress, international tension and political instability.

Changes: three scenarios

How will the contradictions play out over the decades ahead? We cannot know, of course, because the future is inherently uncertain. However, rather than resorting to the usual trite conclusion that 'only time will tell', it is useful to consider three possible scenarios. The authors of *The World Inequality Report 2018* (Alvaredo et al. 2018) use this device too, but base their scenarios on specific statistical assumptions. What follows here is different. It is based on the exercise of different political judgements – broadly, conservative, liberal and radical – that influence how we might be faring, say, fifteen years from now.

First, consider a world in which the inequalities between rich and poor have continued to widen as they did during the first two decades of this century. People in positions of power have ignored exhortations to 'mind the gap': nothing significant has happened to address the trends and problems described in this book. Indeed, the distribution of incomes, wealth and power has become increasingly lop-sided in the affluent nations, and even more so in all the BRICs and most of the poor nations. The global capitalist class is even more closely integrated, creating a prodigious concentration of political economic power. The exercise of this power, compounded by collusive and sometimes corrupt practices, makes any vestigial egalitarian social ambitions seem quite unrealistic. The widespread use of tax havens to hide wealth and reduce tax liabilities undercuts the capacity of governments to redistribute incomes and wealth for beneficial public purposes. The climate change problem is biting hard, disrupting regional economies and increasing the flows of refugees – but to where? Neoliberal ideologies continue to provide a self-justifying rationale for wealthy elites avoiding responsibilities for less fortunate people or the public interest. Resentment against the plutocracy is commonly expressed but there is much support for policies of austerity targeted at the poor. Not for the first time in human history, the fallout from frustrated economic aspirations has turned on even more disadvantaged people. The resulting social conflicts among the middle and lower social strata recurrently spill over into violence, resulting in ever-increasing resources allocated for social control. A new edition of George Orwell's dystopian novel *Nineteen Eighty-Four* experiences a surge of sales…

A second scenario exhibits similar tensions but more ameliorative responses. Some formerly poor nations have significantly closed the gap between their prosperity and the rich nations but their own distributional inequalities have intensified, creating the economic basis for more acute class conflict. The richer nations have low rates of economic growth and continuing wage stagnation, stumbling along with sporadic and half-hearted attempts at modest redistribution. Liberal democratic governments alternate with right wing populist regimes. International summits make some progress in setting targets for dealing with climate change but many national governments fail to comply in practice: 'too little, too late' is the phrase on everyone's lips. Some reform-inclined governments try to make the tax system rather more progressive – together with recurrent rhetoric about the need to crack down on tax cheats. However, their successors usually reverse the reforms – while referring to their own policies as 'reforms' too. Nothing significant has happened to create structural changes that would create greater equity and a clearer path to sustainability, although it is often thought to be a good idea. People have grown generally more disillusioned with mainstream politics as the gulf between promises and outcomes becomes increasingly evident. Policies of 'muddling through' look increasingly inadequate, but that is all that is on offer.

The third scenario is one in which more radical change occurs. In the wealthier countries, a broad stratum of working-class and middle-income people say, in effect, enough is enough. Strong movements motivated by egalitarian goals have increasing influence and had significant success with introducing radical reforms. A number of countries introduce basic income as a comprehensive means of poverty prevention, setting a floor to inequality. Countries that did not previously have inheritance taxation introduce it, while those that already had it have significantly raised the tax rate or rolled it together with income tax, as proposed by an obscure political economist in a book published in 2019. Land tax, substantially funding better provision of public housing and infrastructure, has also become a common feature of public finance in many countries. Some nations impose pay ratios that limit the gap between high and low incomes, including caps on CEO salaries. Most have equity assessments and distributional accounts linked to their budgets. All the affluent nations commit to the target of allocating at least 1% of their national income to international development aid – and actually give it. Poorer countries take the opportunity to introduce basic income schemes too, using the increased development assistance for this purpose and for improving their social infrastructure. In both rich and poor countries, activists and political leaders are committed to making a full transition to democratic eco-socialist arrangements, fundamentally changing the capitalistic political economic priorities that most people had passively accepted before. The triple goals of equity, stability and sustainability are universally agreed. Countries that try to be 'free riders' by not doing their share to reduce climate change are subject to global economic sanctions. People are starting to take the goal of a steady-state economy seriously. Social conflicts continue in various forms – and there is vigorous public debate – but there is also sufficient commonality of purpose to provide a basis for progress towards an equitable and sustainable future.

Making a difference

The prospect of the third of these options coming to fruition requires a coherent view of how progressive social change can occur. For this purpose, we can identify four essential elements in an effective, activist politics: critique, vision, strategy and organization (as posited in Stilwell 2000, 2015, 2016). First, a critique of the existing situation is necessary in order to identify what is wrong and needs to be changed. Second, proponents of change need a vision of the alternative situation to which they aspire. Third, there must be a political strategy for getting from the present to that preferred future. Finally, there must be effective organization to implement that transition.

Critique is the obvious starting point. All concerned citizens have the capacity to identify what they regard as the key social problems of the era and the underlying causes that need redress. The current extremes of income and wealth inequality are already stimulating this sort of critique, although, as ever, people perceive the nature of the problems in different ways. Political economists can play an important role in helping to develop serious intellectual engagement and critical analysis. I hope this book helps.

Vision is also something in which everyone can healthily engage. It is a process of imagining an ideal society or, at least, a better state of affairs than currently exists. More than that, it is a systematic process of working out what is desirable and attainable. Great thinkers throughout literary and political history have made memorable contributions. A vision of a more egalitarian society is not difficult to develop, taking account of what we now know about human behaviour and wellbeing, technological possibilities and environmental constraints. For people in highly unequal societies, looking at the Nordic nations is not a bad place to start.

Strategy is the third key ingredient of social change. People sharing the same critique and vision may strongly disagree about the best way forward. Indeed, strategy has always been the most difficult issue for political activists. There are alternative avenues (not to mention alleys, crossroads and dead-end streets) on the journey. Debating the relative merits of alternative strategies and making collective choices is seldom easy. Wrestling with the bigger questions about reform and revolution – and much else besides – is yet tougher going. Should we be putting all our eggs in the basket of reform to deal with inequality? If so, which of those policies listed in chapters 10–12 of this book should have priority? Should we be thinking of more long-term social transformation? If so, how can the reforms build momentum for those more fundamental changes?

Posing such questions leads into considering the appropriate forms of *organization*. Some see this as a matter of building and working with political parties that have egalitarian values and the capacity to create momentum for progressive social change. The trade union movement, representing the interests of labour, can also be a player. Some people may choose to act through NGOs and faith-based institutions in pursuit of radically redistributive goals. Many social movements are committed to gender equality, indigenous rights, fighting poverty, tax justice and other egalitarian aims. Some such organizations often have only a local focus, but others, such as Oxfam, Greenpeace, the World Social Forum and the Fight Inequality Alliance seek influence and global impact. To call for a 'party of the 99%' (Di Muzio 2015: ch. 6) is laudable but almost certainly unrealistic, given the diverse histories, social bases and concerns. However, it is equally clear that success can only come from a cooperative, multi-pronged effort by a range of progressive organizations working together.

On each of these four aspects of social change, there are inevitably diverse views. The obstacles discussed in the preceding chapter are ever-present. Yet the march of circumstances creates new opportunities as well as threats. When economic stresses intensify, political responses usually follow. If knowledge has a role in driving enlightened public policy, there is further basis for hope. While global progress on all fronts is hard to envisage, some countries can take the lead with progressive policy initiatives; laggards can be shamed. A new paradigm and new political practices can emerge. Then we may achieve something close to the ideal of an equitable society that does not lock some people into vicious cycles of disadvantage while others monopolize the cumulative benefits of privilege.

Conclusion

The observations in this final chapter indicate principles, practices and prospects for progressive political economic change. The priorities for radical reforms listed on the following page point to possible focal points for progress. While not comprehensive, this is an indicative agenda.

Powerful institutions with a vested interest in perpetuating economic inequalities will always resist changes like these. Pervasive populist beliefs, expressed in mantras like 'greed is good', 'markets know best', 'leave business to businesspeople' and 'trickle-down economics', also impede better understanding of how social wealth is created and shared. However, all such institutions, interests and ideologies are open to challenge and change. That is why it is important to develop principles, analyses, strategies and policies aimed at reducing economic inequalities. Onward . . .

Priorities for Radical Reform

- *Public investment* to enhance equality of opportunity, social mobility and quality of life.

  A *strong public sector*, providing universal access to good-quality public education, public health, public housing, public transport and public child care.

- *Unconditional basic income* to provide an income floor, eliminate poverty and create opportunities for creative and socially usefully work.

  Basic income to be at a level sufficient to lift all persons out of poverty, according to the standards of each nation.

- *Progressive, broadly based tax* to fund public sector investment, basic income and other social programmes.

  Progressive rates of tax on incomes from capital, land and labour, inheritance and large gifts; capture of more economic surplus through land tax, resources tax and capital gains tax; emphasis on reduction of tax evasion.

- *Economic and industry planning* to spread gains from productivity and transition to a more equitable and sustainable economy.

  Coordinating incomes policies, macroeconomic, regional, industrial, labour, education and environmental policies.

- *Constraints on corporate power* to reduce the intensity of the processes driving inequality.

  Caps on CEO salaries; development of cooperative enterprises; extending the commons.

- *International compact for a new egalitarian world order* to tackle inequality, enhance economic insecurity and facilitate global sustainability.

  Provision of development assistance directed to funding public investment and provision of basic income.

  Development of distributional accounts, setting new indicators of economic performance, nationally and globally.

Progress in these six broad policy areas could contribute to the reduction of economic inequality within and between nations.

References

Abdih, Y. & Danninger, S. (2017) *What Explains the Decline in the US Labour Share of Income? An Analysis of State and Industry Level Data*, International Monetary Fund, IMF Working Paper WP/17/167, *https://www.imf.org/en/Publications/WP/Issues/2017/07/24/What-Explains-the-Decline-of-the-U-S-45086*.

Alvaredo, F. (2011) A Note on the Relationship Between Top Income Shares and the Gini Coefficient, *Economic Letters*, 110, pp. 274–7.

Alvaredo, F., Chancel, L., Piketty, T, Saez, A. & Zucman, G. (2018) *World Inequality Report 2018*, Belknap Press, Cambridge, MA.

Anderson, T. (2013) *Aid: Is It Worth it? Communicating New Research on Timor-Leste*, Swinburne Press, Hawthorn, Victoria.

Anderson, T. (2015) *Land and Livelihoods in Papua New Guinea*, Australian Scholarly Publishing, North Melbourne.

Argyrous, G. (2011) Economic Evolution and Cumulative Causation, in Argyrous, G. & Stilwell, F. (eds), *Readings in Political Economy: Economics as a Social Science*, 3rd edition, Tilde University Press, Melbourne, pp. 144–51.

Atkinson, A. (2015) *Inequality: What Can Be Done?*, Harvard University Press, Cambridge, MA.

Baland, J.-M., Bardhan, P. & Bowles, S. (eds) (2007) *Inequality, Cooperation, and Environmental Sustainability*, Russell Sage Foundation, New York.

Barnes, T. (2015) *Informal Labour in Urban India: Three Cities, Three Journeys*, Routledge, Abingdon.

Bartolini, S. & Saraccino, F. (2015) The Dark Side of Chinese Growth: Declining Social Capital and Well-Being in Times of Economic Boom, *World Development*, 74, pp. 333–51.

Bateman M. (2010) *Why Doesn't Microfinance Work? The Destructive Rise of Local Neoliberalism*, Zed Books, London.

Becker, G.S. (1964) *Human Capital: An Empirical and Theoretical Analysis*, University of Chicago Press, Chicago.

Becker, G.S. (1971) *The Economics of Discrimination*, University of Chicago Press, Chicago.

Beckles, H. (2013) *Britain's Black Debt: Reparations for Caribbean Slavery and Native Genocide*, University of West Indies Press, Kingston.

Beckles, H. (2016) Rise to Your Responsibility, *Africology: The Journal of Pan African Studies*, 9:5, August, pp. 8–14.

Beder, S. (2006) *Free Market Missionaries: The Corporate Manipulation of Community Values*, Earthscan, London.

Benson, P. & Kirsch, S. (2010) Capitalism and the Politics of Resignation, *Current Anthropology*, 51:4, pp. 459–83.

Berg, G. & Ostry, J. (2011) *Inequality and Sustainable Growth: Two sides of the same coin?* International Monetary Fund, IMF Staff Discussion Note SDN/11/08, *https://www.imf.org/external/pubs/ft/sdn/2011/sdn1108.pdf*.

Berg, G., Ostry, J. & Zettlemeyer, J. (2012) What Makes Growth Sustained? *Journal of Development Economics*, 98:2, pp. 149–66.

Berry, M. (2017) *Morality and Power: On Ethics, Economics and Public Policy*, Edward Elgar, Cheltenham.

Bezemer, D. & Hudson, M. (2016) Finance is Not the Economy, *Progress*, Winter, pp. 3–32.

Blau, F.D. & Kahn, L.M. (2017) The Gender Wage Gap: Extent, Trends, and Explanations, *Journal of Economic Literature*, 55:3, pp. 789–865.

Block, S. (2016) *Income Inequality and the Intracorporate Pay Gap*, MSCI ESG Research Inc, April, *https://www.msci.com/documents/10199/b94ae705-4d36-49e5-8873-b6fe42fdd291*.

Bloomberg (2018) Bloomberg Billionaires Index, *https://www.bloomberg.com/billionaires/*.

Bose, S. (2013) Teaching Poverty: A Poverty of Perspective, *International Journal of Pluralism and Economics Education*, 4:4, pp. 371–86.

Bourgignon, F. (2015) *The Globalization of Inequality*, Princeton University Press, Princeton.

Bowles, S. (2012) *The New Economics of Inequality and Redistribution*, Cambridge University Press, Cambridge.

Bregman, R. (2016) Why Garbagemen Should Earn More Than Bankers, Evonomics, *http://evonomics.com/why-garbage-men-should-earn-more-than-bankers/*.

Bronk, R. (1998) *Progress and the Invisible Hand: The Philosophy and Economics of Human Advance*, Warner Books, London.

Bryan, D. & Rafferty, M. (2018) *Risking Together: How Finance is Dominating Everyday Life in Australia*, Sydney University Press, Sydney.

Bulman, D., Eden, M. & Nguyen, H. (2014) Transitioning from Low-Income Growth to High-Income Growth: Is There a Middle-Income Trap?, World Bank Group, Washington, DC, Policy Research Working Paper WPS 7104, *http://documents.worldbank.org/curated/en/229641468180252928/pdf/WPS7104.pdf*.

Burgmann, V. (2016) *Globalization and Labour in the Twenty-First Century*, Routledge, Abingdon.

Burroughs, J.E. & Rindfleisch, A. (2002) Materialism and Well-Being: A Conflicting Values Perspective, *Journal of Consumer Research*, 29:3, pp. 348–70.

Cahill, D. (2014) *The End of Laissez Faire: On the Durability of Embedded Neoliberalism*, Edward Elgar, Cheltenham.

Cahill, D., Cooper, M., Konings, M. & Primrose, D. (eds) (2018) *The Sage Handbook of Neoliberalism*, Sage, London.

Cahill, D. & Konings, M. (2017) *Neoliberalism*, Polity, Cambridge.

Carroll, W.K. (2010) *The Making of a Transnational Capitalist Class: Corporate Power in the 21st Century*, Zed Books, London and New York.

Causa, O. & Hermansen, M. (2017) Income Redistribution Through Taxes and Transfers Across OECD Countries, OECD Economics Department Working Papers 1453, *http://dx.doi.org/10.1787/bc7569c6-en*.

Cederman, L.-E., Weidmann, N.B. & Gleditsch K.S. (2011) Horizontal Inequalities and Ethnographic Civil War: A Global Comparison, *American Political Science Review*, 105:3, pp. 487–9.

Chang, H.-J. (2002) *Kicking Away the Ladder: Development Strategy in Historical Perspective*, Anthem Press, London.

Chetty, R., Hendren, N., Jones, M.R. & Porter, S.R. (2018) Race and Economic Opportunity in the United States: An Intergenerational Perspective, US Census Bureau, April, *https://scholar.harvard.edu/hendren/publications/race-and-economic-opportunity-united-states-intergenerational-perspective*.

Chossudovsky, M. (1997) *The Globalisation of Poverty: Impacts of World Bank and International Monetary Fund Reforms*, Third World Network, Penang.

Christophers, B. (2018) Intergenerational Inequality: Labour Capital and Housing Through the Ages, *Antipode*, 50:1, pp. 101–21.

Clark, J.B. (1965 [1899]) *The Distribution of Wealth*, Augusta M. Kelley, New York.

Clark, A.E. & Oswald, O.J. (1996) Satisfaction and Comparison Income, *Journal of Public Economics*, 1:3, pp. 359–81.

Cleary, P. (2016) *Trillion Dollar Baby: How Norway Beat the Oil Giants and Won a Lasting Fortune*, Black Inc., Melbourne.

Cohen, A.J. & Harcourt, G.C. (2003) Whatever Happened to the Cambridge Capital Theory Controversies? *Journal of Economic Perspectives*, 17:1, pp. 199–214.

Colander, D. (2014) Piketty's Policy Proposals: How to Effectively Redistribute Income, *Real-World Economics Review*, 69, pp. 161–6.

Collins, C., Asante-Muhammed, D., Nieves, E. & Hoxie, J. (2016) The Ever-Growing Gap: Without Change, African-American and Latino Families Won't Match White Wealth for Centuries, Institute for Policy Studies, Washington, *https://ips-dc.org/wp-content/uploads/2016/08/The-Ever-Growing-Gap-CFED_IPS-Final-1.pdf*.

Collins, J. (2016) Putting a Mining Tax Back on the Agenda, *Australian Options*, 84, Spring, pp. 12–15.

Collins, J. (2018) Class Antagonism and Landed Property in the Functional Distribution of Income in Australia, *Journal of Australian Political Economy*, 81, pp. 144–65.

Constantini, M., Meco, I. & Paradiso, A. (2018) Do Inequality, Unemployment and Deterrence Affect Crime over the Long Run? *Regional Studies*, 52:4, pp. 558–71.

Cook, E. (2018) The Great Marginalization: Why Twentieth-Century Economists Neglected Inequality, *Real-World Economics Review*, 83, pp. 20–34.

Corlett, A. (2017) Diverse Outcomes: Living Standards by Ethnicity, Resolution Foundation, *https://www.resolutionfoundation.org/app/uploads/2017/08/Diverse-outcomes.pdf*.

Credit Suisse (2017a) Global Wealth Databook 2017, *http://publications. credit-suisse.com/tasks/render/file/index.cfm?fileid=FB790DB0-C175-0E07-787A2B8639253D5A*.

Credit Suisse (2017b) Global Wealth Report 2017, *http://publi cations.credit-suisse.com/tasks/render/file/index.cfm?fileid=12DF FD63-07D1-EC63-A3D5F67356880EF3*.

Czech, B. (2013) *Supply Shock: Economic Growth at the Crossroads and the Steady State Solution*, New Society Publishers, Gabriola Island.

Daly, H. (2014) *From Uneconomic Growth to the Steady State Economy*, Edward Elgar, Cheltenham.

Darity, W.A., D. Hamilton & Stewart, J.B. (2015) A Tour de Force in Understanding Intergroup Inequality: An Introduction to Stratification Economics, *Review of Black Political Economy*, 42, pp. 1–6.

Das, R.J. (2017) *Marxist Class Theory for a Skeptical World*, Brill, Leiden.

Dauvergne, P. (2016) *Environmentalism of the Rich*, MIT Press, Cambridge, MA.

Davidson, K. (1987) J.K.Galbraith and the New Economics, *Sydney Morning Herald*, 24 February.

de Graff, J. Wann, D. & Naylor, T.H. (2005) *Affluenza: The All-Consuming Epidemic*, 2nd edition, Barrett-Koehler Publications, San Francisco.

de Neve, J.-A. & Powdthavee, N. (2016) Income Inequality Makes Whole Countries Less Happy, *Harvard Business Review*, January 12, *https://hbr.org/2016/01/income-inequality-makes-whole-countries-less-happy*.

Dean, H. (2009) Critiquing Capabilities: The Distractions of a Beguiling Concept, *Critical Social Policy*, 29:2, pp. 261–73.

Dean, M. & Broomhill, R. (2018) From Post-Fordism to 'Post-Holdenism': Responses to Deindustrialisation in Playford, South Australia, *Journal of Australian Political Economy*, 81, Winter, pp. 166–92.

Deighton, A. (2015) *The Great Escape: Health, Wealth and the Origins of Inequality*, Princeton University Press, Princeton.

Demaria, F., Schneider, F., Sekulova, F. & Martinez-Alier, J. (2013) What is Degrowth? From an Activist Slogan to a Social Movement, *Environmental Values*, 22, pp. 191–215.

Di Muzio (2015) *The 1% and the Rest of Us: A Political Economy of Dominant Ownership*, Zed Books, London.

Doran, C. (2007) A Militarised Neoliberalism: Australia's Economic Policy in Iraq, *Journal of Australian Political Economy*, 59, June, pp. 48–73.

Dorling, D. (2017) *The Equality Effect: Improving Life for Everyone*, New Internationalist Publications, Oxford.

Dow, G. (2002) Neoliberal Corporate Governance of the Australian Economy, in Bell, S. (ed.), *Economic Governance and Institutional Dynamics*, Oxford University Press, Melbourne, pp. 53–75.

Drache, D., Rioux, M. & Longhurst, P. (2016) The Rich List: The Global Corporate Race to be Number One, Transnational Law Institute, TLI Think! Paper 12/2016, Kings College, London, *http://www.ieim. uqam.ca/IMG/pdf/12_-_drache_rioux_longhurst_vf.pdf*.

Dunkley, G. (2016) *One World Mania: A Critical Guide to Free Trade, Financialization and Over-Globalization*, Zed Books, London.

Easterlin, R.A. (1974) Does Economic Growth Improve the Human Lot? Some Empirical Evidence, in David, P.A. & Reder, M.W. (eds), *Nations and Households in Economic Growth: Essays in Honour of Moses Abromovitz*, Academic Press, New York, pp. 89–126.

Easterlin, R.A. (1985) Will Raising Incomes for All Increase the Happiness for All? *Journal of Economic Behaviour and Organisation*, 27, pp. 35–47.

Elsenhans, H. & Babones, S. (2017) *BRICS or Bust? Escaping the Middle-Income Trap*, Stanford University Press, Stanford.

Engel, S. (2010) *The World Bank and the Post-Washington Consensus in Indonesia and Vietnam: Inheritance of Loss*, Routledge, London.

England, P. (2005) Gender Inequality in Labour Markets: The Role of Motherhood and Segregation, *Social Politics*, 12:2, pp. 264–88.

Ennis, S, Gonzaga, P. & Pike, C (2017) Inequality: A Hidden Cost of Market Power, *http://www.oecd.org/daf/competition/inequality-a-hidden-cost-of-market-power.htm*.

Errasti, A., Bretos, I. & Nunez, A. (2017) The Viability of Cooperatives: The Fall of the Mondragon Cooperative Fagor, *Review of Radical Political Economy*, 49:2, pp. 191–7.

Fanon, F. (1961) *The Wretched of the Earth*, Grove Press, New York.

Federici, S. (2004) *Caliban and the Witch: Women, the Body and Primitive Accumulation*, Autonomedia, Brooklyn, NY.

Federici, S. (2012) *Revolution at Point Zero: Housework, Reproduction and Feminist Struggle*, PM Press, Oakland, CA.

Felipe, J., Abdon, A. & Kumar, U. (2012) Tracking the Middle-Income Trap: What Is It, Who Is in It, and Why?, Levy Economics Institute of Bard College, Working Paper 715, *http://www.levyinstitute.org/pubs/wp_715.pdf*.

Ferguson, C. (1969) *The Neoclassical Theory of Production and Distribution*, Cambridge University Press, Cambridge.

Ferguson, J. (2009) The Uses of Neoliberalism, *Antipode*, 41:S1, pp. 168–84.

Fine, B. (2010) *Theories of Social Capital: Researchers Behaving Badly*, Pluto Press, London.

Fioramonti, L. (2013) *Gross Domestic Problem: The Politics Behind the World's Most Powerful Number*, Zed Books, London and New York.

Fioramonti, L. (2017) *The World After GDP: Politics, Business and Society in the Post-Growth Era*, Polity, Cambridge.

FitzRoy, F. & Jin, J. (2018) Basic Income and a Public Job Offer: Complementary Policies to Reduce Poverty and Unemployment, *Journal of Poverty and Social Justice*, 26:2, pp. 191–206.

Fix, B. (2018) A Hierarchy Model of Income Distribution, York University, Working Papers in Capital as Power2018/02, *http:// www.capitalaspower.com/2018/04/2018-02-fix-a-hierarchy-model-of-income-distribution/*.

Flynn, L.B. & Schwartz, H.M. (2017) No Exit: Social Reproduction in an Era of Rising Income Inequality, *Politics and Society*, 45:4, pp. 471–503.

Folbre, N. (2012) The Political Economy of Human Capital, *Review of Radical Political Economics*, 44:3, pp. 281–92.

Folbre, N. (2018) The Care Penalty and Gender Inequality, in Averett, A.L., Argys, L.M. & Hoffman, S.D. (eds), *The Oxford Handbook of Women and the Economy*, Oxford University Press, Oxford and New York, pp. 749–66.

Foster, J.B. (2008) The Financialization of Capitalism and the Crisis, *Monthly Review*, 62:5, *https://monthlyreview.org/2008/04/01/the-financialization-of-capital-and-the-crisis/*.

Frank, R.H. (1999) *Luxury Fever: Why Money Fails to Satisfy in an Era of Success*, The Free Press, New York.

Frank, R.H. (2016) *Success and Luck: Good Fortune and the Myth of Meritocracy*, Princeton University Press, Princeton.

Frank, R.H. & Cook, P. (1995) *The Winner-Take-All Society*, The Free Press, New York.

Fraser, N. (1995) From Redistribution to Recognition? *New Left Review*, 212, July–August, pp. 68–93.

Fraser, N. & Honneth, A. (2003) *Redistribution or Recognition? A Political-Philosophical Exchange*, Verso, London.

Frey, B. & Stutzer, A (2002) *Happiness and Economics*, Princeton University Press, Princeton.

Frey, C.B. & Osborne, M. A. (2013) *The Future of Employment: How Susceptible are Jobs to Computerisation?*, Oxford Martin School Working Papers.

Friedman, M. (1962) *Capitalism and Freedom*, University of Chicago Press, Chicago

Friedman, M. & Friedman, R. (2011 [1980]) The Power of the Market, in Argyrous, G. & Stilwell, F. (eds) *Readings in Political Economy: Economics as a Social Science*, 3rd edition, Tilde University Press, Melbourne, pp. 77–81.

Fullbrook, E. (2016) *Narrative Fixation in Economics*, WEA and College Publications, Bristol and London.

Gaffney, M. & Harrison, F. (1994) *The Corruption of Economics*, Shepheard-Walwyn, London.

Galbraith, J.K. (1962) *The Affluent Society*, Penguin, Harmondsworth.

Galbraith, J.K. (1974) *Economics and the Public Purpose*, Andre Deutsch, London.

Galbraith, J.K. (1976) Economics as a System of Belief, in Wheelwright, E.L. & Stilwell, F. (eds), *Readings in Political Economy*, Vol. 2, ANZ Book Co., Sydney, pp. 32–43.

Galbraith, J.K. (2014a) Kapital in the Twenty-first Century, *Dissent Magazine*, 61:2.

Galbraith, J.K. (2014b) Unpacking the Fundamental Law, *Real-World Economics Review*, 69, pp. 145–8.

Gasparini, L. & Lustig, N. (2011) The Rise and Fall of Income Inequality in Latin America, Society for the Study of Economic Inequality, ECINEQ WP 2011–213, *http://www.ecineq.org/milano/wp/ecineq2011-213.pdf*.

George, H. (1879) *Progress and Poverty*, Schalkenbach Foundation, New York.

George, S. (2004) *Another World is Possible If...*, Verso, London.

Gibiliso P. (2014) *The Politics of Disability: A Need for a Just Society Inclusive of People with Disabilities*, CCB Publishing, British Columbia.

Gilens, M. (2005) Inequality and Democratic Responsiveness, *Public Opinion Quarterly*, 39:5, pp. 778–96.

Gittins, R. (2010) *The Happy Economist: Happiness for the Hard Headed*, Allen & Unwin, Sydney.

Gleeson-White, J. (2014) *Six Capitals*, Allen & Unwin, Sydney.

Godechot, O. (2017) Inequality: A Piketty et al. Moment in the Social Sciences, *Economic Sociology*, 19:1, pp. 1–6.

Gore, C. (2017) Late Industrialisation, Urbanisation and the Middle-Income Trap: An Analytical Approach to the Case of Vietnam, *Cambridge Journal of Regions, Economy and Society*, 10, pp. 35–57.

Griffiths, P. (2011) The Creation of Income Inequality: The Impact of Government Policies in Australia and Other OECD Economies, paper presented to the International Conference on Income Distribution Theory and Policy, Xhongnan University, China.

Hamermesh, D. (2011) *Beauty Pays: Why Attractive People Are More Successful*, Princeton University Press, Princeton.

Hamilton, C. (2003) *Growth Fetish*, Allen & Unwin, Sydney.

Hamilton, C. & Denniss, R. (2005) *Affluenza: Why Too Much is Never Enough*, Allen & Unwin, Sydney.

Hardin, G. (1968) The Tragedy of the Commons, *Science*, 162:3858, pp. 1243–8.

Harrington, M. (1976) *The Twilight of Capitalism*, Simon & Schuster, New York.

Hart-Landsberg, M. (2018) The US is a World Leader in Income and Wealth Inequality, MR Online, 30 June, *https://mronline.org/2018/06/30/the-u-s-is-a-world-leader-in-income-and-wealth-inequality/*.

Harvey, D.M. (1982) *The Limits to Capital*, Basil Blackwell, Oxford.

Harvey, D.M. (1989) *The Urban Experience*, Basil Blackwell, Oxford.

Harvey, D.M. (2010) *A Companion to Marx's Capital*, Verso, London and New York.

Harvey, D.M. (2014) *Seventeen Contradictions and the End of Capitalism*, Profile Books, London.

Hauser, O.P. & Norton, M.I. (2017) (Mis)perceptions of Inequality, *Current Opinion in Psychology*, 18, pp. 21–5.

Hayek, F.A. (1944) *The Road to Serfdom*, University of Chicago Press, Chicago.

Hayter, T. (1981) *The Creation of World Poverty*, Pluto Press, London.

Headey, B. & Wooden, M. (2004) The Effect of Wealth and Income on Subjective Well-being and Ill-being, *The Economic Record*, 80:S1, pp. 24–33.

Hein, E., Dunhaupt, P., Alfageme, A. & Kulesza, M. (2017) Financialisations and Distribution in the US, the UK, Spain, Germany, Sweden and France – Before and After the Crisis, Institute for International Political Economy, Berlin, Working Paper 85/2017, *http://www.ipe-berlin.org/fileadmin/downloads/Papers_and_Presentations/IPE_WP_85.pdf*.

Herrera, D. (2004) Mondragon: A For-Profit Organisation That Embodies Catholic Social Thought, *Review of Business*, 25:1, pp. 56–68.

Hewitson, G.J. (1999) *Feminist Economics: Interrogating the Masculinity of Rational Economic Man*, Edward Elgar, Cheltenham and Northampton.

Hickel, J. (2016) The True Extent of Global Poverty and Hunger: Questioning the Good News Narrative of the Millennium Development Goals, *Third World Quarterly*, 37:5, pp. 749–67.

Higgins, W. & Dow, G. (2013) *Politics against Pessimism: Social Democratic Possibilities since Ernst Wigforss*, Peter Lang, Bern.

Hill, J. (2014) *Good Times, Bad Times: The Welfare Myth of Them and Us*, Bristol University Press, Bristol.

Hirsch, F. (1977) *Social Limits to Growth*, Routledge & Kegan Paul, London.

Hobsbawm, E. (1962) *The Age of Revolution: Europe 1789–1984*, Weidenfeld & Nicolson, London.

Hodgson, G.M. (2014) What is Capital? Economists and Sociologists Have Changed Its Meaning: Should It be Changed Back?, *Cambridge Journal of Economics*, 38, pp. 1063–86.

Holmberg, S. & Schmitt, M. (2016) The Milton Friedman Doctrine is Wrong: Here's How to Rethink the Corporation, Evonomics, *http:// evonomics.com/milton_friedman_doctrine_wrong_heres_rethink_cor poration/*.

Holt, R. & Pressman, S. (2009) Nicholas Kaldor and Cumulative Causation: Public Policy Implications, in Berger, S. (ed.), *The Foundations of Non-Equilibrium Economics: The Principle of Circular and Cumulative Causation*, Routledge, Abingdon, pp. 77–90.

Holtwell, F (2018) Bringing Back the Lucas Plan, *The Bullet*, 6 April, Socialist Project California, *https://socialistproject.ca/2018/04/brin ging-back-the-lucas-plan/*.

Hunt, E.K. (1990) *Property and Prophets: The Evolution of Economic Institutions and Ideologies*, 6th edition, Harper & Row, New York.

ILO (2016) *World Employment Social Outlook 2016: Transforming Jobs to End Poverty*, International Labour Organization Office, Geneva.

Islam, M.R., Madsen, J.B. & Doucouliagos, H. (2018) Does Inequality Constrain the Power to Tax? Evidence from the OECD, *European Journal of Political Economy*, 52, March, pp. 1–17.

Jacobs, J. (1969) *The Economy of Cities*, Random House, New York.

Jerven, M. (2015) *Africa: Why Economists Got It Wrong*, Zed Books, London.

Jessop, B. (2016) *The State: Past, Present, Future*, Polity, Cambridge.

Jones, C.I. & Clenow, P.J. (2016) Beyond GDP? Welfare across Countries and Time, *American Economic Review*, 106:9, pp. 2426–57.

Karabarbounis, L. & Neiman, B. (2013) The Global Decline of the Labour Share, *Quarterly Journal of Economics*, 129:1, pp. 61–103.

Kaur, R. & Wahlberg, A. (eds) (2014) *Identity, Inequity and Inequality in India and China: Governing Difference*, Routledge, Oxford and New York.

Keen, S. (2001) *Debunking Economics: The Naked Emperor of the Social Sciences*, Pluto Press, Sydney.

Kentikelinis, A.E, Stubbs, T.H & King, L.P. (2016) International Monetary Fund Conditionality and Development Policy Space, *Review of International Political Economy*, 23:4, pp. 543–82.

Kelsey, J. (2015) *The FIRE Economy*, Bridget Williams Books, Wellington.

Keynes, J.M. (2018 [1936]) *The General Theory of Employment, Interest, and Money*, Palgrave Macmillan, Basingstoke.

King, J. (2017) The Literature on Piketty, *Review of Political Economy*, 29:1, pp. 1–17.

Klein, N. (2007) *The Shock Doctrine*, Allen Lane, New York.

Komlos, J. (2018) Employment in a Just Economy, *Real-World Economics Review*, 83, pp. 87–98.

Kraus, M.W., Rucker, J.M. & Richeson, J.A. (2017) Americans Misperceive Racial Economic Inequality, *Proceedings of the National Academy of Sciences, https://doi.org/10.1073/pnas.1707719114.*

Krugman, P. (2011) Oligarchy, American Style, *New York Times*, 4 November.

Kunst, J.R., Fischer, J., Sidanius, R. & Tomsen, L. (2017) Preferences for Group Dominance Track and Mediate the Effects of Macro-level Socio-economic Inequalities and Violence across Societies, *Proceedings of the National Academy of Science*, 114:21, *http://www.ncbi.nlm.nih.gov/pmc/articles/PMC5448166/.*

Kuttner, R. (1984) *The Economic Illusion: False Choices Between Economic Prosperity and Social Justice*, Houghton Mifflin, New York.

Kuznets, S. (1955) Economic Growth and Income Inequality, *American Economic Review*, 45, March, pp. 1–28.

Lane, R. (1991) *The Market Experience*, Cambridge University Press, New York.

Lane, R. (2000) *The Loss of Happiness in Market Democracies*, Cambridge University Press, New York.

Layard, R. (2003) *Happiness: Has Social Science a Clue?* Lionel Robbins Memorial Lectures, London School of Economics, London.

Layard, R. (2005) *Happiness: Lessons for a New Science*, Penguin, New York.

Layard, R., Mayraz, G. & Nickell, S. (2008) The Marginal Utility of Income, *Public Economics*, 92:8, pp. 1846–57.

Legge, J.M. (2016) *Economics Versus Reality*, Transaction Publishers, New Brunswick and London.

Leigh, A. (2013) *Battlers and Billionaires*, Black Inc. Redback, Melbourne.

Leigh, A. (2015) *The Luck of Politics: True Tales of Disaster and Outrageous Fortune*, Black Inc., Collingwood, Victoria.

Leiman, M. (2010) *The Political Economy of Racism*, Haymarket, Chicago.

Lewis, R. (2014) Britain's Black Debt: Review, *Journal of Interdisciplinary History*, 44:3, Winter, pp. 420–1.

Lind, M. (2017) The New Class War, *American Affairs Journal*, 1:2, *https://americanaffairsjournal.org/2017/05/new-class-war/.*

Linder, S. (1970) *The Harried Leisure Class*, Columbia University Press, New York.

Lord, B. (2015) Can Philanthropy Fix our Inequality? Inequality.org, 24 January, *Inequality.org/great-divide/philanthropy-solution-inequality/.*

Lipton, M (1977) *Why Poor People Stay Poor: Urban Bias in World Development*, Harvard University Press, Cambridge, MA.

Lustig, R. (2017) *The Hacking of the American Mind: The Science behind the Corporate Takeover of our Bodies and our Brains*, Avery, New York.

Mankiw, N.G. (2015) *Principles of Economics*, Cenage Publishing, Boston.

Marmot, M. (2016) *The Health Gap: The Challenge of an Unequal World*, Bloomsbury Publishers, London.

Maslow, A. (1943) A Theory of Human Motivation, *Psychological Review*, 50:4, pp. 370–96.

Mason, P. (2016) *Postcapitalism: A Guide to our Future*, Penguin Books, Harmondsworth.

Matthews, J. (2017) *Global Green Shift: When Ceres Meets Gaia*, Anthem Press, London.

McCain, R.A. (2017) *Approaching Equality: What Can be Done about Wealth Inequality?* Edward Elgar, Cheltenham.

McDonald, K. & Marshall, S. (eds) (2010) *Fair Trade, Corporate Accountability and Beyond: Experiments in Globalising Justice*, Ashgate, Farnham.

McMichael, P. (2008) *Development and Social Change: A Global Perspective*, 4th edition, Pine Ford Press, Thousand Oaks, CA.

Meadows, D., Meadows, M., Randers, J. & Behrens, W.W., III (1972) *The Limits to Growth*, Earth Island, London.

Mijs, J. (2018) Inequality is Getting Worse but Fewer People Than Ever are Aware of It, The Conversation, 3 May, *http://theconversation. com/inequality-is-getting-worse-but-fewer-people-than-ever-are-aware-of-it-76642*.

Mikler, J. (2018) *The Political Power of Global Corporations*, Polity, Cambridge.

Mikucka, M., Sarracino, F. & Dubrow, J.K. (2017) When Does Economic Growth Improve Life Satisfaction? *World Development*, 97, pp. 447–59.

Milanovic, B. (2012) Global Income Inequality by the Numbers: In History and Now – An Overview, World Bank, Washington, DC, Policy Research Working Paper WPS 6259, *http://documents.world bank.org/curated/en/959251468176687085/pdf/wps6259.pdf*.

Milanovic, B. (2016) *Global Inequality: A New Approach for the Age of Globalization*, Belknap Press, Cambridge, MA.

Milanovic, B. (2018) Europe's Curse of Wealth, *Social Europe*, 6 June, *http://socialeurope.eu/europes-curse-of-wealth/*.

Mills, C.W. (2002 [1951]) *White Collar: The American Middle Class*, Oxford University Press, Oxford.

Mineau, D. (2016) How Economists Duped Us into Attacking Capitalism Instead of Parasitic Rent-Seeking, Evonomics, *http://evonomics.com/economists_duped_attacking_capitalism/*.

Mishan, E.J. (1967) *The Costs of Economic Growth*, Praeger, New York and Washington.

Mishel, L. & Schieder, J. (2017) CEO Pay Remains High Relative to the Pay of Typical Workers and High-Wage Earners, Economic Policy Institute, 20 July, *https://www.epi.org/publication/ceo-pay-remains-high-relative-to-the-pay-of-typical-workers-and-high-wage-earners/*.

Mitchell, W. & Watts, M. (2002) Restoring Full Employment: The Job Guarantee, in Carlson, E. & Mitchell, W. (eds), *The Urgency of Full Employment*, Centre for Applied Economic Research, UNSW Press, Sydney, pp. 95–114.

Mohan, G. (2013) Beyond the Enclave: Towards a Critical Political Economy of China and Africa, *Development and Change*, 44:6, pp. 1255–72.

Mohan, G., Lampert, B., Tan-Mullins, M. & Chen, D. (2014) *Chinese Migrants and Africa's Development: New Imperialists or Agents of Change?* Zed Books, London.

Morgan, J. (2015) Piketty's Calibration Economics: Inequality and the Dissolution of Solutions? *Globalizations*, 12:5, pp. 803–23.

Murray, G. (2012) *Financial Elites and Transnational Business: Who Rules the World?* Edward Elgar, Cheltenham.

Myrdal, G. (1944) *An American Dilemma: The Negro Problem and Modern Democracy*, Harper, New York.

Myrdal, G. (1957) *Economic Theory and Undeveloped Regions*, Methuen, London.

Myrdal, G. (1968) *Asian Drama: An Inquiry into the Poverty of Nations*, Pantheon, New York.

Nelson, C., Pike, D. & Ledvinka, G. (2015) *On Happiness: New Ideas for the Twenty-First Century*, UWA Publishing, Crawley.

Nozick, R. (1974) *Anarchy, State and Utopia*, Basil Blackwell, Oxford.

Nunn, A. & White, P. (2016) The IMF and a New Politics of Inequality? *Journal of Australian Political Economy*, 78, Summer, pp. 186–231.

Nurske, R. (1952) *Some Aspects of Capital Accumulation in Underdeveloped Countries*, Commemoration lecture, National Bank of Cairo.

Nussbaum, M. (2000) *Women in Human Development: The Capabilities Approach*, Cambridge University Press, Cambridge and New York.

Obeng-Odoom, F. (2015a) Africa: On the Rise, but to Where?, *Forum for Social Economics*, 4:3, pp. 234–50.

Obeng-Odoom, F. (2015b) The Social, Spatial, and Economic Roots of Urban Inequality in Africa: Contextualizing Jane Jacobs and

Henry George, *American Journal of Economics and Sociology*, 74:3, pp. 550–86.

Obeng-Odoom, F. (2017) The Myth of Economic Growth in Africa, *Review of African Political Economy*, 44, pp. 466–75.

Obeng-Odoom, F. (2018) Transnational Corporations and Urban Development, *American Journal of Economics and Sociology*, 77:2, March, pp. 447–510.

OECD (2016) *The Productivity–Inclusiveness Nexus*, OECD, Paris, 1–2 June, *https://www.oecd.org/global-forum-productivity/library/The-Pro ductivity-Inclusiveness-Nexus-Preliminary.pdf*.

OECD (2018) *Taxation of Household Savings*, OECD Tax Policy Studies, No. 25, Paris, *https://read.oecd-ilibrary.org/taxation/taxation-of-house hold-savings_9789264289536-en#page1*.

Okun, A. (1975) *Equality and Efficiency: The Big Trade-off*, Brookings Institute, Washington, DC.

O'Rourke, P.J. (1998) *Eat the Rich: A Treatise on Economics*, Pan Macmillan, Sydney.

Østby, G. (2016) Rural–Urban Migration, Inequality and Urban Social Disorder: Evidence from African and Asian Cities, *Conflict Management and Peace Science*, 33:5, pp. 491–515.

Ostrom, E. (1990) *Governing the Commons: The Evolution of Institutions for Collective Action*, Cambridge University Press, Cambridge.

Ostry, J.D., Berg, A. & Tsangarides, N. (2014), *Redistribution, Inequality and Growth*, IMF Staff Discussion Note SDN/14/02, *https://www.imf.org/external/pubs/ft/sdn/2014/sdn1402.pdf*.

Ostry, J.D., Loungani, P. & Furceri, D. (2016) Neoliberalism: Oversold? *Finance and Development*, June, pp. 38–41.

Panayotakis, C. (2011) *Rethinking Scarcity: From Capitalist Economic Inefficiency to Economic Democracy*, Pluto Press, London.

Parr, A. (2013) *The Wrath of Capital: Neoliberalism and Climate Change Politics*, Columbia University Press, New York.

Peck, J. & Tickell, A (2007) Conceptualizing Neoliberalism, Thinking Thatcherism, in Leitner, H., Peck, J. & Sheppard, E.S. (eds), *Contesting Neoliberalism: Urban Frontiers*, Guilford Press, New York and London, pp. 26–50.

Peetz, D. (2018) The Labour Share, Power and Financialisation, *Journal of Australian Political Economy*, 81, Winter, pp. 33–51.

Pen, J. (1971) *Income Distribution: Facts, Theories, Policies*, Praeger, New York.

Petach, L. (2017) Politics, Preferences and Prices: The Political Consequences of Inequality, *Real-World Economics Review*, 80, pp. 2–13.

Philipsen, D. (2015) *The Little Big Number: How GDP Came to Rule the World and What to Do about It*, Princeton University Press, Princeton and Oxford.

Piekalkiewicz, M. (2017) Why Do Economists Study Happiness?, *Economic and Labour Relations Review*, 60:1, pp. 3–22.

Pigou, A.C. (1928) *The Economics of Welfare*, 3rd edition, Cambridge University Press, Cambridge.

Piketty, T. (2014a) *Capital in the Twenty-first Century*, trans. A. Goldhammer, Harvard University Press, Cambridge, MA.

Piketty, T. (2014b) Dynamics of Inequality: Interview, *New Left Review*, 85, pp. 105–16.

Piketty, T. (2015) Putting Distribution Back at the Centre of Economics: Reflections on *Capital in the Twenty-First Century*, *Journal of Economic Perspectives*, 29:1, pp. 67–88.

Piketty, T. (2016) Panama Papers: Act Now. Don't Wait for Another Crisis, *Guardian*, 10 April, *https://www.theguardian.com/commentis free/2016/apr/09/panama-papers-tax-havens-thomas-piketty/*.

Piketty, T. (2018) Brahmin Left vs Merchant Right: Rising Inequality and the Structure of Political Conflict, World Inequality Working Paper, *http://piketty.pse.ens.fr/files/Piketty2018. pdf*.

Piketty, T., Saez, E. & Zucman, G. (2018) Distributional National Accounts: Methods and Estimates for the United States, *Quarterly Journal of Economics*, 133:2, pp. 553–609.

Plant, J. (1967) The Origins and Development of Australia's Policy Posture at the United Nations Conference on International Organization, San Francisco, 1945, unpublished PhD thesis, Australian National University.

Pressman, S. (2015) *Understanding Piketty's Capital in the Twenty-first Century*, Routledge, London.

Rasch, R. (2017) Measuring the Middle Class in Middle-Income Countries, *Forum for Social Economics*, 46:4, pp. 321–36.

Rawls, J. (1971) *A Theory of Justice*, Harvard University Press, Cambridge, MA.

Reardon, J., Madi, M. & Cato, M. (2018) *Introducing a New Economics: Sustainable and Progressive*, Pluto Press, London.

Redden, G. (2017) John Howard's Investor State: Neoliberalism and the Rise of Inequality in Australia, *Critical Sociology*, 43, December, pp. 1–16.

Rogers, J. & Streek, W. (2009) *Works Councils, Consultation, Representation and Cooperation in Industrial Relations*, University of Chicago Press, Chicago and London.

Rodgers, D. (2018) The Uses and Abuses of Neoliberalism, *Dissent*, January, pp. 2–9.

Roll, E. (1973) *History of Economic Thought*, Faber & Faber, London.

Rooke, D. (2018) *One Last Spin*, Scribe, Melbourne and London.

Roth, S. (2018) Capital's Share of Income is Way Higher Than You Think, *Evonomics*, *http://evonomics.com/capitals-share-of-income-is-way-higher-than-you-think/*.

Rothwell, J. (2016) Make Elites Compete: Why the 1% Earn So Much and What to Do About It, Brookings, 25 March, *https://www.brookings.edu/research/make-elites-compete-why-the-1-earn-so-much-and-what-to-do-about-it/*.

Ruccio, D. (2011) *Development and Globalisation: A Marxian Class Analysis*, Routledge, Abingdon.

Ruccio, D. (2016) Financial Globalization and Inequality, *http://anticap.wordpress.com/2016/10/10/financial-globalization-and-inequality/*.

Russell, B. (1917) *Roads to Freedom*, George Allen & Unwin, London.

Ryan-Collins, Lloyd, T. & McFarlane, L. (2017) *Rethinking the Economics of Land and Housing*, Zed Books, London.

Schneider, M., Pottinger, J. & King, J. (2016) *The Distribution of Wealth: Growing Inequality?* Edward Elgar, Cheltenham.

Schofield-Georgeson, E. (2018) Regulating Executive Salaries and Reducing Pay Disparities: Is Pay Disclosure the Answer? *Journal of Australian Political Economy*, 81, Winter, pp. 96–120.

Schroeder, S. (2015) *Public Credit Rating Agencies: Increasing Capital Investment and Lending Stability in Volatile Markets*, Palgrave Macmillan, New York.

Schroeder, S. (2018) Just How Fragile is the Australian Economy? *Australian Options*, 87, pp. 18–22.

Schroeder S. & Chester, L. (eds) (2014) *Challenging the Orthodoxy*, Springer, Heidelberg.

Schumpeter, J.A. (1934) *The Theory of Economic Development: An Inquiry into Profits, Capital, Interest and the Business Cycle*, Harvard University Press, Cambridge, MA.

Schumpeter, J.A. (1942) *Capitalism, Socialism and Democracy*, Harper & Row, New York.

Scitovsky, T. (1976) *The Joyless Economy: An Inquiry into Human Satisfaction and Consumer Dissatisfaction*, Oxford University Press, Oxford.

Seabrook, J. (1988) *The Race for Riches: The Human Costs of Wealth*, Marshall Pickering, Basingstoke.

Selwyn, B. (2017) *The Struggle for Development*, Polity, Cambridge.

Sen, A.K. (1980) Equality of What? In Harrison, R. (ed.), *Rational Action: Studies in Philosophy and Social Science*, Cambridge University Press, Cambridge, pp. 115–32.

Sen, A. (1999) *Commodities and Capabilities*, 2nd edition, Oxford University Press, Delhi and New York.

Serr, K. (2017) Understanding Poverty: Conceptualising Human Needs, in Serr, K. (ed.), *Thinking about Poverty*, 4th edition, The Federation Press, Sydney, pp. 90–107.

Sharp, R. & Broomhill, R. (2002) Budgeting for Equality: The Australian Experience, *Feminist Economics*, 8:1, pp. 25–47.

Sheil, C. (2014/15) Piketty's Political Economy, *Journal of Australian Political Economy*, 74, pp. 19–37.

Shields, J. (2005) Setting the Double Standard: Chief Executive Pay the BCA Way, *Journal of Australian Political Economy*, 56, December, pp. 299–324.

Shiva, V. (2005) *Earth Democracy: Justice Sustainability and Peace*, Zed Books, London.

Sklair, L. (2001) *The Transnational Capitalist Class*, Wiley-Blackwell, Oxford.

Smith, A. (1976 [1776]) *An Inquiry into the Nature and Causes of the Wealth of Nations*, University of Chicago Press, Chicago.

Smith, N. (2007) Nature as Accumulation Strategy, *Socialist Register*, 43, pp. 16–36.

Soldatic, K. & Sykes, D. (2017) Poverty and People with a Disability, in Serr, K. (ed.), *Thinking about Poverty*, 4th edition, The Federation Press, Sydney, pp. 189–207.

Spies-Butcher, B., Paton, J. & Cahill, D. (2012) *Market Society: History, Theory, Practice*, Cambridge University Press, Melbourne.

Standing, G. (2011) *The Precariat: The New Dangerous Class*, Bloomsbury Academic, London.

Standing, G. (2017) *Basic Income: And How We Can Make It Happen*, Penguin, London.

Stanford, J. (2017) US Private Capital Accumulation and Trump's Economic Program, *Real-World Economics Review*, 79, pp. 74–90.

Stanford, J. (2018) The Declining Labour Share in Australia: Definition, Measurement and International Comparison, *Journal of Australian Political Economy*, 81, Winter, pp. 11–32.

Stevenson, B. & Wolfers, J. (2008) Economic Growth and Happiness: Reassesssing the Easterlin Paradox, National Bureau of Economic Research, Cambridge, MA, NBER Working Paper 14282, *http://www.nber.org/papers/w14282.pdf*.

Stevenson, B. & Wolfers, J. (2013) Subjective Well-Being and Income: Is There Any Evidence of Satiation? National Bureau of Economic Research, Cambridge, MA, NBER Working Paper 18992, *http://www.nber.org/papers/w18992.pdf*.

Stiglitz, J.E. (2002) *Globalization and Its Discontents*, W.W. Norton, New York.

Stiglitz, J.E. (2013) *The Price of Inequality: How Today's Divided Society Endangers Our Future*, Norton, New York.

Stiglitz, J.E. (2015) *The Great Divide: Unequal Societies and What We Can Do about Them*, Norton, New York.

Stiglitz, J.E. (2016) Standard Economics is Wrong: Inequality and Unearned Income Kills the Economy, Evonomics, *http://evonomics.com/joseph-stiglitz-inequality-unearned-income/*.

Stiglitz, J.E., Sen, A. & Fitoussi, J-P. (2009) Report by the Commission on the Measurement of Economic Performance and Social Progress, *http://ec.europa.eu/eurostat/documents/118025/118123/Fitoussi+Commission+report*.

Stilwell, F. (1993) *Economic Inequality: Who Gets What in Australia*, Pluto Press, Sydney.

Stilwell, F. (2000) *Changing Track*, Pluto Press, Sydney.

Stilwell, F. (2011) The State: Competing Perspectives, in Argyrous G. & Stilwell, F. (eds), *Readings in Political Economy: Economics as a Social Science*, 3rd edition, Tilde University Press, Melbourne, pp. 274–7.

Stilwell, F. (2012) Marketising the Environment, *Journal of Australian Political Economy*, 68, pp. 108–27.

Stilwell, F. (2013) *Political Economy: The Contest of Economic Ideas*, Oxford University Press, Melbourne.

Stilwell, F. (2015) Towards a Political Economy of the Possible, in Sprague, J. (ed.), *Globalization and Transnational Capitalism in Asia and Oceania*, Routledge, London, pp. 303–17.

Stilwell, F. (2016) Sustainable, Equitable, Secure: Getting There? in Washington, H. & Twomey, P. (eds), *A Future Beyond Growth: Towards a Steady State economy*, Routledge, Abingdon, pp. 146–57.

Stilwell, F. (2019) From Economics to Political Economy: Contradictions, Challenge and Change, *American Journal of Economics and Sociology*, 47:1, pp. 35–62.

Stilwell, F. & Jordan, K. (2007) *Who Gets What: Analysing Economic Inequality in Australia*, Cambridge University Press, Melbourne.

Stilwell, F., Jordan, K. & Pearce, A. (2008) Crises, Interventions and Profits, *Global Change, Peace and Security*, 20:3, October, pp. 263–74.

Stockhammer, E. (2012) Rising Inequality as a Root Cause of the Present Crisis, Political Economy Research Institute, Working Paper, University of Massachusetts, Amherst, *https://www.peri. umass.edu/publication/item/464-rising-inequality-as-a-root-cause-of-the-present-crisis.*

Sullivan, L., Meschede, T., Dietrich, L., Shapiro, T., Traub, A., Ruetschlin, C. & Draut, T. (2015) *The Racial Wealth Gap: Why Policy Matters*, Demos, New York.

Syll, L. (2014) Piketty and the Limits of Marginal Productivity Theory, *Real-World Economics Review*, 69, pp. 36–43.

Tae-Hee, J., Chester, L. & D'Ipolitti, C. (eds) (2018) *The Routledge Handbook of Heterodox Economics*, Routledge, London and New York.

Tawney, R. (1931) *Inequality*, Allen & Unwin, London.

Taylor, C. (1994) The Politics of Recognition, in Gutman, A. (ed.), *Multiculturalism*, Princeton University Press, Princeton, pp. 23–73.

Thornton, T. (2017) *From Economics to Political Economy: The Problems, Promises and Solutions of Pluralist Economics*, Routledge, Abingdon.

Thurbon, E. & Weiss, L. (2016) The Developmental State in the Late Twentieth Century, in Reinart, E.S., Ghosh, J. & Kattel, R. (eds), *Handbook of Alternative Theories of Economic Development*, Edward Elgar, Cheltenham, pp. 637–50.

Thurow, L. (1996) *The Future of Capitalism*, Nicholas Brearley, London.

Tsounta, E. & Osueke, A.I. (2014) What is Behind Latin America's Declining Income Inequality? IMF Working Paper WP/14/124, *https://www.imf.org/external/pubs/ft/wp/2014/wp14124.pdf.*

Turnbull, S. (1973) Time-Limited Corporations, *Abacus*, 9:1, pp. 28–43.

UNRISD (2010) Combating Poverty and Inequality: Structural Changes, Social Policies and Politics, United Nations Research Institute for Social Development, Geneva, *http:// www.unrisd.org/unrisd/website/document.nsf/(httpPublications)/ BBA20D83E347DBAFC125778200440AA7?OpenDocument.*

Valiente-Reidl, E. (2013) *Is Fair Trade Fair?* Palgrave Macmillan, Eastbourne.

van Parijs, P. & Vanderborght, Y. (2017) *Basic Income: A Radical Proposal for a Free Society and a Sane Economy*, Harvard University Press, Cambridge, MA.

van Treek, T. (2009) The Political Economic Debate on Financialization - A Macroeconomic Perspective, *Review of International Political Economy*, 16:5, pp. 907–44.

Varoufakis, Y. (2016) How Do the Economic Elites Get the Idea That They Deserve More? Evonomics, *http://evonomics.com/why-eco nomic-elite-believe-they-deserve-more/*.

Varoufakis, Y, Halevi, J. & Theodorakis, N.J. (2011) *Modern Political Economy: Making Sense of the Post-2008 World*, Routledge, Abingdon.

Veblen, T. (1970 [1989]) *The Theory of the Leisure Class*, Unwin Books, London.

Wachtel, H.M. (1971) Looking at Poverty from a Radical Perspective, *Review of Radical Political Economy*, 3:1, pp. 1–19.

Wachtel, P.L. (1983) *The Poverty of Affluence: A Physiological Portrait of the American Way of Life*, The Free Press, New York.

Wade, R. (2002) Globalisation, Poverty and Income Distribution: Does the Liberal Argument Hold?, in Gruen, D., O'Brien, T. & Lawson, J. (eds), *Globalisation, Living Standards and Inequality: Proceedings of a Conference Held in Sydney on 27–28 May, 2002*, Reserve Bank of Australia and Australian Treasury, Canberra, pp. 37–65.

Wang, C., Caminada, K. & Goudswaard, K. (2014) Income Redistribution in 20 Countries Over Time, *International Journal of Social Welfare*, 23, pp. 262–75.

Washington, H. (2016) Introduction: Why The Growth Economy is Broken, in Washington, H. & Twomey, P. (eds), *A Future Beyond Growth: Towards a Steady State Economy*, Routledge, Abingdon, pp. 1–14.

Weaver, C. (2008) *Hypocrisy Trap: The World Bank and the Poverty of Reform*, Princeton University Press, Princeton.

Weeks, J. (2014) *Economics of the 1%: How Mainstream Economics Serves the Rich, Obscures Reality and Distorts Policy*, Anthem Press, London and New York.

Williamson, J.G. (1965) Regional Inequality and the Process of National Development, *Economic Development and Cultural Change*, 13, pp. 1–84.

Wilkinson, R. (1996) *Unhealthy Societies: The Afflictions of Inequality*, Routledge, London and New York.

Wilkinson, R. (2005) *The Impact of Inequality: How to Make Sick Societies Healthier*, W.W. Norton, New York.

Wilkinson, R. & Pickett, K. (2009) *The Spirit Level: Why More Equal Societies Almost Always Do Better*, Allen Lane, London.

Wilkinson, R. & Pickett, K. (2018) *The Inner Level: How More Equal Societies Reduce Stress, Restore Sanity and Improve Everyone's Well-being*, Allen Lane, London.

Woods, N. (2006) *The Globalizers: The IMF, the World Bank and Their Borrowers*, Cornell University Press, Ithaca., NY and London.

Wray, L.R. (2015) *Modern Money Theory: A Primer on Macroeconomics for Modern Monetary Systems*, Palgrave Macmillan, Basingstoke and New York.

Wray, L.R. (2016) Taxes for Redemption, not Spending, *World Economics Review*, 7, pp. 3–11.

Wright, E.O. (2005) *Approaches to Class Analysis*, Cambridge University Press, Cambridge.

Wright, E.O. (2010) *Envisioning Real Utopias*, Verso, London.

Wright, E.O (2016) How to be an Anti-capitalist for the 21st Century, *Journal of Australian Political Economy*, 77, Winter, pp. 5–22.

Yunus, M. (with Jolis, A.) (2003) *Banker to the Poor: The Story of Grameen Bank*, Aram Press, London.

Yunus, M. (2007) *Creating a World without Poverty: Social Business and the Future of Capitalism*, Public Affairs: Perseus Books, Philadelphia, PA.

Zucman, G. (2014) Taxing Across Borders: Tracking Personal Wealth and Corporate Profits, *Journal of Economics Perspectives*, 28:4, pp. 121–48.

Zucman, G. (2015) *The Hidden Wealth of Nations: The Scourge of Tax Havens*, University of Chicago Press, Chicago.

Zucman, G. (2016) A Top Expert On Tax Havens Explains Why the Panama Papers Barely Scratch the Surface (in conversation with Libby Nelson), *Vox*, 8 April, *http://www.vox.com/2016/4/8/11371712/panama-papers-tax-haven-Zucman*.

Index

countervailing forces reducing,
131–6, 238–40
defining, 22–6
democracy and, 155–6
dimensions and intersections, of
5–7, 13
drivers, 7, **131**
efficiency-equity trade-off, 142,
242
environment and, 151–3, 248–9
factors driving, 115–31
framework to analyse, 11–13
global measures, 49–53, 211
happiness and, 162–8
human rights and, 156–7
impacts, economic and social, **158**
income and wealth matter, 22–6,
37
inter-generational, 85, 117, 148–9
international, 41–5, 211
intra-national, 46–9, 139
market distortions, 98–103
measuring, 22–6, 27, 37, 55–67
national economic growth and,
140–5
neoliberalism as ideology of,
122–5, 135, 208, 233–6, 241
patterns of, 7, 14–15, 54–67
peace and, 153–4
Piketty's research, 108–13
political economic themes, 14–17
productivity and, 93–8, 140–1
prospects for change, 15, 251–6
reasons for, competing
viewpoints, 7–11
reducing poverty and, 223–6, 228
regional, 72–4
shifting share, 54–65
social cohesion, 149–51, 189–91
social intersections of, **72**
social mobility and, 147–9
social problems and, 145–7
technological change, 128–31
urbanization, 126–8
why it matters, 15

see also income inequality; wealth
Inequality-Adjusted Human
Development Index, *see* IAHDI
information and market distortion,
100
inheritance, 19, 86, 87, 117, 186–8
Inner Level, The (Wilkinson and
Pickett), 33, 69, 133, 134, 135,
147, 233
innovation, 99, 129, 140–1
institutional economics, 10, 116–17
interest payments, 28
interest groups
capture, 238
power, 236–7, 243
inter-generational inequality, 85, 117,
148–9
interlocking directorates, 106
international aid policies, 223–4, 225,
253
international capital levy, 185
international inequality, 41–5,
211–18
global measures of, 49–53
income distribution, 42–5, **62**
shifting shares, 55–65, 211
see also inequality
international institutions, poverty
alleviation and, 212, 216, 219,
226–7
International Labour Organization
(ILO), 215, 239
International Monetary Fund (IMF)
labour share, decline of, 26–7, 123,
124, 142
reforming, 226–7
role in reducing inequality, 211,
220
international reparations, 224
interpersonal utility comparisons,
168
intra-generational inequality, 85–7,
148–9
intra-national inequality, 46–9, 139
Italy, 42, 73